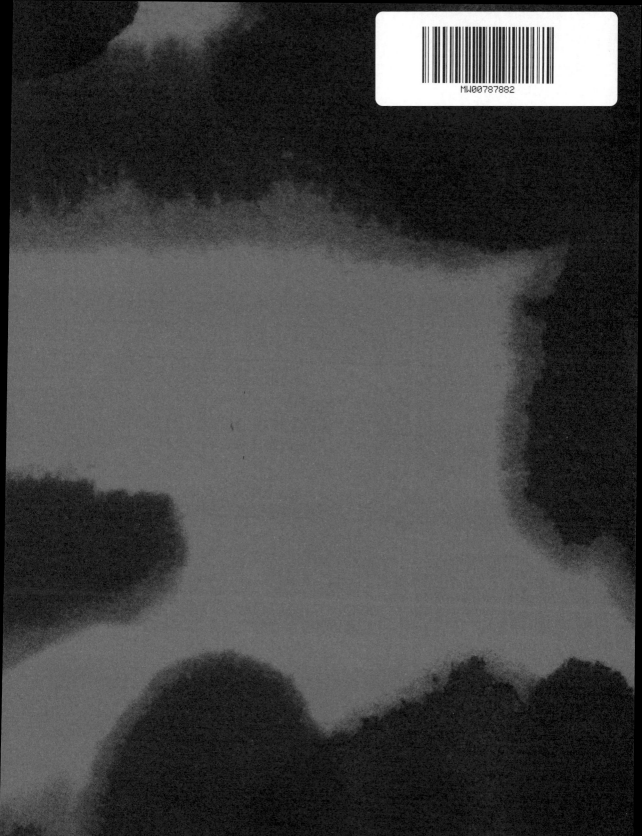

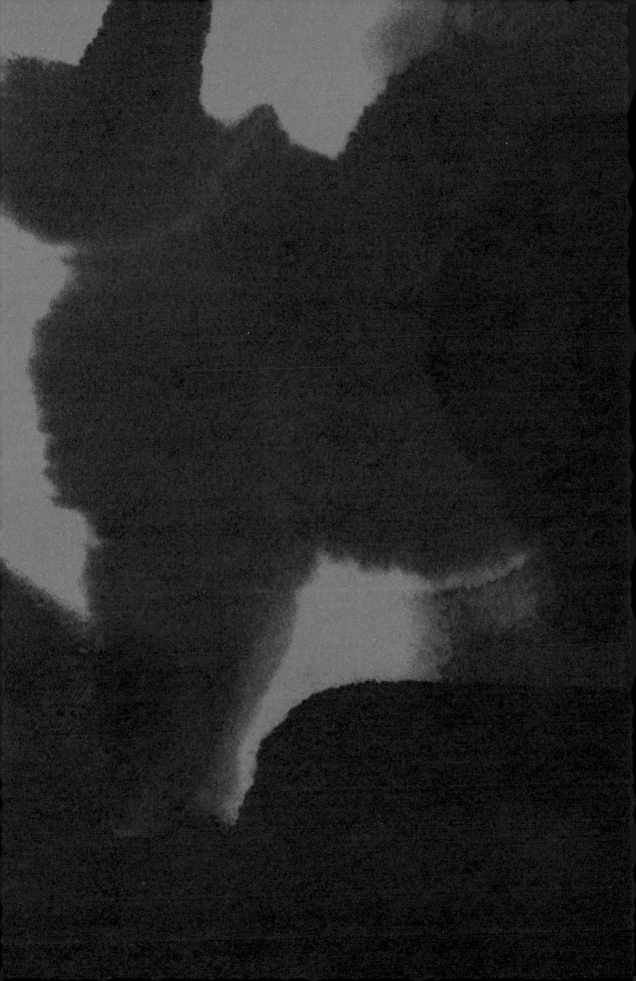

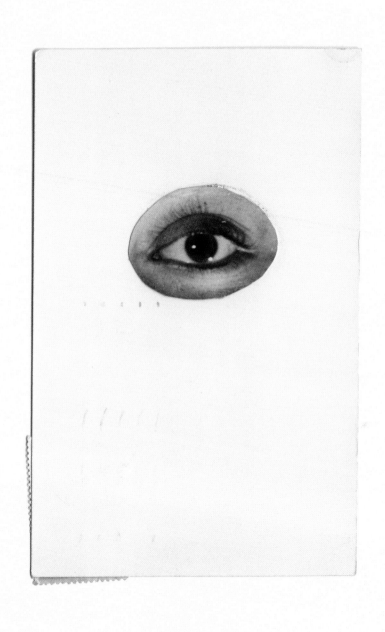

Roger Luckhurst

PRINCETON

HIC

An Illustrated History

with over 350 illustrations

Book I	Chap 1 — the lawyers letters &c
Styria & London	" 2 — (clerk visits Styria Transylvania) Munich
London	" 3 — the journey — ? — blue flame
	3 & 4 — arrival the Castle
	" 5 — loneliness the Kiss "this man belongs to
	5 Dr Seward's diary
	" 6 — old chapel burying earth — Sortes Virgil
	(notes in letter)
	7 — The purchase of London Estate
	Dr Seward's diary — fly patient — bowed down

Book II	Chap 1 the auctioneer Whitby — argument uncanny things
Tragedy	" 2 the Doctor Whitby — the storm — ship arrives
	" 3 the lawyers clerk Whitby They walk in sleep —
	" 4 a shift of ? London Mina's wedding
	" 5 a medical impasse A target of terror (wolf rising)
	Seward visits asylum
	" 6 The Tragedy A medical impasse dog dies
	" 7 The Vow Opening vault. The Vow

Book III	Chap 1 The Suspicion — Harker's diary
Discovery	" 2 Inquiries — the Dinner — re Vampires
	" 3 Diaries &c Mina custody Dracula Town to t Transylvania
	" 4 On the track Texan in Transylvania
	" 5 Strange clues — Count's house searched bloodred
	" 6 — a test of sanity (?)
	" 7 — Conviction Harker sees the Count — Disappearance of the

Book IV	Chap 1 a Dinner of thirteen
Punishment	" 2 a Vigilante Committee
	" 3 Disappearance
	" 4 a choice of dwellings
	" 5 closing the net (removing earth
	" 6 Back to Styria Transylvania
	" 7 a Tourists Tale
	(one killed & wolf (wehr?)

Dog in the Texan

The Shape
of the Gothic

It used to be easy to define the Gothic. A castle on a precipice, silhouetted against a gibbous moon. Next door, a ruined church with arched windows, the gravestones at crazy angles. Something unholy and transgressive stirring in the shadows under the twisted yew tree. The mist would be optional, but the bats and screech-owl compulsory.

This makes the Gothic a product of northern European climes: the alpine heights where Frankenstein's monster roams; the wild forests of Scandinavia; the bleak cemeteries of London or Edinburgh, where body-snatchers lurk. But if these are some of its places of origin, it has since exploded across the planet. The Gothic now speaks in many languages. In a single evening, one might play a level of a Japanese survival horror game while plugged into a doomy 1980s soundtrack from The Sisters of Mercy or The Cure, then stream an episode of any number of horror series from America, or France, or Egypt, while flicking through a few stanzas of 'Graveyard Poetry' from the 1740s, before hitting the streets in un-glad rags in order to watch the latest Korean or Italian or Thai or Australian horror film at the local cinema. The global spread of the Gothic has been swift and overwhelming – as uncontainable as a zombie virus.

Some complain that the term 'Gothic' is now so ubiquitous that its original meaning has been entirely hollowed out. But I prefer to see it as a collection of 'travelling tropes' that, while they originate in a narrow set of European cultures with distinct meanings, have embarked on a journey in which they

1

are both transmitted and utterly transformed as they move across different cultures. Sometimes the Gothic keeps a recognizable shape, but more often it merges with local folklore or beliefs in the supernatural to become a weird, wonderful new hybrid.

The pointed arch that defines Gothic architecture maintains its distinctive shape, yet transforms in meaning and significance as it passes from Islamic to northern European to American settings, to the 'Bombay Gothic' of buildings in colonial India or the white settler churches of Australia and Aotearoa New Zealand. The vampire, meanwhile, starts in rumours of foul undead things unearthed on the borders of eastern Europe, but as it travels by print from Prague to Vienna, and on to Paris and London, it is transformed and translated from place to place. *Dracula* emerges from the very specific context of late-Victorian London, but Bram Stoker's masterpiece quickly reappeared in very free adaptations in Turkey and Iceland, the meaning moulded to local contexts. The vampire has since become a recognizable trope, wildly re-drawn as it arrives in Spain or Italy or West Africa or South Korea.

As the Gothic ages, it has also moved beyond its origins in architecture and the printed page to become fully transmedial, its tropes and motifs recurring in novels, films, television, fine art, comics, fashion, computer games and the dark web of the internet itself. Gothic plots often revolve around ideas of transgression, the breaching of boundaries of life and death, good taste and bad, knowledge and belief, and this restless transformation makes it a privileged place for many to explore foundational questions of self and other. No wonder the Gothic has become a place where unspeakable stories might find voice, whether in the metamorphoses of man into animal or the splitting of self and other. Unspoken or suppressed desires have shaped the genre from the very beginning. The Gothic has provided space for the expression of female desire, from Mary Shelley's monstered creation to Sarah Waters's queer spectral visitors, and what is now termed the Trans Gothic builds on Susan Stryker's evocation, in 1993, of Frankenstein's creature as a place to rethink the transgressive trans body. The 'transing Gothic', as Jolene Zigarovich calls it, is 'a persistent venue for transgressive non-normative sexualities and gender identities.'

This transgression is also figured in the Gothic's spatial and geographic imagination. Dracula resides in Transylvania, that place beyond the trees; the horrors beyond the mountains animate the shattering visions of H. P. Lovecraft's *At the Mountains of Madness* (1931) or the Donner Party, marooned in the California mountains, resorting to survival cannibalism. If the fear of what lies beyond is part of the American frontier imagination, the transatlantic slave trade, the Middle Passage forged between Africa, Europe and the Americas, binds the world together around atrocity. This repressed history continually leaks from the Gothic, from the over 500 enslaved Africans registered to *The Monk* author Matthew Lewis's Jamaican plantations and the slave fortune that built William Beckford's Fonthill Abbey, to the Southern ghosts of Toni Morrison's *Beloved* and the suburban nightmare of Jordan Peele's *Get Out*. The migration of refugees can become their transmigration into spectres, drowned in transit and left haunting, as in Mati Diop's Senegalese film *Atlantics* (2019) or the Sudanese couple in Remi Weekes's *His House* (2020).

Gothic: An Illustrated History takes up the challenge of building a global history of the Gothic, attempting to glimpse this protean creature as it shape-shifts. It follows the trajectory of twenty 'travelling tropes', grouped into four sections of five essays each: 'Architecture & Form', 'The Lie of the Land', 'The Gothic Compass' and 'Monsters'. We begin with the disorienting transformation of rural traditions in the eighteenth century: the Gothic as a register of crisis. In the modern world, the city begins to pulse with the energy of a dynamic present, while depictions multiply of the countryside as a backwater, a place where things slow and swirl and the Old Ways linger on. Paths move outwards from the village, into the forest and further into the trackless wilderness before returning to the sketchy in-between edgelands. From there, the Gothic travels the world. Since its origins with the northern Goths and Visigoths, we have become familiar with a 'Southern Gothic', whether in horrific projections of what lies in the unknown terrain of the Antarctic, or in the American South, steeped in genocidal history. An Eastern Gothic has also emerged, where the hordes of the 'Yellow Peril' haunt the colonial imaginary. Cosmic horror brings us glimpses of the vast, incomprehensible terrors in which the whole of our fragile planet bathes. Here, the Gothic achieves escape velocity: in space, no one can hear you scream.

The protean creatures that populate the Gothic imagination shape the final quarter of this book. As ideas of humanity shift, so the shape and size of our monsters alters: sea monsters, krakens, wendigos, dinosaurs, *kaiju* (Godzilla and his prehistoric chums), pixies and fairies that hover on the edges of perception. Medieval chimerae were reported by travellers in distant regions – griffins, manticores, hydras – spliced together, with clear moral and allegorical functions. Meanwhile, a tentacular imagination opens up to further boundless forms: the mists, oozes, slimes, blobs, grey goo and toxic clouds that spill over fixed boundaries and invade us all. There is nowhere this insidious Gothic cannot travel. But for all this pursuit of the other, we secretly know that the monster is the one who looks exactly like us: the changeling, the fetch, the double, the robotic replica. We look in the mirror and see an utter stranger there, even as it reflects back to us the shape we thought we knew best.

The Gothic is endlessly transitive, always moving, shifting and changing as it goes. It requires us to be flexible readers, supple in our definitions and our responses. Here it comes, beetling along the street like that shocking Mr Hyde, who, Robert Louis Stevenson tells us, moves with the speed of a Juggernaut, vanishing around the corner so quickly that we cannot quite grasp the weird sense of transgression he leaves in his wake. If this journey takes us back to the beginning, to ourselves, *Gothic: An Illustrated History* registers just some of the transformations undertaken as we hurtle back to a place that we can never again quite call home.

1. An early Victorian storage jar for medical leeches.

I

ARCHITECTURE
&
FORM

The Pointed Arch

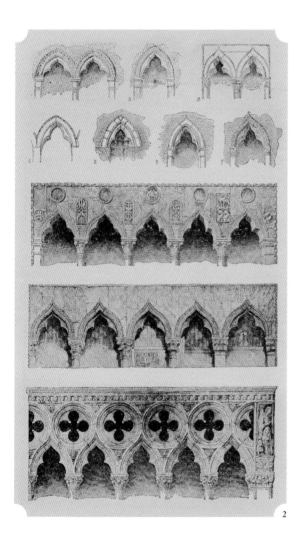

2

'Monstrous and barbaric', cried the Renaissance historian Vasari in 1550, of buildings in what he called 'the German manner'. A century later, the Neoclassicist John Evelyn found that Greek and Roman architecture 'answer[s] all the perfection required in a faultless and accomplished building'. The Goths and Vandals, meanwhile, had introduced 'in their stead a certain fantastical and licentious manner of building, which we have since called modern or Gothic: – congestions of heavy, dark, melancholy and monkish piles, without any just proportion, use, or beauty, compared with the truly antient'. 'Monkish' speaks volumes: this was the style of the churches and monasteries of the old, popish religion that Evelyn's England had overthrown under King Henry VIII.

Evelyn's close friend and ally was Sir Christopher Wren, who, in the early eighteenth century, resurrected St Paul's Cathedral in London, but replaced its old medieval plan with a triumphant, rational dome. Wren speculated in his own writings that the Gothic was a suspiciously foreign style, introduced from the 'Saracenic' East 'after the fall of the Greek Empire, by the prodigious success of those people who adhered to Mahomet's doctrine'. To identify this foreign, Islamic imposition, he noted 'the sharp-heeled arch', which would be further elaborated into rows and tiers of arches, traceries, spires and pinnacles, 'unbounded fancies', he said, in damning tones, that 'induced much mincing of the stone'. Wren's origin story was long considered wild and speculative, but his knowledge of 'the Arabic, Saracenic, or Mooresque', as he called it, was good, part of a revived interest in Islamic culture in his time. The first French Gothic cathedrals took inspiration from the Hagia Sofia in Istanbul, and, as Diana Darke notes in *Stealing from the Saracens* (2020),

1. [opposite] Imam Mosque, Isfahan, Iran, built in 1611–29.
2. John Ruskin, Windows of the Early Gothic Palaces, from *The Stones of Venice* (1851–53).

their towers, arches and rose windows were borrowed from ancient Christian and Islamic structures in Syria and Israel. It is thrilling to find that the pointed arch, that defining shape of European Gothic architecture, holds this hybrid origin.

What does the pointed arch *do*? There is a spiritual, symbolic answer and a more prosaic, technical answer. Pointed arches stretch up towards God, flooding the interior with divine light and inspiring solemn awe, what one commentator called 'an artificial infinite'. Even secular tourists might still experience this feeling as they enter the nave of cathedrals in Salisbury, Rouen or Milan. In 1760, the writer and Bishop of Gloucester William Warburton speculated:

> For this northern people having been accustomed, during the gloom of paganism, to worship the Deity in groves (a practice common to all nations), when their new religion required covered edifices, they ingeniously projected to make them resemble groves as nearly as the distance of architecture would permit.

Sadly, the theory that Gothic vaulting repeated the interlocking branches of avenues of trees was completely wrong, but the notion of the Gothic style embodying natural patterns and inherent numinous feelings remained influential – unless, of course, you were a sixteenth-century Protestant or Puritan, taught to despise elaborate ornamentation.

The pointed arch results from a mundane but rather brilliant technical breakthrough. Flat stone lintels or beams can only carry so much weight before they collapse under their own mass. Egyptian, Greek and Roman buildings can only span so far because of this; but later, semi-circular arches above windows and doors used a large keystone to spread the weight either side of the opening, down through the arch, which sits on an impost. In an arcade of arches, all springing from imposts resting on the top of columns, the weight is taken by the end columns or walls, which can be further buttressed outside – hence the buttresses and, later, highly decorative 'flying' buttresses that are typical signs of Gothic exteriors.

This weight management opened up interiors in a wholly new way. Some have suspected that the Gothic pointed arch emerged merely in the intersection of rows

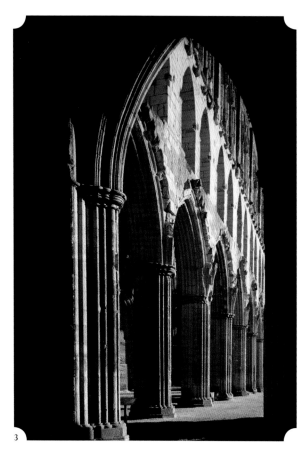

3

A term of reproach, a barbarous appellation, an invidious designation, a vulgar epithet, an ignorant by-word, a low nick-name.

3. The ruins of Rievaulx Abbey, North Yorkshire, UK, built in 1132 and destroyed in 1538–39 during the dissolution of the monasteries.
4. The Stone Screen at York Minster, UK, photographed by George Washington Wilson in 1865.
5. Victorian stereoscopic photograph of the ribbed ceiling and central pillar of Salisbury Cathedral's Chapter House, UK.
6. Victorian stereoscopic photograph of the arched entrance to Salisbury Cathedral's Chapter House.

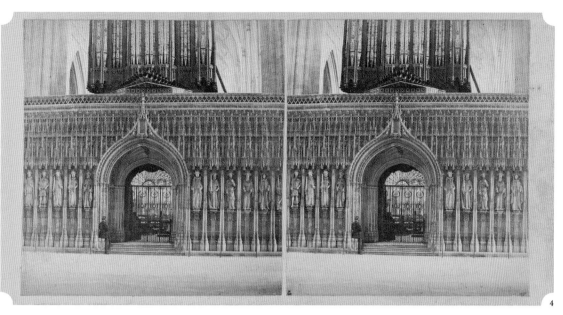

4

5

6

of semi-circular arches. But in fact, the engineers of these buildings had realized that the pointed arch, with a much smaller keystone, could nevertheless still direct the weight down through slender columns and thence to the ground. Under the keystone, windows and doors could be opened up to light and glass; interiors were now flooded with divine rays. The spaces in between the arches (called spandrels) could also be decorated with patterned stone or religious images. Vasari and Evelyn may have associated the Gothic with feudal tyranny, ignorance and superstition, but these buildings were conjured by a masterly understanding of physics and mathematics, often borrowed from Arabic sources.

The naming and classification of medieval buildings as 'Gothic' that took place in the eighteenth and nineteenth centuries was not only the affair of pedantic antiquarians. From the 1720s, there were the beginnings of a Gothic Revival. Styles abused since the Renaissance began to return to use. It was the height of the Gothic Revival, which spread from Britain across Europe in the nineteenth century, that saw the most sustained use of the pointed style. Three passionate supporters can tell us why.

In 1798, John Carter, a draughtsman, began a series of important columns in the *Gentleman's Magazine*. As France experienced a fierce and bloody revolution, through regicide, radical republicanism and finally a militarist empire under Napoleon Bonaparte, Carter

7

An artificial infinite.

was determined to see pointed architecture as England's 'National Architecture' – a way of grounding the English state in a deep, stable political and religious history distinct from the chaos just over the water. At first hesitant about the term 'Gothic', which, he wrote in 1801, was 'a term of reproach, a barbarous appellation, an invidious designation, a vulgar epithet, an ignorant by-word, a low nick-name, given to hold up to shame our ancient English architecture', in 1802 he nonetheless published the important anthology *Essays on Gothic Architecture*, which pulled together many obscure antiquarian sources to track the emerging appreciation of this form. At a time of political and military panic, Carter fused the Gothic with Englishness, using the style as a vehicle for British patriotism. He was apoplectic when historians began to suggest that, actually, the pointed arch was first used in France, in the church of St Denis in 1145, which had, in turn, borrowed elements from Middle Eastern architecture.

7. The Decorated Gothic of York Minster's southern transept, photographed by J. Draffin in 1860.
8. A ribbed ceiling in the twelfth-century nave of Notre-Dame Cathedral, Paris, France.
9. Gothic echoes in the distant future, on the set of *Dune* (David Lynch, 1984).

8

9

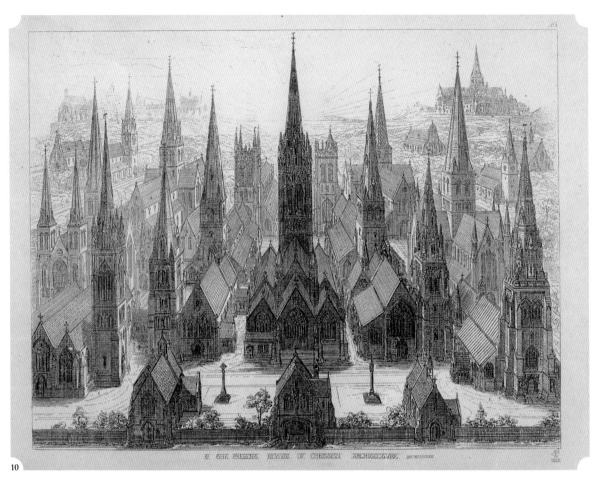

10

11

France had in fact built a large number of magnificent Gothic cathedrals in the twelfth century, among them Notre-Dame and Chartres. In his 1831 novel, *Notre Dame de Paris*, Victor Hugo waxes lyrical about its façade, its 'recessed and pointed doorways', the rose window and flanking towers, the 'flimsy gallery of trefoiled arches' on 'slender colonnettes', all rising to create an effect of 'tranquil grandeur'.

Only a few decades after the Napoleonic Wars ended at Waterloo, the architect, designer and critic Augustus Welby Pugin began to exert his influence in England through a series of beautifully executed records of old buildings, polemical essays and lectures, and his own Gothic Revival church buildings. Pugin, who collaborated with Charles Barry to rebuild the Houses of Parliament in the Perpendicular Gothic style,

The divine awe of the cathedral cunningly turned into political awe for the power of the colonizers.

saw pointed architecture as an expression of religious devotion: '*Height*, or the *vertical principle*, emblematic of the resurrection, is the very essence of Christian architecture.' This coincided with a major evangelical revival in England, a huge phase of church building for rapidly expanding cities and much angst-ridden public debate about modern life and ancient beliefs. Pugin's book *Contrasts* (1836) worked as a series of satirical comparisons between the degraded modern world and an idealized fantasy of organic medieval life. Gothic Revival spaces were not just a question of style to Pugin, but a matter of rescuing souls. At times, he could sound as nationalistic as Carter: 'We are not Italian,' he said of the trend for villa-style domestic housing. He called the Gothic style the 'absolute duty' of the English architect. But his nationalism was complicated: Pugin was the son of a French refugee, and converted to Roman Catholicism. He got into trouble for being too suspiciously Catholic in his designs for the medieval hall at the Great Exhibition of 1851. The nationalist and Catholic aspects of the Gothic were not really compatible; the range of meanings in the Gothic Revival were never stable.

After Pugin, the most important Victorian influence on the Gothic Revival was John Ruskin. In the wake of the revolutionary shocks that rocked Europe in 1848, when even in England the workers of the Chartist movement threatened the old establishment order, Ruskin began to pour out a series of essays, lectures and books that argued for a restoration of organic, harmonious, pious medieval life, as embodied in its architecture.

10. The heavenly city in Augustus Pugin's *An Apology for the Revival of Christian Architecture* (1843).
11. Three decorative grille designs for the Palace of Westminster, London, UK, designed by Augustus Pugin, *c.* 1845–59.

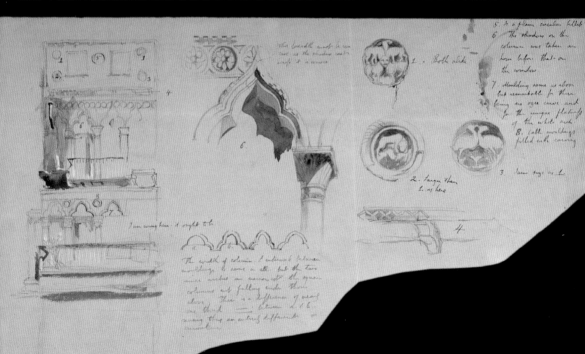

14

He found this dreamy ideal hanging on beneath the spires of Oxford and Cambridge, with their (all-male) medieval communities of monkish scholars, but it was best embodied in Venice. His mammoth three-volume book, *The Stones of Venice* (1851–53), was a celebration of an ideal, but also a record of the decline of the great city, from its imperial and Gothic heights in the thirteenth and fourteenth centuries to its modern, shattered state as a bauble casually passed between greater powers, left to rot and ruin. This was clearly meant as a moral warning for Great Britain, then at the beginning of its own imperial heyday. But even Ruskin had to acknowledge that Venice was also important because it had been the great cosmopolitan city, one of the crucial meeting points of East and West, Europe and its Others.

Ruskin, an astonishing draughtsman and pioneering user of photography, visited Venice several times to record its decaying masterpieces. He sketched pointed arches obsessively, working out sequences of the rise towards perfection and fall away into decadent Mannerism. He categorized Byzantine arches, Saracenic arches, Gothic arches – the Palazzo Moroni incorporated them all. He adored the Ducal Palace and the church of St Mark's, next to each other in Venice's central square, considering them the finest buildings in the world. But his writing boils with almost comical fury at the destruction or reworking of churches and palazzos when the Renaissance arrived in Vienna, a rage that knocks chunks out of his earnest morality.

A certain fantastical and licentious manner of building, which we have since called modern or Gothic: – congestions of heavy, dark, melancholy and monkish piles.

In the most important chapter of *The Stones of Venice*, 'On the Nature of the Gothic', he identified the mode in six mildly eccentric categories. *Savageness* was the mark of its origins in the North, the 'rude and wild' in building. *Changefulness*, or *Variety*, marked the delightful irregularity and asymmetry of Gothic buildings; this allowed him to praise the 'authentic' artisanal labour of the medieval world over the soulless symmetries of both Classicism and the entire modern world of factory production, its alienated labour forces and blandly identical commodities. *Naturalism* was central: he argued that the decoration was taken from the proper observation of natural forms, and revived the old idea that Gothic churches derived from forest groves. The fourth quality was the *Grotesque*. Rather than using this as a term of abuse, Ruskin made it a virtue, a tendency towards the 'fantastic'.

12. [opposite above] The Gothic revival staircase of the St Pancras Renaissance Hotel, London, UK, designed as the Midland Grand by George Gilbert Scott, 1865–73.
13. [opposite below] Ruskin's Venetian notebooks, sketch study towards *The Stones of Venice* (1851–53).
14. The Gothic fantasy of *Dark Souls III* (2016), a video game series first designed by Hidetaka Miyazaki.

His next category, *Rigidity*, sought to praise the massy, cold, spiky, pointed Northern rigour of the Early Gothic typical of England, Germany or northern France, contrasted with 'the languid submission' that he found in southern Europe. Lastly, he adored exactly the *Redundance* of ornament that rationalists like Wren had condemned.

'On the Nature of the Gothic', often extracted from the sprawling volumes of *The Stones of Venice*, had a huge impact on Victorian architects, artists, writers and political thinkers. The cultural interests of William Morris (if not his socialism) were all Ruskinian – his anti-capitalist writings, his poetry of northern sagas, his love of medieval chivalry and his revival of artisanal 'Gothic' designs for books and furniture from his own workshop. And there would have been no Walter Pater, the writer who inspired the aesthetes of the fin de siècle to their dalliances with naughty Catholic ritual and transgressive desire, without Ruskin.

The most significant difference between Ruskin and Carter or Pugin is, as his praise of the north suggests, that he understood the Gothic in a much more international, European way. In a different, more cosmopolitan period, when Britain was more open to the world, Ruskin was happy to take stylistic echoes from the French and German Gothic. His main practical impact on Revival architecture was to introduce the polychromatic decorations in exterior and interior brickwork that typified Venice. The buildings of the Gothic Revival in England most directly inspired by Ruskin explode in polychromy. All Saints Church, on Margaret Street, London, was the model church for the very high Anglican Ecclesiological Society, an influential Cambridge group that pushed the religious revival of Gothic architecture. The exterior is in brightly patterned brick, the huge spire competing with Westminster Abbey and the interior glimmering with light and colour among an eclectic array of different kinds of pointed arches. The style was soon exported across the empire, to Australia, Canada and India. A distinctive 'Bombay Gothic' style, for instance, appears in the nineteenth-century civic buildings and railway terminus of Mumbai, used to assert British control over the native population, the divine awe of the cathedral cunningly turned into political awe for the power of the colonizers.

So pervasive was the Ruskinian Gothic that by 1872, Ruskin professed that he was being forced to move from his south London retreat in Denmark Hill because suburban sprawl was drowning his neighbourhood in mock-Venetian villas: 'it is surrounded everywhere by the accursed Frankenstein monsters of my own making', he lamented, in a telling use of a Gothic classic with a very different meaning. There had been an inevitable degeneration of the Gothic into an ornamental style with none of Ruskin's moral earnestness. By 1890, even the mere fashion for pointed porches on semi-detached surburban villas had died off. The Gothic Revival was finished.

Pugin got into trouble for being too suspiciously Catholic in his designs.

15. [opposite] All Saints Church, Margaret Street, London, UK, designed in High Victorian Gothic style by William Butterfield, 1850–59.

Ruins

In the 1720s, a weird craze swept England's aristocracy: building fake ruins. Baron Bathurst built Alfred's Hall, one of the very first, in the grounds of his estate in the Cotswolds between 1721 and 1732, part of a cult of celebrating the Anglo-Saxon king. This artificial ruin has since fallen into actual ruin. Garden designers (with fantastic names like Batty Langley) began to privilege the 'Gothick' style in country house landscapes, its stark silhouettes especially suited to contemporary theories of the picturesque and sublime. Some suggested that existing ruins could do with being knocked about a little more to make them look more picturesque; in some cases, as at Hagley Hall, Worcestershire, real ruins were pulled down to make space for sham ones.

The most famous of these follies was the Gothic Temple in the garden at Stowe, designed by James Gibbs for Sir Richard Temple in 1741. The imposing Temple was three storeys high, with pointed arches and castellated parapets, fancifully decorated with statues of seven Saxon deities representing the ancient liberties of the British race. The craze for fake ruins took off to such an extent that in the 1776 comedy *The Clandestine Marriage*, one character complains: 'It has cost me a hundred and fifty pounds to put my ruins in thorough repair.'

In art, the *capriccio* genre first developed in the Renaissance, but boomed again in the 1700s. Fantastical, dream-like compositions of impossible or composite buildings, often ancient ruins hurled into elaborate piles, the *capriccio* mixed up styles and actual historical buildings, overloading them with crazy detail and dizzying perspectives. These constructed fantasies were made popular in Italy and Greece among the travellers following the Grand Tour,

2

The Gothic ruin is a symbol of the rubble of history, its ghosts emblems 'of all dead generations.'

1. [opposite] The ruin of Eastern State Penitentiary, a model prison in Philadelphia, USA, which opened in 1829 and closed in 1971.
2. The Gothic Temple folly in the gardens at Stowe, UK, built as a ruin in 1741.

by painters like Giovanni Paolo Panini and Giovanni Battista Piranesi. Piranesi's fine drawings of ruins and impossible structures fed directly into the Gothic Revival in England, where ruin paintings by Gainsborough, Turner and others became a whole sub-genre. In Germany, the brooding ruins painted by Caspar David Friedrich evoke such a melancholic atmosphere that he remains the go-to Gothic land-scape painter.

There is a vast library of works that speculate on the hidden springs of what the Germans call *Ruinenlust* (the desire for ruins) or *Ruinensehnsucht* (the longing or yearning for ruins). The classic argument is that ruins allow for bittersweet contemplation of the tran-sience of all things, perhaps a little of the piquancy of living on in the rubble, but also moral instruction on human vanity. In 1767, the Enlightenment philosopher Denis Diderot wrote: 'The ideas ruins evoke in me are grand. Everything comes to nothing, everything perishes, everything passes, only the world remains, only time endures.'

For eighteenth-century thinkers, the ruin also featured in discussions of the imagination. Some-thing about incompleteness or fragmentation invited the mind to actively complete the ruin, stimulating the highest speculative faculties as the viewer imagined themselves into the incomplete structure and its remote past. But this stretch of the mind's powers can also tilt into other, less enlightened modes of thought. In his essays on the imagination, the essayist, playwright and critic Joseph Addison used the example of a night-time walk in a ruined abbey to explore how 'the night heightens the awfulness of the place, and pours out her supernumerary horror upon everything in it'. He concluded that 'I do not at all wonder that weak minds fill it with spectres and apparitions', providing the ammunition for those who would later denounce the Gothic as a dangerous, corrupting stimulant that unseats reason.

Ruins might evoke these con-ventionalized sets of complex feelings and responses, but to understand the Gothic ruin-craze of the eighteenth century we need to get much more historically specific. The ruin is a sign that nearly always points to a political and religious meaning. After Henry VIII's 1536–40 dissolution of the monasteries, Britain and Ireland were dot-ted with the ruins of vanquished and humiliated Catholic institutions, destroyed in a sometimes bloody

3

4

Ruin contemplation very often cuts out political and social dynamics.

3. J. M. W. Turner, *Tintern Abbey: The Crossing and Chancel, Looking Towards the East Window*, 1794.
4. Giovanni Paolo Panini, *Architectural Capriccio with figure among Roman Ruins*, c. 1630.
5. Yves Marchand and Romain Meffre, *Ballroom, Lee Plaza Hotel*, 2006, from *The Ruins of Detroit* (2010).
6. Giovanni Battista Piranesi, *Ancient Intersection of the Via Appia and Via Ardeatina*, from *The Antiquities of Rome* (1756).

5

6

7

8

and traumatic usurpation of their wealth and power; another wave of violent destruction followed during the Civil War. Ruins are the trace of murderous struggle across the world, emblems of power and glory lost, pulled down into the rubble, from the deserts of Egypt to the pyramids of Central America.

Gothic ruins can also mark a desire to appeal to ancient continuity. Alfred's Hall bore the legend 'In memory of Alfred, Restorer of Religion' – a statement of the persistence of the old religion, not the new. These ideals of stability could go even further back: in 1740, William Stukeley published his study of the ruins at Stonehenge, in which he hoped to prove that ancient druids were proto-Christian worshippers, suggesting thousands of years of hidden continuity.

Many early Gothic novelists were didactic writers who used ruins to suggest the corruption of superstitious, Catholic Europe. Anna Laetitia Aikin wrote in 1773 that when she walked through abbey ruins she 'began to indulge a secret triumph in the ruin of so many structures, which I had always considered the haunts of ignorance and superstition'. In Ann Radcliffe's bestselling Gothic romances of the 1790s, ruined castles denote foreign tyrannical excesses, ancient political disorders and menacing libertines waiting to corrupt female virtues. Radcliffe's Protestant heroines usually end up married and living in rationally designed, modest villas, with not a single trace of a mouldering grave or screech-owl.

By the end of the eighteenth century, different kinds of politics had begun to influence the contemplation of ruins. In the fevered first years of the French Revolution, the radical Count de Volney published *The Ruins, or, Meditation on the Ruins of Empires* (1792), which opens amid the classical ruins of Palmyra to contemplate the overthrow and destruction of entrenched power:

> Solitary ruins, sacred tombs, ye mouldering and silent walls, all hail!... A while ago the whole world bowed the neck in silence before the tyrants that oppressed it; and yet in that hopeless moment you already proclaimed the truths that tyrants hold in abhorrence: mixing the dust of the proudest kings with that of the meanest slaves, you called upon us to contemplate this example of Equality.

Volney's revolutionary lesson about Equality still persists – as does the iconic status of the ruins at Palmyra.

9

7. Andrew Moore, *Courtyard, Cass Tech High School, Detroit*, 2008, from *Detroit Disassembled* (2010).
8. Thomas Cole, *Effect for Newstead Abbey, Nottinghamshire*, 1830.
9. Ruins of Pripyat, Ukraine, the city hurriedly abandoned after the 1986 nuclear catastrophe at Chernobyl, photographed in 2019.

10

11

Perhaps this was why, in 2015, ISIS forces occupying central Syria, committed to the establishment of a fundamentalist Islamic caliphate, actively set out to blow up the surviving ruined temples there.

In England, Edward Gibbon's *The History of the Decline and Fall of the Roman Empire* (1776–89), which opened contemplating the ruins of the Forum in Rome, exerted a massive political and imaginative effect on anxieties about the inevitable waning of political power with the passage of time. Could ruminating on ruins save empires from degeneration and decline?

The most famous contemplation of ruins in English Romantic poetry is William Wordsworth's 'Lines Composed a Few Miles above Tintern Abbey' (1798). The old Cistercian abbey, founded in 1098 and left to ruin in 1536 on the orders of Henry VIII, was a much-visited picturesque site. The fragile pointed arches and remains of the east window had been painted by J. M. W. Turner in 1794. Wordsworth's opening lines set the 'wild secluded scene', but rapidly abandon close detail to become a poem about the 'tranquil restoration' in memory of a location 'In which the heavy and weary weight / Of all this unintelligible world, / Is lightened'. Some critics of this quintessential illustration of Wordsworth's theory of 'emotions recollected in tranquillity' observe that by 1798 the poet had to erase the evidence of an iron foundry bellowing smoke nearby and impoverished workers squatting in the ruins of the abbey. The industrial revolution had already taken hold in the Wye Valley, but ruin contemplation very often cuts out such political and social dynamics.

The pleasant shivers evoked by ruined abbeys have been replaced by the horrific vastness of modern militarized destruction.

The Gothic ruin is a symbol of the rubble of history, its ghosts emblems 'of all dead generations' – as Karl Marx put it – 'that weigh like a nightmare on the brains of the living'. The past always threatens to return, undead. Yet ruins have a strange relationship to time: we might get a pleasurable frisson of our survival into the present as we contemplate old stones, but they also make us project our own future ruination. When architect and antiquarian Sir John Soane designed the current Bank of England, he asked his painter friend Joseph Gandy to depict it as a future ruin. Perhaps this was in the tradition of the *capriccio*, but it was a weird thing to do in 1798, at the height of Terror at the threat of revolutionary France.

Future ruins shatter the complacency of every contemporary age, breaking open the self-satisfaction

10. Etching of the ruins of Palmyra, Syria, plate 71 from *Picturesque journeys of Syria, Phenicia, Palestine and Lower Egypt* (1798). Designed by Berthault, after L. F. Cassas.
11. The iconic ruin of the Industrial Promotion Hall in Hiroshima, destroyed after a nuclear bomb was dropped on the Japanese city in August 1945.
12. Browsing in the library at Holland House in London, UK, after damage by a firebomb dropped in October 1940.
13. An abandoned video store after the nuclear meltdown at the Daiichi power plant near Fukushima, Japan, 2011.

12

13

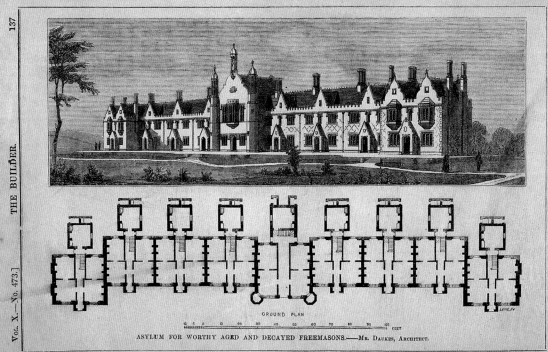

137

GROUND PLAN

10 5 0 10 20 30 40 50 60 70 80 90 100 FEET

ASYLUM FOR WORTHY AGED AND DECAYED FREEMASONS.——Mr. DAUKES, ARCHITECT.

of its sense of superiority over the past. It is another version of *sic transit gloria mundi* (so pass the glories of the world), and it has, if anything, intensified since 1939, when humanity invented a slew of brand new ways to bring about ruination.

Rose Macaulay's brilliant reflections in *The Pleasure of Ruins*, published in 1953, conclude with a brief afterword on the ruined spaces of British cities, blitzed by German bombs in 1940 and 1944–45. The complete destruction of German cities by the Allies and the nuclear annihilation of Hiroshima and Nagasaki in 1945 gave us our iconic images of post-war ruins. These were not Wordsworthian picturesque scenes recollected in tranquillity. The war ruins were too near in time, brutal reminders of the realities of disfigurement and 'murdered bodies', Macaulay said. The writer W. G. Sebald remained blisteringly angry about the mass murders of Allied bombing raids on Germany, speaking in graphic terms about an atrocity covered up in 'ruin literature' in his lectures *On the Natural History of Destruction* (1999). Oddly, Hitler's favoured architect for the Third Reich, Albert Speer, also thought of his plans as future ruins, theorizing what he called 'ruin value'. In these instances, the pleasant shivers evoked by ruined abbeys have been replaced by the horrific vastness of modern militarized destruction, the old sublime obscenely updated by the US Air Force's display of 'Shock and Awe'. The ruins of Mosul or Idlib are emblems of catastrophic mass murder, not aesthetic pleasure.

But the most evocative modern ruins are those of institutions that once promised social transformation, and whose mouldering remains now signal melancholic failure. Vast, radial penitentiaries, built by idealistic evangelists and modernizers who believed that prisoners could be reformed partly by the influence of architectural design, are now either overcrowded and crumbling, or standing empty and falling into ruin. The model for this prison plan, replicated around the world, was the Eastern State Penitentiary, opened in Pennsylvania by Quaker reformers in 1829 and finally closed in 1970. It survives only as a cult ruin for atrocity tourism and Halloween parties. The same fate befell the monster asylums built from the 1850s – one for each county in England, one for each state in America – and closed down from the 1960s onward. Their corridor plans promised the treatment and reintegration of the insane, but they instead became cruel and isolating, dystopian 'total institutions' that devoured individuals and created hopeless dependants.

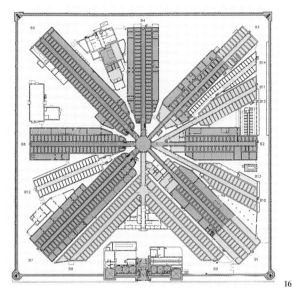

16

17

14. [opposite above] Spiral staircase, Western State Asylum, West Virginia, USA, opened in 1828 and abandoned on closure in 2003.

15. [opposite below] Floorplan and sketch for an asylum for 'Worthy Aged and Decayed Freemasons' in Croydon, UK, 1852.

16. The rational plan for the Eastern State Penitentiary in Philadelphia, crowded by additional structures at the time it closed in 1971.

17. The derelict Denbigh Asylum in Wales, UK, which housed patients from 1848 until its closure in 1995.

These survivals stand as totemic ruins on the edges of towns, magnets for urban 'place-hackers'. There is even a whole sub-genre of photography of abandoned and ruined asylums, and they are regularly used as horror film locations.

The capital city of this trend in 'ruin porn' is Detroit, Michigan. An early centre for the car industry, which employed hundreds of thousands of people, before the 1929 economic crash Detroit had built vast tracts of housing estates and a downtown of Art Deco skyscrapers. From the 1930s, car firms started to disperse to smaller factories, partly to break the power of unionized labour. Automation and globalization finished off these gigantic plants, mostly by the early 1970s. Detroit was also a centre for African Americans escaping the segregated South, and with heightened racial tensions, combined from the 1970s with drugs flooding the inner cities and corruption in city government, large sections of the city began falling into ruin. It became an emblem of the failure of industrial modernity.

The city features heavily in the documentarian Camilo José Vergara's photobook *American Ruins* (1999); he had previously proposed a 'ruins preserve' in downtown Detroit, as though urban decay had to be fixed for aesthetic contemplation for all time. French photographers Yves Marchand and Romain Meffre produced a book of large-format pictures, *The Ruins of Detroit* (2008), which worked through abandoned warehouses, the famous ruin of Michigan Central Station (itself modelled on a classical ruin), and abandoned cinemas, ballrooms, grand mansions and tract housing. Andrew Moore followed up in *Detroit Disassembled* (2009), rushing to capture the ruins before they were finally cleared away or collapsed under their own weight. Most of these images, like Wordsworth's 'Tintern Abbey', erase the people who continue to live amid the ruins. Inevitably, Detroit has also been a setting for horror films, the ruins put to work in, for instance, David Robert Mitchell's *It Follows* (2013).

The ruin, then, is the defining shape of the built Gothic. It shares its melancholic sensibility with the literary notion of the fragment, to which we now turn.

Everything comes to nothing, everything perishes, everything passes, only the world remains, only time endures.

18. Ruin of the 1893 William Livingstone House in Brush Park, Detroit, photographed by Yves Marchand and Romain Meffre for *Ruins of Detroit* in 2006. The house has since been demolished.
19. Maika Monroe as Jay in the Detroit-set horror film *It Follows* (David Robert Mitchell, 2014).

18

19

Fragment

The Gothic Revival in architecture tends towards ruin and ruination; in literature, the Gothic favours the fragment. The antiquarians of the eighteenth century rooted around in the rubble, prospected among graves and sought clues in mouldering manuscripts, spinning elaborate theories about the enigmatic past. Travellers on the Grand Tour visited the famous fragments of classical sculpture in Athens or Rome or stood in the courtyard of the Uffizi Gallery and contemplated the surviving pieces of the Colossus of Constantine, the hand pointing skyward, the giant foot, the severed head. This was a statue built in imperial triumph and brought low, but rescued for artistic contemplation. There was a whole programme for the aesthetic study and imitation of classical fragments, and the Torso of Belvedere, rediscovered in Italy in 1430 and much admired by Michelangelo, became a symbol for art itself.

Soon enough, wealthy European travellers began bringing ancient stone fragments home. Lord Elgin hurriedly collected up fallen fragments of the Parthenon frieze in Athens, then actively encouraged his agents to saw off more pieces from the ruined building itself. When he finally displayed them in London in 1807, the fragments had a sensational cultural effect.

In 1765, Bishop Thomas Percy published *Reliques of Ancient English Poetry*, which gathered together what he saw as the last surviving fragments of 'the ancient Bards...of Celtic or Gothic race' that had barely survived into the medieval period. These northern ballads came from 'the same common Teutonic stock' and shared 'the same Gothic language', in which they communicated 'a romantic wildness' that modern English civilization had now lost.

He was inspired by the fragmentary *Poems of Ossian*, published by the Scottish antiquarian James Macpherson to great enthusiasm in 1762. These short, enigmatic poetic pieces were translations of the 'lost' Gaelic poet Ossian, all bleak, blasted landscapes and lonely graves where the ghosts of fallen Scottish clansmen 'shine' at night 'like a moon-beam from a cloud'. The broken bardic pieces of a once fiercely independent nation, they spoke to Scots suffering

'If you want to see me whole, you have to sew me together yourself,' she says.

defeat and dispossession by the English, who had suppressed the Scottish rebellion at Culloden in 1745. In the following year, Macpherson published his rediscovery of a long poem by Ossian, *Fingal*. It turned out that Ossian was largely an invention, a Homeric figure who could unite disparate fragments of a culture under one identity. Macpherson was not quite perpetrating a hoax, but an act of salvation for fragments that he had hunted out in obscure parts of the Highlands and creatively reunified. Only a few years later, in 1770, the young teenage poet Thomas Chatterton died by suicide after the revelation that he had fabricated a medieval poet and monk, 'Thomas Rowley', and forged his purported manuscripts. Chatterton became one of the defining emblems of the doomed poet, and the 'fragmentary manner' is seen as one of the key elements of Romanticism. As the German Romantic philosopher Friedrich Schlegel wrote in his own collection of fragments and epigrams: 'Many of the works of the ancients have become fragments. Many modern works are fragments as soon as they are written.'

1. [opposite] *Two Studies of the Belvedere Torso*, an eighteenth-century sketch by Joseph Highmore.

The fragment device was used most influentially in 1773, when the siblings John and Anna Aikin published the essay 'On the Pleasure Derived from Objects of Terror' along with a squib of a Gothic terror tale, 'Sir Bertrand: A Fragment', meant to illustrate the key idea or sensation of 'terror'. In a series of breathless, disconnected scenes, the knight Sir Bertrand is lost and overtaken by nightfall on a blasted heath, finds his way to 'a large antique mansion', and enters into its pitch dark, his 'blood chilled'. He follows a spectral blue flame that casts a paradoxical 'dismal gleam' up ever higher stairs, a cold dead hand falling on his, to a vault where a spectral armoured defender vanishes at the swipe of a sword and allows passage into a large apartment, where an open coffin, flanked by menacing Moorish statues, reveals the corpse of a woman in a black veil who sits up suddenly and compels a kiss from Sir Bertrand, at which point the house collapses yet somehow transforms into a sumptuous banqueting suite. The fragment ends:

> After the banquet was finished, all retired but the lady, who, leading back the knight to the sofa, addressed him with these words: ----------- -- --

to face page 288.

2

In a few short pages, the Aikins build the generic elements of the Gothic Romance: its heightened tone, its fever pitch, its topography of ruins and spatial labyrinths, its sacrifice of coherence for intensity and dreamlike elaboration. 'Sir Bertrand' hurls itself forward, barely in control of its own disorderly desires – but also breaks off at the impossible prospect of a woman about to talk. The dash, the broken-off sentence, hint at the unspeakable. Like the ruin, the fragment compels the imagination to complete it – and the blank space beyond the dash is often more terrifying than any words could be.

'Sir Bertrand' was intended to illustrate the Aikins's rather dry exposition of the sublime, that mix of terror with pleasure theorized by Edmund Burke in his book *A Philosophical Enquiry into the Sublime and Beautiful* (1757), an important touchstone for the development of the Gothic. But it became very influential in Gothic and Romantic literature. There were direct imitations, as in Mary Hays's 'A Fragment' (1793) or Nathan Drake's 'Montmorenci: A Fragment' (1798). The young William Wordsworth spent much energy

2. An engraving of one of the pages of the fifteenth-century manuscript faked by the poet and forger Thomas Chatterton, with a poem by 'William Canynge'.
3. Henry Wallace, *The Death of Chatterton*, c. 1856.
4. Yinka Shonibare, *Fake Death Picture (The Death of Chatterton – Henry Wallace)*, 2011.

trying to emulate it, in poems that survive only as fragments. His 'Gothic Tale' features a castle on a precipice in moonlight, the walls 'a stony heap', and a man led through the ruins down perilous steps to a dungeon to awful sights 'that obey the dead, or phantoms of a dream'. The poem breaks off there, aghast. Samuel Taylor Coleridge's 'Christabel' also borrows from 'Sir Bertrand', despite Coleridge's public disapproval of terror novels. 'Christabel' is one of his many broken-backed, fragmentary, incomplete poems, first published alongside perhaps the most famous literary fragment of all, 'Kubla Khan', the opium-dream poem left incomplete by the arrival of the mundane, legendary 'man from Porlock' at Coleridge's front door. 'Christabel', with the arrival at night, through a dark wood to a tumbledown castle, and the encounter with another undead, entrancing woman, is cut from the same cloth as the Aikins's story.

Coleridge was encouraged to publish 'Christabel' and 'Kubla Khan' by Lord Byron, another writer who embraced the fragmentary and incomplete. Famously, the gathering of the circles of Byron and Shelley at the Villa Diodati in 1816, where they read the collection of German ghost stories *Tales of the Dead* (translated into French) and began a competition to emulate them, produced the bones of Mary Shelley's *Frankenstein* and Byron's doctor William Polidori's 'The Vampyre'. Polidori's tale, published in 1819, was actually an elaboration of Byron's abandoned fragment from that competition, 'Augustus Darvell', about a man who dies from a wasting disease and is buried in the ruins of an old Turkish cemetery in Smyrna, having commanded his companion to conceal all knowledge of his death. He is set to return, as in the vampire legends of Greece that fascinated Byron. The fragment ends, typically, with a broken-off sentence: 'Between astonishment and grief I was tearless –'. Byron consented to publish the fragment in 1819, in part to try to reclaim the source of 'The Vampyre', which was widely presumed to be a true confession of his scandalous life as a libertine. Our compulsion to complete the story is such that small fragments can produce whole Gothic subcultures.

Mary Shelley's *Frankenstein* (1818), a story told in criss-crossing, fragmentary testimonies, has inspired retellings that emphasize its mosaic-like structure. Shelley Jackson's *The Patchwork Girl* (1995) is a hypertext fiction that exists only on a computer screen, told in short, disconnected sections of prose navigated by clicking on sections of a female body loosely stitched together.

5

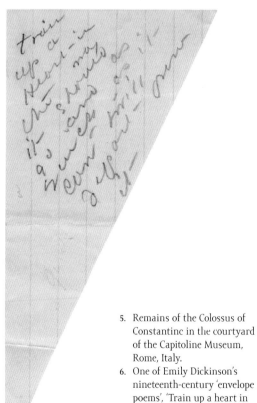

6

5. Remains of the Colossus of Constantine in the courtyard of the Capitoline Museum, Rome, Italy.
6. One of Emily Dickinson's nineteenth-century 'envelope poems', 'Train up a heart in the way'.
7. William Orme, mezzotint of *Sir Bertrand in the Haunted Castle*, 1798.

The fragments begin to tell the unspoken history of the creature's female companion, abandoned and 'torn apart' by Victor in utter disgust. 'If you want to see me whole, you have to sew me together yourself,' she says. In 2003, Jackson began work on *SKIN*, a narrative told in fragmentary phrases tattooed across the bodies of volunteers. Tactics like this allow silenced 'monsters' a voice in the opened cracks of language: the 'found' fragments of Jordy Rosenberg's *Confessions of the Fox* (2018), for instance, give both voice and privacy to London's eighteenth-century folk hero Jack Sheppard, presented by Rosenberg as an enigmatic transgender man, variously called 'Daemon. Sphinx. Hybrid. Scitha, man-horse, deep-water Kraken, Monster-flower' by his lover, Edgeworth Bess.

Stories and texts break off; detached fragments travel to wildly different destinations. Thus, the Gothic spread through Europe. In the 1740s, Edward Young's long, devout *Night Thoughts*, which includes meditations over the grave of a dead girl, was picked up, shortened, revised and fragmented into ever-freer translations across France, Germany and beyond, sparking a craze for 'Graveyard Poetry'. In return, the German ballad 'Lenore' (1796), by Gottfried August Bürger, about a girl whose lover returns from war an animated corpse, was also freely translated across Europe. Germany's great Romantic writer J. W. Goethe read *The Castle of Otranto* so often his copy had to be rebound, while Ann Radcliffe's 'explained supernatural' was clearly influenced by Friedrich von Schiller's *Schauerroman* ('shudder-novel') *The Ghost-Seer* (1789), which introduced the idea of a shocking conjuration of the dead only to explain it as a confidence trick. Meanwhile, the blasphemous transgressions of Matthew Lewis's *The Monk* (1796) prompted the Marquis de Sade, then imprisoned, to write of the revolutionary nature of Gothic sex and violence. *The Monk* had already incorporated into its ragged structure the fragment of a tale from Germany called 'The Bleeding Nun', and was itself freely translated, its startling incidents cut up and re-edited into an ever-wilder international composite.

The early novels of the French writer Honoré de Balzac were saturated with occult, supernatural and Gothic tropes; like Victor Hugo, he contributed to the school of melodramatic, shocking fiction condemned in the 1820s for its *frénétique* style. The quintessential French decadent Charles Baudelaire expended significant energy translating the American horror stories of Edgar Allan Poe, and even later,

7

THE MONK,

A Romance;

IN WHICH IS DEPICTED THE

Wonderful Adventures of Ambrosio,

FRIAR OF THE ORDER OF CAPUCHINS,

WHO WAS DIVERTED FROM THE TRACK OF VIRTUE BY THE

Artifices of a Female Demon,

That entered his Monastery disguised as a Novice, and after seducing
him from his

VOW OF CELIBACY,

PRESENTED HIM WITH

A Branch of Enchanted Myrtle,

TO OBTAIN THE PERSON OF THE BEAUTIFUL

Antonia of Madrid;

HOW HE WAS

DISCOVERED IN HER CHAMBER

BY

HER MOTHER, WHOM HE MURDERED,

To keep his Crime a Secret;

And the Particulars of the Means by which he caused the

Body of Antonia

To be conveyed in a Sleep to the

DREARY VAULTS OF HIS OWN CONVENT,

WHERE HE

ACCOMPLISHED HIS WICKED MACHINATIONS

On the Innocent Virgin, whom he then

ASSASSINATES WITH A DAGGER,

PRESENTED HIM BY HIS ATTENDANT FIEND,

Who afterward Betrays him to the

Judges of the Inquisition,

In the Dungeons of which he is Confined, and suffers Tortures;
and how, to Escape from thence, he Assigns over his

Soul and Body to the Devil,

Who Deceives him, and Inflicts a

MOST IGNOMINIOUS DEATH.

LONDON:
PRINTED AND PUBLISHED BY W. MASON,
21, CLERKENWELL GREEN.
SIXPENCE.

See p. 35.

8. Frontispiece to an 1818 edition of
   The Monk, the scandalous Gothic novel
   by Matthew Lewis.
9. A fragment of marble relief from the first
   century AD in New York's Metropolitan
   Museum of Art, USA.
10. Emily Dickinson, 'envelope poem',
   'One note from one Bird'.

the Irish-Greek-American writer Lafcadio Hearn collected stories of zombies in the Caribbean, voodoo in New Orleans, and vengeful spirits in Japan and China. Masaki Kobayashi's *Kwaidan* (1965), an influential horror-anthology film, adapts Hearn's English transpositions of Japanese folktales for Japanese screens. The fragmented, protean shape of the Gothic has been there from the beginning. Like the bleeding nun, the vampire or the zombie, these fragments spread across the planet in an endless play of combined and re-combined stories, staying recognizable yet transforming with every cultural shift.

Many central Gothic novels are composed of fragments – or, like fake ruins, *pretend* to be fragments. Mary Shelley's *Frankenstein*, Emily Brontë's *Wuthering Heights*, Robert Louis Stevenson's *The Strange Case of Dr Jekyll and Mr Hyde* and Bram Stoker's *Dracula* are all composed of interlocking, fragmentary testimonies. No one character holds the complete truth, and the horror leaks from the gaps in between. As Jonathan Harker observes at the end of *Dracula*, in 'the mass of material of which the record is composed, there is hardly one authentic document! nothing but a mass of type-writing'. Arthur Machen's nasty, transgressive story, 'The Great God Pan' (1895) uses this strategy to skate very close to speaking the unspeakable. In fragmentary texts, the reader glimpses a deadly she-devil, born of some obscure congress with the old pagan god Pan. Helen, it seems, drives men to sexual ecstasy and suicide in the back-streets of scandal-ridden late Victorian London. The last section is even called 'The Fragments', broken-off testimonies retrieved from a dead man's notes scrawled 'in Latin, much abbreviated', the manuscript 'only deciphered with great difficulty, and some of the words have up to the present time evaded all the efforts of the expert employed'. This story, condemned upon publication as 'a nightmare incoherence of sex' by one alarmed reviewer, had a direct influence on how H. P. Lovecraft composed 'The Call of Cthulhu' (1926), in which the tentacular, Medusoid god is approached through a patchwork of testimonies and reports that break off when they reach the limits of what sanity can bear. The device has persisted into the twenty-first century, in the elliptical textual fragments of China Miéville's story 'Reports of Certain Events in London' (2005), which purports to be the broken remnants of testimonies about phantom 'trap' streets that appear and disappear in the city, delivered anonymously through the author's letterbox.

The tales in the Edwardian writer M. R. James's *Ghost Stories of an Antiquary* (1904) and its sequel, written as Christmas entertainment for his academic friends, turn on bluffly complacent old dons who turn up fragmentary or lost manuscripts, old etchings or buried antiquities best left where they're found. But it is his contemporary Henry James who began to use the broken-off sentence, the dash, as his signature device, from his late unnerving ghost stories in the 1890s until his final, unfinished tale, *The Sense of the Past* (published the year after his death, in 1917). *The Turn of the Screw* (1898), which was to become an opera by Benjamin Britten and Myfanwy Piper

Many of the works of the ancients have become fragments. Many modern works are fragments as soon as they are written.

(1954), several films (*The Innocents*, 1961; *The Turning*, 2020) and a Netflix show, *The Haunting of Bly Manor* (2020), is a notoriously indeterminate Gothic story, leaving the reader forever unsure if the young governess at its centre is seeing ghosts that menace the young children in her charge, or projecting spectral appearances from the hidden springs of her own mental pathology. 'The story *won't* tell', warns the frame narrator, 'not in any literal vulgar way'. Inside the frame narrative, the status of the haunting at Bly pivots on incomplete exclamations, narrative ellipses and unfinished exchanges – the dialogue full of dashes that actively maintain the ambiguity. The mounting threat of these malignant ghosts – if that is what they are – ends with the death of the young boy, Miles. The boy's last exclamation before he dies – of fright or suffocation, it's not clear – is 'Peter Quint – you devil'. Either he sees the ghost (you *devil*) or he berates the governess for her absurdity (*you* devil), and the loose syntax of the dash means that one can never quite decide which. An early reader of James's story, his near neighbour H. G. Wells, was so enraged by this indeterminacy that he went around to James's house to demand an explanation, a means of closing up these loose sutures that make the text bleed meaning.

The American writer Emily Dickinson typically composed her short, spare poem-fragments using only dashes as punctuation – some posthumous editors have found as many as sixteen variants in her manuscripts, of different lengths, heights and jaunty angles. Her Gothic fragments tell minimal tales of terror about sacred groves, haunted houses, deathbed scenes and the smothered agony of her experience as a woman in straight-laced New England. The critic Daneen Wardrop talks of Dickinson's 'Gothic gapping' leaving readers 'dangling in the filaments of dashes', as evident in, for example, 'Poem #407', sometimes known as 'One need not be a Chamber to be Haunted'. Between the dashes stalk narrative stubs of the Gothic iconography of abbeys and ruins, this now familiar repertory of the external forms compared to inner, subjective states of self-haunted agony: agony: 'Far safer, through an Abbey gallop...Than unarmed, one's a'self encounter – / In lonesome Place –'.

And all the time, the dashes distend the lines, stretching the possible meanings, inserting visual passages or literal spatial corridors between the stubs. They open wounds that for decades her posthumous editors tried to stitch up and transform into conventional grammar. But the poem's final, brusque line, 'Or More –', suggests incalculable spectres that wait in the space at the end of the line, the terrors that tarry in the blank whiteness at the bottom of the page, where the fragment breaks off at its limit.

11. [opposite] Fragments of a Roman fresco from the first century AD in the Getty Museum, Los Angeles, USA.

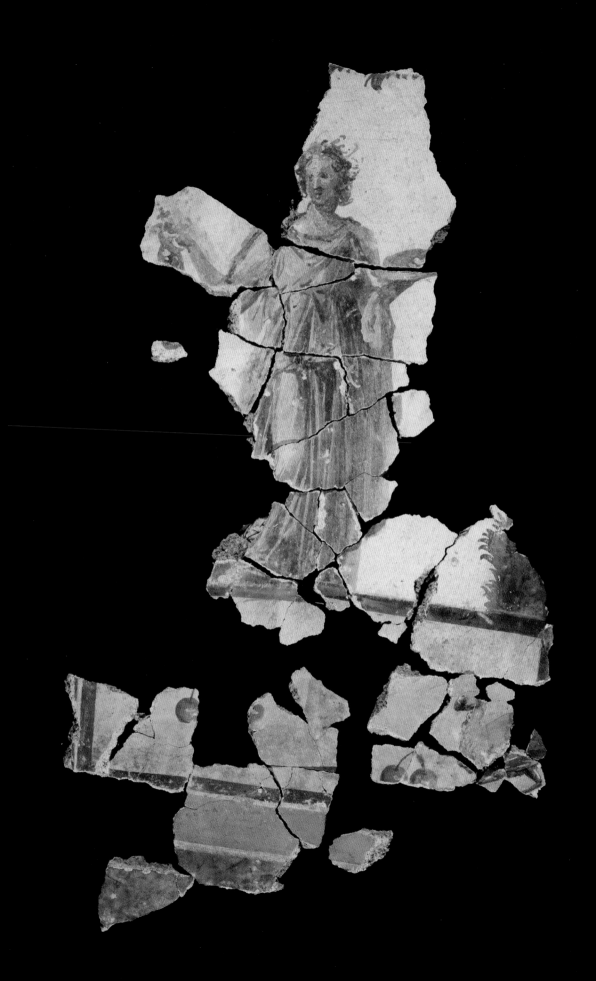

Labyrinth

The Gothic breaks off and fragments, but it also envelops, suffocates and enfolds. It lures you in, then slams the heavy door behind you. One persistent device from the very beginning of the Gothic romance is the secret or winding passage, the bewildering network of rooms, hallways and dark corridors that can build out further into a nightmare city of tangled streets. These spaces unfold in Gothic tales with the logic of dreams, impossibly improvising an architecture that disobeys every law of geometry. In Horace Walpole's *The Castle of Otranto* (1764), the menaced couple Theodore and Isabella evade tyranny using dungeons and tunnels and a 'labyrinth of caverns' full of 'secret recesses' that open into a forest (another kind of maze) outside the walls of the castle. In Ann Radcliffe's *The Mysteries of Udolpho* (1794), Emily, kept captive by the dastardly Montoni, takes an extended candlelit journey at night through the castle's vaulted galleries, spiral staircases, ruined crypts and twisting passages, which exteriorize her confounded psychic state. The elaboration of multiple plotlines and perspectives, the lengthy digressions and inserted parallel stories make long novels like Matthew Lewis's *The Monk* (1796) or Charles Maturin's *Melmoth the Wanderer* (1820) take on the shape of a labyrinth. It is a device that persists all the way up to Mark Danieleweski's *House of Leaves* (2000), a bewildering exploration of a vast labyrinth that impossibly opens inside a small domestic house. The labyrinth remains a defining Gothic trope.

2

Many cultures have used the symbol of the labyrinth, or have actually built them for ritualistic purposes, from the ancient Egyptians at Fayoum to the man in the maze of the Tohono O'odham Nation; and from the ancient Chinese *Migong* (Perplexing Buildings), built in imperial compounds and gardens, to the formal hedge maze laid out at Hampton Court Palace by King William III in 1690. But the most influential labyrinth story is the ancient Minoan myth of the labyrinth built by King Minos to house the monstrous spawn of his wife, Pasiphae, and a bull: the Minotaur. The ingenious Dedalus builds a labyrinth to confine the beast and doom the tribute of young Greeks sent into the maze every seven years, sacrificed to the Minotaur's hunger in the twisting dark. Theseus, one such young man, is secretly aided by Ariadne, Minos's daughter, and kills the monster. She leaves him a sword and a ball of thread to find his way out once the deed is done. Having sailed away, Theseus and his men perform a ritual dance that, in a stylized way, repeats the pattern of the labyrinth. All the way down to the 'turf mazes' that are found etched into the ground across Britain, these spaces are associated with rituals and dances of commemoration.

The story of the Minotaur and the labyrinth is told many times in classical literature, not least by Ovid in *The Metamorphoses*, and by Virgil in the opening to Book VI of *The Aeneid*, the descent into the Underworld. It has echoed down the millennia, but truly came alive again in 1900, when the British

1. [opposite] Danny Lloyd as Danny Torrance in the corridors of the Overlook Hotel, *The Shining* (Stanley Kubrick, 1980).
2. A Cretan coin depicting the labyrinth of Knossos.

3

4

archaeologist Arthur Evans, excavating at Knossos in Crete, claimed to have found the Palace of Minos, a vast building complex with over 300 chambers that he declared was the legendary labyrinth itself. Evans had in fact imposed a mazy structure on the ruins he uncovered, building up walls with concrete and confidently giving chambers grand names that actualized elements of the myth. Back in England, Evans built a vast country house at Youlbury, also designed as a labyrinth. The cultural effect of his six-volume study *The Palace of Minos*, completed in 1935, was massive. Picasso drew endless variations on the Minotaur throughout the 1930s, an emblem of male sexual virility trapped in the maze of its own desire. The French Surrealists published thirteen issues of their journal *Minotaure* (1933–39), embracing this impossible chimera of man and beast. Man Ray's disturbing photograph *Minotaur* (1934) is an image of a naked female torso, the arms bent to echo bullish male horns, articulating the sexual monstrosity of this hybrid creature that had led the philosopher Michel Foucault to call the labyrinth 'the place of modern perversity'.

The influence of the discoveries at Knossos continued throughout the twentieth century, returning in Francis Bacon's studies of bulls, powerful symbols of brutish male sexual aggression. In Stanley Kubrick's film of Stephen King's novel *The Shining* (1980), set in the labyrinth of the Overlook Hotel, the monstrous father Jack Torrance is constantly associated with images of the Minotaur; his son, Danny, must confound and kill him to survive, which he does by trapping the monster in the hedge maze outside.

Historians sometimes distinguish between a labyrinth, which is *unicursal* – that is, with only one route to the centre, its course folded and confounding yet easy to follow if patient – and the maze, which is *multicursal* – a design that introduces multiple routes, tricks and dead ends and which is designed to bewilder or entertain. The labyrinth houses the aggressive Minotaur, while Edmund Burke, in one of the foundational works of the Gothic theory of terror, called the female body 'a deceitful maze'. These distinctions are sometimes useful, but not always easy to sustain.

Greek pottery frequently portrayed Theseus slaying the Minotaur, and labyrinths were also used to represent the powerful defences of legendary cities like Troy. Roman literature retold the myth, and the symbol

Multicursal and unbounded, where each and every tunnel branches and branches again.

3. An Akimel O'odham (Pima) labyrinth from Southwest America, 1910.
4. Artist Mark Wallinger designed a labyrinth for each of the 270 stations in the London Underground system. This is *Labyrinth #142/270, Bank*, 2013.
5. Mark Wallinger, *#59/270, Regent's Park*, in Regent's Park station.
6. Man Ray, *Minotaur*, 1933.

5

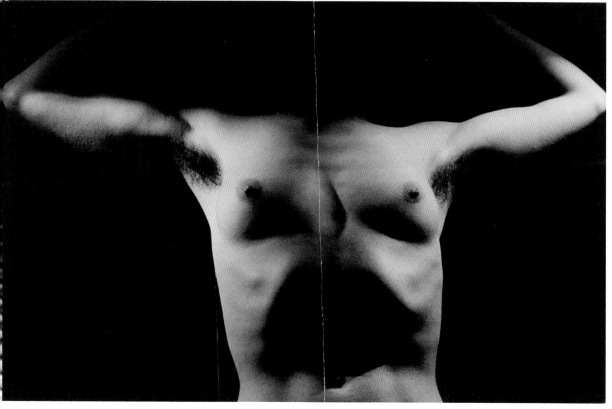

6

7

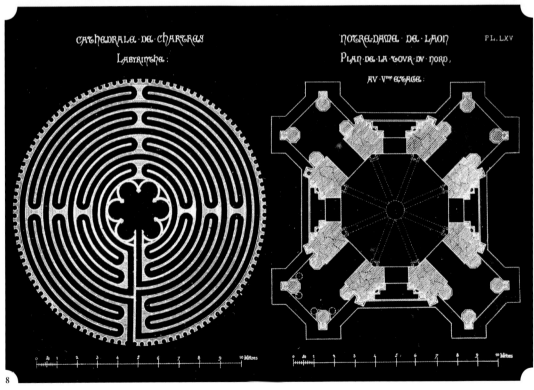

8

of the labyrinth was also sometimes used at doorways and thresholds to confound intruders. It was picked up in early Christian art, where the story of Theseus in the labyrinth could be transposed to Christ and the devil, or the struggle of the pilgrim to stay on the one true path of faith. Early Christian churches started to lay out images of labyrinths on their floors, often with the devilish Minotaur at the centre, showing how pagan stories could be transposed. The earliest survives from AD 324. As a text from the early Christian writer Gregory of Nyssa explains: 'Those who wander, caught in a labyrinth, do not know how to find the way out; but if they meet someone who knows this maze well, they undertake to follow him to the end, through the complicated and misleading turns of the edifice.'

The earliest extant monastic manuscripts to include labyrinth designs date from the eighth century, but it is a peculiarity of northern France that the vast Gothic cathedrals built in the thirteenth century often had labyrinths embedded in their stone floors. The cathedral at Chartres (rebuilt very quickly after a fire, from 1194 to 1221) has the largest and most famous of these labyrinths, situated inside the western entrance. At thirteen metres across, it fills the whole width of the nave. It is circular (expressing the perfection of God's design), with eleven circular layers or courses, and it echoes very precisely the shape and size of the stained-glass window opposite. But while that depicts Christ and his disciples, for centuries the labyrinth had a raised brass plaque at the centre that depicted the Minotaur (it was destroyed during the French Revolution).

The Chartres labyrinth plays an important symbolic role in the Gothic architecture of the cathedral. Worshippers enter at the west door from the mundane world beyond, a maze of sin, and head east, towards the holy altar, towards purity and transcendence. Labyrinths are sometimes called *Chemins de Jerusalem*, tracing out the twists and turns of the difficult pilgrimage to the holy city, the aim of every pious medieval Christian, many of whom could not make the arduous physical journey and so used symbolic means of pilgrimage. On Easter Sunday, the labyrinth was used to act out Jesus's harrowing of hell, between his death on the Cross and his resurrection. In a darkened church, the priest, carrying a candle, would lead the choir through the labyrinth and back towards the holy sanctum, the passage out of hell and towards union with God.

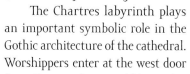

Those who wander, caught in a labyrinth, do not know how to find the way out.

7. Mike Nelson's immersive installation, *The Coral Reef*, 2000.
8. Floorplan of the labyrinth in the nave of Chartres Cathedral, France.
9. The Chartres Cathedral labyrinth.

Yet these labyrinths are evidently pagan remainders, which perhaps explains why many were eventually destroyed by Church authorities worried by associations they could not control. Isn't the circular labyrinth much like the magic circle drawn in chalk, from which the magus invokes his demons? Labyrinths are enigmatic, like the turf mazes in England that seem to have some association with monasteries nearby, perhaps used as ritual pathways of penance. No one is quite confident in their explanation for the figures who were trapped in the octagonal labyrinth once laid out in the Gothic Cathedral in Reims, for example: perhaps the four masters who built the Gothic masterpiece over the course of the thirteenth century? But who was the figure at the centre of the folded paths? The whole thing was erased in 1779, as though no longer bearable to the Church authorities. The sense that church labyrinths are puzzles, with hidden clues or messages to be worked out, also drives their continued use in bestsellers of historical fiction like Umberto Eco's *The Name of the Rose* (1980) or Kate Mosse's novel about Chartres, *Labyrinth* (2005). In France, the complex legacies of *patrimoine* ('heritage') are symbolized in the labyrinth logo used to mark a *Monument Historique*.

A chimera of horns and hoofs that stands at the centre of the labyrinth, doling out punishment to every wannabe Theseus.

10

Multicursal mazes disturb us because inside them our agency must submit to a hidden power, which directs our steps for capricious sport. The Victorian scientist John Lubbock started to send ants through mazes in the 1880s to test their distributed memory and intelligence. The rat mazes first used by Willard Small at Clark University in 1901 were actually initially modelled on the Hampton Court maze, as if to reinforce the sense that these designs have shed some of their sacred meanings to become laboratories.

Modern installation artists such as Mike Nelson plunge the visitor into enclosed labyrinthine spaces, a taut folding of plywood corridors, abandoned rooms and a wilderness of doors that evoke feelings of dread and mounting panic as one searches for the way out. A little more benignly, in 2014 the artist Mark Wallinger produced 270 unique labyrinth designs on small square enamel plaques, one for each station of the London Underground. They are placed at different points in each station, prompting a hunt to find them. Some overtly echo their locale: a fortress style for Bank, more fluid lines for watery Embankment.

10. *Pan's Labyrinth* (Guillermo del Toro, 2006).
11. [opposite above] Jason Rohrer's experimental video game *Passage* (2007).
12. [opposite below] The dark corridors of the seminal video game *DOOM* (1993).

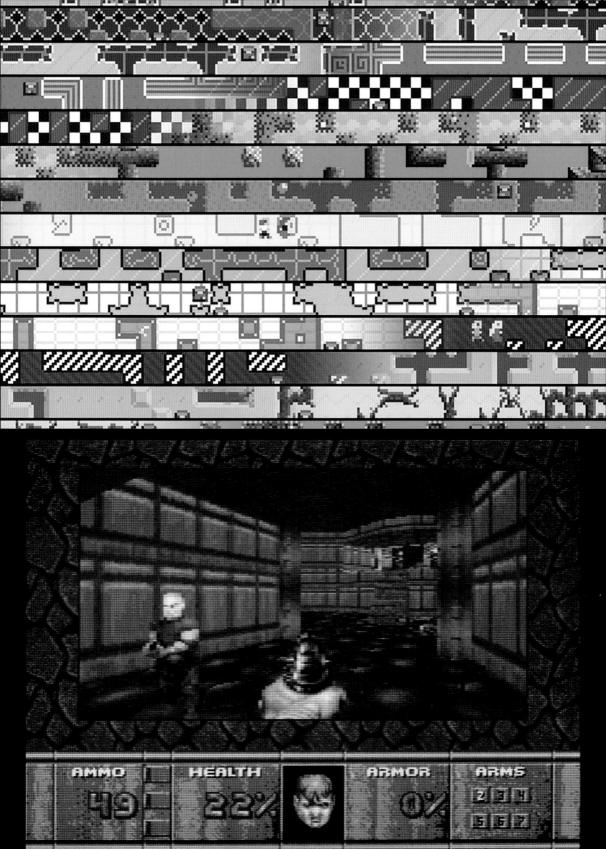

AMMO 49   HEALTH 22%   ARMOR 0%   ARMS 2 3 4 5 6 7

'London is undoubtedly a labyrinth for those who live and work in it: we move, for the most part, along predetermined pathways,' Will Self reflects on Wallinger's intervention. Self contrasts this with the experience of tourists, for whom the Underground becomes a bewildering maze, 'multicursal and unbounded, where each and every tunnel branches and branches again'. The straight lines of Harry Beck's famous topological map of the Underground always verge on merging with the actual topographical chaos of the city above.

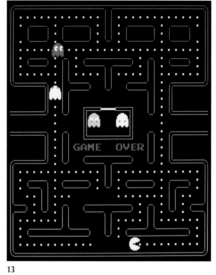

But the contemporary space most imbued with the Gothic sensibility of the maze is not real, but virtual: the video game. In 1980, the Japanese arcade game Pac-Man used a simple top-down view of a square maze where the player is chased by a stylized version of the *gaki* (hungry ghosts in the Buddhist tradition), rendered as cute, bed-sheeted menaces. It was hardly terror-inducing, but that changed with the arrival of more immersive, three-dimensional computer game spaces in the early 1990s. In *Wolfenstein 3D* (1992), *Alone in the Dark* (1992) and especially *DOOM* (1993), the player navigates a complex of corridors, threatened by supernatural enemies that loom out of voids or wait around corners. *DOOM* levels seem at first like mazes, but in fact always hide a single path to the end of the level – providing the player survives the onslaught of demonic beings that appear through a hell-portal in *DOOM*'s setting, a military base on one of the moons of Mars.

The *DOOM* games (sequels appeared in 1994 and 2004) were revolutionary in their exploitation of the maze as a panicky, constricted space where the first-person player encounters a series of demons that steadily escalate in their resistance to the weapons available. The myth endures: the culmination of the game is an encounter with the 'boss', the Minotaur itself, a chimera of horns and hoofs that stands at the centre of the labyrinth, doling out punishment to every wannabe Theseus.

Like *DOOM*, the 'survival horror' genre – a term coined by designer Shinji Mikami in 1996 – favoured a labyrinthine structure. It was first associated with the *Resident Evil* franchise of games and films,

which featured another mazy corporate complex, this time overrun by zombies. In the early explosion of personal console gaming, the maze married limited processing power with the menacing form of a labyrinth encountered hallway by hallway, room by room. It has continued with games like *Passage* (2007) and *The Path* (2009). As computer processing power has increased, the multicursal possibilities have increased prodigiously, exploding the labyrinth. But since constriction and containment are part of the essential experience of anxiety (a term derived from the feeling of constricted breath), immersion in a maze remains a quintessential game design, the labyrinth persisting and mutating across media.

13. The fixed maze of the arcade game *Pac-Man* (1980).
14. [opposite] Labyrinth in the Silos Apocalypse, a tenth-century Spanish manuscript.

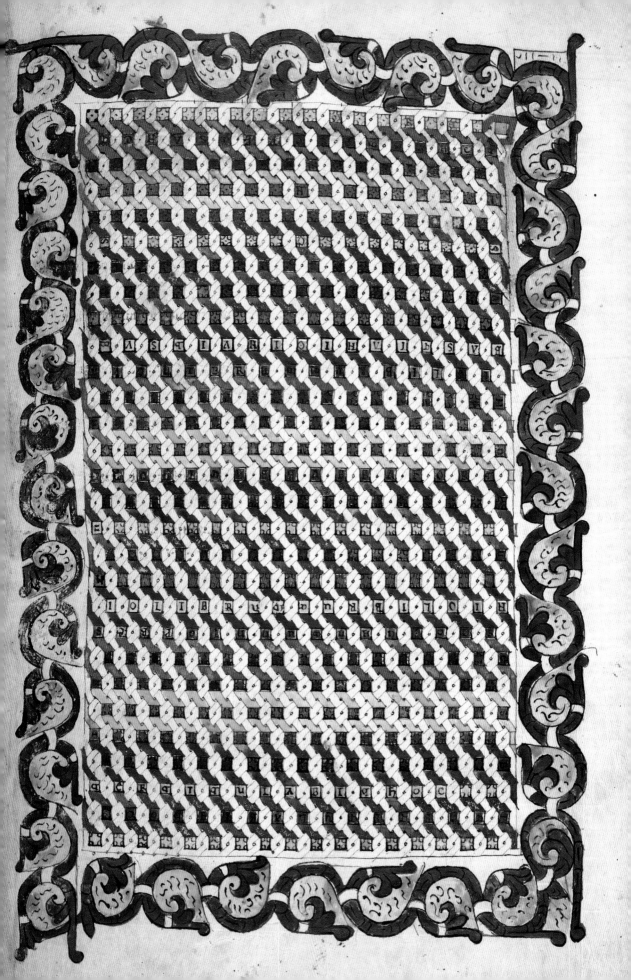

House

Turrets, basements, hungry ghosts: the house is where the Gothic comes home, but only to undermine the very foundations of the concept of 'home'. Domestic Gothic architecture, with its pointed roofs and arched windows, can become dream-like, fragmentary or labyrinthine. Houses can feature as abandoned ruins full of unresolved trauma, or perfectly bland modern spaces nevertheless stuffed with awful secrets or hidden annexes, basements or attics.

The Gothic romance was powered by hundreds of 'terror novels' that began pouring from the presses in the 1790s. The Gothic Revival in architecture had begun thirty years earlier, but these intertwined in the lives of two very strange, scandalous gentlemen, who each used the shape of the Gothic in language and built form to express a fugitive, transgressive identity.

Two Queer Houses

Horace Walpole published *The Castle of Otranto* in 1764, first as a fake found manuscript and then under his own name. He wrote to his friend William Cole of its origins in a dream, 'of which, all I remember was, that I had thought myself in an ancient castle (a very natural dream for a head filled like mine with Gothic story), and that on the uppermost banister of a great staircase I saw a gigantic hand in armour. In that evening, I sat down, and began to write.' Walpole had the dream in the bedchamber of his house in Strawberry Hill, which he had spent the last seventeen years turning into a miniature Gothic castle. It was so famous by the 1780s that he wrote a guidebook, *A Description of the Villa of Mr. Horace Walpole*, for the visitors who came from far and wide to view the elegant state rooms and his extensive collection of paintings and artefacts. The guide pointed to certain objects, such as a portrait in the long gallery, which had featured in *Otranto*: house and text were inextricably linked.

Standing on the lawn below Strawberry Hill, the visitor looks up at a range of Gothic styles that stretch from the eleventh to the fifteenth century. It is a clump of battlements, round and hexagonal towers, pointed finials, lancet and ogee windows and ancient stained glass (much of which was shattered when a nearby gunpowder factory blew up and broke all the windows for miles around). These elements were sourced from England, Germany, France and Spain. It was designed to resemble an organic accumulation of various styles built up over the centuries, but everything is a confection, a fake, like the framing of the trick preface in *The Castle of Otranto*.

1. [opposite] *The Amityville Horror* (Stuart Rosenberg, 1979).

2

On the uppermost banister of a great staircase I saw a gigantic hand in armour.

2. Gothic lantern designed for Horace Walpole's house Strawberry Hill, *c.* 1755.
3. Sketch of the Cabinet in *A Description of the Villa at Strawberry Hill* (*c.* 1784).
4. Gothic chair designed for Horace Walpole by William Hallett, *c.* 1755.
5. William Beckford's Fonthill Abbey, as drawn by John Rutter for *Delineations of Fonthill and its Abbey* (1823).

Walpole had bought the small villa as a pastoral retreat from London, with a picturesque view of the Thames (now entirely obscured). In 1764, it became a full-time retreat from politics. The youngest son of the Whig politician and Britain's first Prime Minister Robert Walpole, he was targeted by his Tory opponents after defending a cousin and ally from the arbitrary exercise of power by the King. For his pains, Walpole was accused of harbouring an 'unsuccessful passion' for this young man and memorably denounced as a 'hermaphroditic horse'. This accusation veered close to sodomy, then a crime punishable by death. Walpole would not have recognized himself as homosexual, but he surrounded himself with the male advisors on his 'Committee of Taste' and had several intense attachments to men, often safely expressed through the passionate letters that he sent in their thousands. He was a man with a vulnerable, dissident identity and disposition. No wonder, given these experiences, that *The Castle of Otranto* was a fevered nightmare centred on the tyranny and violence of a murderous lord. No wonder its author built battlements and towers and lancet windows.

The story of William Beckford would probably be more famous than Walpole, if the wildly grand folly of his giant house, Fonthill Abbey, had not fallen down not once, but three times, leaving only the barest of traces behind. In Beckford's case, his Gothic romance, the Orientalist fantasia *Vathek*, appeared first, written in 1782 when he was twenty-one years old; the Abbey followed at the turn of the century.

Beckford's grandfather had made a vast fortune from slave labour on the twenty sugar plantations that he owned in Jamaica. At his death, he owned 1,200 slaves and held £1.5 million in bank stock. When his son eventually returned from Jamaica to England in the 1760s, he bought a large country estate at Fonthill in Wiltshire and had a house built there in the classical Palladian style. The garden had fashionable Gothic follies, including tunnels, grottos, and some brand-new ruins of pointed arches.

The grandson to this bloody estate, William Beckford, born in 1760, was educated at home and began to write fantastic fictions based on the landscape at Fonthill. His mother had prepared him for a life in national politics; instead, the boy acquired an eccentric education in Paris, Geneva, Venice and elsewhere, developed a passion for the Orientalist fantasies

3

4

5

Drawn by W. Foster. Engraved by John Hoggarth. Ornamented by R. Winterbottom Arch.

INTERIOR OF St MICHAEL'S GALLERY,
Looking across the Octagon into King Edward's Gallery.

of *A Thousand and One Nights*, and at twenty-one inherited a vast fortune that allowed him to indulge any passing fancy. Unlike the elusive Walpole, Beckford declared himself a 'patapouf' – a lover of men – and wrote of his conquests of stable boys and male servants. Later, his daughter spent years being blackmailed over her father's missives.

Beckford published *Vathek*, an extraordinary vision of a Muslim caliph eventually dragged to hell for his life of abandoned bliss and violent transgression, from exile in Switzerland. The follow-up, *Episodes of Vathek*, contained more tales of Vathek and his companions, including the overtly same-sex desires of Prince Alasi. These were read as open confessions: the names Beckford and Vathek became interchangeable. In time, Beckford wandered to Portugal, where he began a relationship with Gregorio Franchi, who was to work as his agent, fixer, lover and procurer of boys. He also saw the sublime Monastery of Santa Maria at Batalha, a huge and imposing Gothic structure. In 1790, on one of his periodic returns to Fonthill, he determined to build himself an Abbey just as imposing and sublime. This Gothic pile was designed to have a tower and spire larger than nearby Salisbury Cathedral, and large portions of it were built using the stones of his father's Palladian house – a symbolic act of patricide.

At its full extent, Fonthill Abbey was an extraordinary mix of Gothic styles, reaching for and sometimes achieving the sublime. John Rutter, in his *Delineations of Fonthill and its Abbey* (1823), called its gallery 'a specimen of the richest combinations, which the genius of Gothic architecture has yet invented' (it is likely Rutter, hired by Beckford, was taking dictation from his boss). Beckford had a Gothic villa built at the end of the south wing, which he moved into in 1807, pulling down the remainder of his father's house; this was then joined by a northern gallery, which he eventually decided to cap with a holy sanctuary (with paintings of the Last Judgment) and a church, where, in dramatic chiaroscuro, his own tomb would lie.

'Some drink to forget their unhappiness,' Beckford wrote. 'I do not drink, I build'. But in the end, even Rutter's fulsome praise of the building admitted that the *ad hoc* extensions meant a 'perpetual change of style'. Of the eighteen bedrooms clustered around the central tower to hold it up, perhaps only three were fit for habitation. The changes of proportion and scale were awkward, offending even Beckford himself. The tower creaked ominously in the wind.

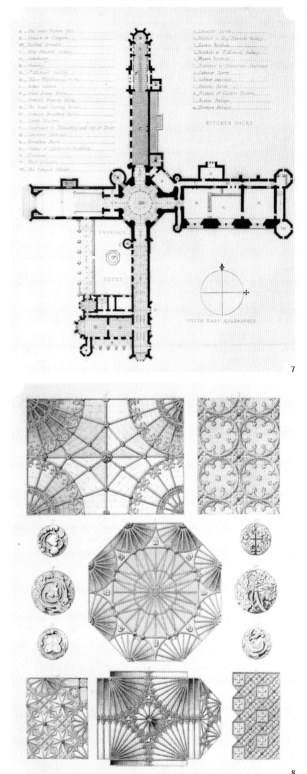

7

8

6. [opposite] John Rutter, the vista of St Michael's Gallery, Fonthill.
7. John Rutter, floorplan of Beckford's grand folly.
8. John Rutter, examples of Fonthill's roof ribbing in the Decorative Gothic style.

Having spent several fortunes, he got bored. His income went into decline in the 1790s as sugar prices fell, and, deeply in debt, by 1822 the only solution was to sell his collections and the house itself. Like Walpole, Beckford prepared a catalogue of his possessions, but this time with an auctioneer. Having carefully fostered the legend of Fonthill Abbey and its association with the orgiastic scenes from *Vathek* with the help of a seven-mile long wall around the estate, Beckford opened its doors to the public for the price of one guinea.

'Fonthill Fever' struck the country. Sixty carriages arrived every day; a special coach service ran from Bath. 'The rage is at its height,' a delighted Beckford wrote. 'They dream only of the Abbey.' But not everyone was impressed: one critic in *The Museum* magazine called 'the whole structure a *solecism*, from beginning to end'. Beckford finally sold the Abbey to the industrialist John Farquhar, who set about breaking up and selling off the collection in 1823. On 21 December 1825, the 300-foot tower toppled, destroying much of the west and south wings as it fell. Legend has it that the foreman of works on the rebuilt tower confessed on his deathbed that he had never built foundations, but pocketed the money instead. Soon, Fonthill was abandoned as a ruin. Twelve years later, when Beckford first went back to survey his destroyed Gothic folly, he declared it 'sublime'.

The memory of Fonthill lived on through the Gothic Revival; it has been suggested that it directly influenced the Gothic styles and grand perspectives of the Houses of Parliament. The shape of that vanished house and Walpole's more modest, domestic fantasia underpin much of what followed.

9

9. An interior set for *The Haunting* (Robert Wise, 1963).

The Haunted House

From Ann Radcliffe's *Mysteries of Udolpho* (1794), via Bly Manor in Henry James's *The Turn of the Screw* (1898) and Shirley Jackson's *The Haunting of Hill House* (1959), to Sarah Waters's *The Little Stranger* (2009) or Michelle Paver's *Wakenhyrst* (2019), the remote, isolated Gothic pile oozes with malignant spirits. But at the same time that Walpole was constructing his rural Gothic fantasia, London was gripped by widely circulated reports of a ghost called Scratching Fanny, who produced loud knocks and bangs and apparitions in a small, three-storey tenement in over-crowded Cock Lane, not far from St Paul's Cathedral. The house drew crowds of spectators – Cock Lane is still visited nightly by the London Ghost Tour bus – and became a test for Enlightenment thinkers, who were dismayed that sceptical rationalism had not yet stamped out base superstition. The satirist William Hogarth mocked the ghost in his engraving *Credulity, Superstition and Fanaticism: A Medley* (1762). But if the Cock Lane ghost was soon ridiculed into silence, the case also signalled that terror had begun to creep up on the present day, into the contemporary family home. The homely, as Sigmund Freud neatly put it, is disrupted by the unhomely, the *unheimlich* or uncanny, 'that class of the frightening which leads back to what is old and long familiar'.

In Victorian fiction, this turn of the Gothic towards uneasy domesticity is illustrated by some of its most enduring classics. In Charlotte Brontë's *Jane Eyre* (1848), awash with uncanny visions and occulted sympathies, the spectral presence at Thornfield Hall is in fact Rochester's first wife, who has been folded into secret rooms on the servants' corridor above. The architecture of the plot comes entirely from Gothic romance, but Bertha Mason is a tortured human trace of colonial violence, not a supernatural presence. She tells her own story in Jean Rhys's spooky prequel, *Wide Sargasso Sea* (1966). In Charlotte Riddell's fiction, such as 'The Old House in Vauxhall Walk' (1882) and *The Uninhabited House* (1875), it is money that haunts everyday London houses. Her stories are full of struggling clerks, lawyers, usurers, businessmen, deeds, invoices and the constant gnawing need for cash to secure respectability; sometimes they tip into the realm of what she called 'weird stories', as if the distortions of capital have bent reality out of shape and produced new kinds of hauntings.

In 1842, Andrew Jackson Downing's book *Cottage Residences* helped to launch a Gothic Revival in the North American medium of wood and batten boards. Pointed roofs and gables were decorated with elaborate Gothic patterns, sometimes called 'gingerbread' or 'jig-saw batten', but eventually known as Carpenter Gothic. This domestic form of the Gothic bled uneasily into the American unconscious, from Hawthorne's *House of the Seven Gables* (1851) to the hooded eyes of the attic windows in *The Amityville Horror* (1977; filmed in 1979), or the pointed style of the Bates house looming on the skyline in Alfred Hitchcock's *Psycho* (1960), inspired by Edward Hopper's haunting painting *House by the Railroad* (1925). This house returned to haunt the roof of New York's Metropolitan Museum of Art in 2016, as Cornelia Parker's *Transitional Object (PsychoBarn)*.

The haunted house has a stratified imagination: the domestic space is menaced from above and below, from bad things in the attic (*Burnt Offerings, Black Christmas, Insidious*) or the basement (*Psycho, Night of the Living Dead, The Shining, The Evil Dead*). Doors and entryways are zones of anxiety. In the film *Paranormal Activity* (2007), we watch the black void of a landing beyond the bedroom door in an anonymous suburban house for what seems like hours, jumping at the slightest unexplained movement of the door. This is the typical experience of the haunted-house computer game, too, whether on edge in the Derceto Mansion of one of the first survival horror games, *Alone in the Dark* (1992), or the tense spaces of Brannenberg Castle in *Amnesia: The Dark Descent* (2010).

In 1848, at the height of fevered millennial movements and evangelical activity in New England, the Fox family moved into a house with a bad reputation in Hydesville, New York. By March 1848, Kate Fox was communicating with an entity they first called Mr Splitfoot (after the cloven foot of the devil) and later identified as the unquiet spirit of a murdered pedlar buried in the cellar. The Fox Sisters became the first 'mediums' of a new religious movement called Spiritualism, which quickly went international. By the 1880s, when some of the sisters confessed to their fraud, Spiritualism was far beyond their control. Millions of followers were ardent in their belief that they could contact departed loved ones from the family parlour. A movement focused on domestic spaces,

10

That class of the frightening which leads back to what is old and long familiar.

10. Mother's house in *Psycho* (Alfred Hitchcock, 1960).
11. Edward Hopper, *House by the Railroad*, 1925.
12. An example of early nineteenth-century American domesticated Gothic, from Andrew Jackson Downing's *Cottage Residences; or, A Series of Designs for Rural Cottages, Adapted to North America* (1842).
13. Cornelia Parker, *Transitional Object (PsychoBarn)* installed at the Metropolitan Museum of Art, New York, 2016.

11

12

13

14

3:08:26 AM

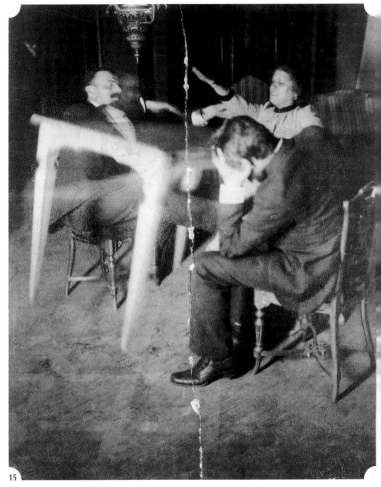

15

it had provided a way for working-class women to become public figures with authority, the spirits themselves comforting presences folded into the bosom of the family.

Yet even for sympathetic Spiritualists, haunted houses could also be possessed by mean spirits. By the early twentieth century, young girls were particularly associated with 'poltergeists' (German for 'noisy spirits'), with some cases flaring into sensational celebrity. Between 1977 and 1979, a small council house in Brimsdown, on the outskirts of London, became the site of poltergeist activity associated with two sisters aged eleven and thirteen, dramatized as the television series *The Enfield Haunting* (2015) and, later, the film *The Conjuring 2* (2016). The bland normality of these domestic spaces jars with cosmic possibilities, the notion that ordinary pubescent girls might be the conduit for unknown forces from the beyond. Like the device of found footage, these 'true' stories place the audience in a delicious zone of uncertainty, common sense stalked by a shiver of fear that this might, after all, be real.

The documenting of haunted houses has changed shape and unveiled new spectres with every advance of technology: fast shutter speeds capture ghostly presences; audio tapes left running in empty rooms pick up the whisperings of the dead; the green hues of night-vision cameras (the standard aesthetic of *Most Haunted*, which has run on British television for over 250 episodes) capture unexplained flares of light. We have been in this zone of uncertainty since the foundation of the Society for Psychical Research in London in 1882. Formed by a group of earnest intellectuals, the SPR developed a whole new language to scientize the marvellous or supernatural, borrowing from cutting-edge physics and psychology. One of the most famous investigations of the SPR's Haunted House Committee was at Ballechin House in Perthshire, Scotland, led by the female psychic Ada Goodrich-Freer, who moved into the place in 1897 for a few months. The controversy surrounding her account, *The Haunting of B---- House*, co-written with the third Marquess of Bute, spilled into the letter pages of *The Times* of London. The story of a psychic sensitive inadvertently bringing a haunted house to life was the direct inspiration for Shirley Jackson's *The Haunting of Hill House*, which in turn served as the basis for *The Haunting* (1963), one of the most effective haunted house films ever made.

London was gripped by widely circulated reports of a ghost called Scratching Fanny.

14. *Paranormal Activity* (Oren Peli, 2007).
15. Photograph of a séance with the famous medium Eusapia Palladino, 1903. Her claims to conjure spirits were investigated by the Society of Psychical Research.
16. *Alone in the Dark* survival horror video game (1992), in which the player moves through a haunted mansion in the American South.

'If we eliminate from our hearts and minds all dead concepts in regard to the house', the arch-Modernist Le Corbusier proclaimed in 1923, 'we shall arrive at the "house-machine".' Surely such a space, by definition, could not be haunted: it had no past. And yet the architectural uncanny erupts even here. In their book *Horror in Architecture*, Joshua Cameroff and Ong Ker-Shing speak of gleaming, white, rational spaces as doubled by 'unspeakable cavities' and 'obscene and recessive spaces' that 'contradict the resolved bourgeois exterior'. In the stories of J. G. Ballard, often set in hyper-rationalized, ultra-modern apartment complexes, bizarre acts of violence erupt, and strange shadow selves or doubles plot murder (as in 'Zone of Terror' or 'Motel Architecture'). The dream of the house as a 'machine for living in', **17**

as the Modernist slogan went, could not escape the dead hand of history. The radical intellectuals, many of them Jewish, who explored these possibilities in the 1920s and 1930s were themselves soon targeted by the fascist state.

The house remains a privileged locale for ghost stories across the world, one of the most mobile of the Gothic's travelling tropes. Hungry ghosts with the energy of implacable furies wait in abandoned houses in the Japanese film *The Grudge* (2004), or the series of books (*Ring*, 1991; *Spiral*, 1995; *Loop*, 1998) by Kōji Suzuki, the basis for the *Ring* films (1998–2000) and *Dark Water* (2002). The secret of *Ring* circles around what is hidden under the floorboards of a house on a remote island, while *Dark Water* is set in a run-down city apartment block, where leaks and stains and mysterious pools of water tell the story of an atrocious murder in the water tower on the roof. These films meld the multitude of spirits in Shintō and Buddhist beliefs with conventions of the Gothic to produce a distinctly material ghost cinema in post-war Japan. They have all been quickly remade for American audiences, accelerating the global circulation of these haunted-house stories.

In *A Tale of Two Sisters* (Kim Jee-Woon, 2003) – one of many film adaptations of the Korean folktale *Janghwa Hongryeon jeon* (*The Story of Janghwa and Hongryeon*),

and another haunted-house film subjected to an American remake (*The Uninvited*, 2009) – a vengeful spirit folds itself into strange corners of the family home. Bong Joon-ho's *Parasite* (2019), meanwhile, has its own very distinct take on the haunted recesses of the gleaming, ultra-modern family house.

Gentler ghosts drift through the domestic spaces of the Thai director Apichatpong Weerasethakul, in *Uncle Boonmee Who Can Recall his Past Lives* (2010) and the surreal, field-hospital-set *Cemetery of Splendour* (2015), in which the protagonists care for a group of soldiers with a mysterious, spirit-inflicted sleeping sickness. The boundary between this world and the next, and between past, future and present, in these trance-like evocations seems entirely erased, a strange, dissociated state in which visitors from the after-life are welcomed and embraced. Yet these spectres are not toothless; Weerasethakul also constructs a sly political commentary on the fragile place of democracy and modernity in contemporary Thailand. The Gothic always comes home, but to a house made *unheimlich* by haunting presences that cry out for their story to be told.

17. *The Uninvited* (Guard Brothers, 2009), an American remake of the 2003 Korean film *A Tale of Two Sisters*.
18. [opposite] Storyboard for the legendary shower scene in *Psycho* (Alfred Hitchcock, 1960), drawn by Saul Bass.

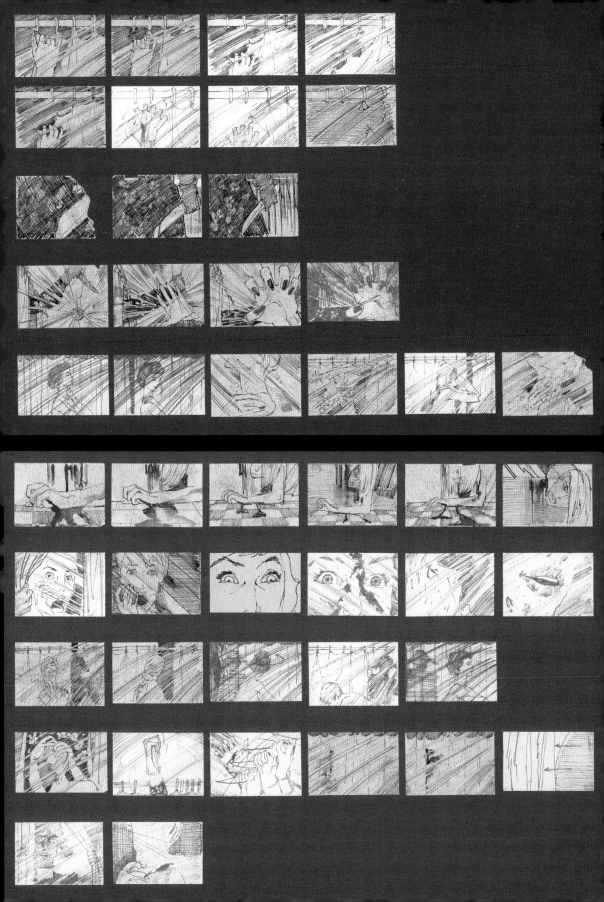

II

THE LIE OF THE LAND

The Country
& the City

Bram Stoker's *Dracula* (1897) begins with the naïve Jonathan Harker travelling from England to the outer limits of Christian Europe. As his peculiar host Count Dracula explains, Transylvania is a border-zone that has changed hands between European and Ottoman empires over long centuries of struggle. The plot of *Dracula* traces a circle: Harker journeys from civilization to this sinister backwater, sunk in feudal dependency, Catholic priestcraft and folkloric beliefs. He does not know that he is clearing a path for the vampire to travel back along the same route, turning it into a vector to infect London. This 'reverse colonization' culminates in Dracula's occupation of the metropolis, his house on Piccadilly just about the closest one can get to Buckingham Palace, at the symbolic centre of empire. Once Professor Van Helsing builds his band of Christian brothers to purge Dracula's pestilence from the civilized world, the journey repeats itself as they pursue Dracula back across Europe.

Beating to and fro in the stony wilderness, entangled...in the endless mazes of unknown streets.

Early Gothic romances tend to be set in the gloomy medieval past, in remote castles in southern, Catholic Europe (Radcliffe's *Mysteries of Udolpho* in southern France and Italy, Lewis's *The Monk* in Spain at the height of the Inquisition). The Gothic is still regularly displaced back in time, invoking dark forces that pre-date modernity, but, like Count Dracula, it also slides slowly into the modern city, the here and now.

The term 'Urban Gothic' is used for this shift from the foreign and Other, to the self-same and contemporary. It is in Dickens's vision of London in *Bleak House* (1853) or *Our Mutual Friend* (1865), a dark labyrinth peopled with grotesques; it recalls the unnerving figure of Mr Hyde, hurtling through

1. [opposite] Illustration by S. G. Hulme Beaman for the 1930 edition of Robert Louis Stevenson's *The Strange Case of Dr Jekyll and Mr Hyde.*

2. An 1832 floorplan of the home of John Hunter, a leading surgeon of the day, in London's Leicester Square: a possible model for Dr Jekyll's house in Stevenson's Gothic tale.
3. *Street of Crocodiles* (Quay brothers, 1986).
4. Eco-monstrous: *The Swarm* (Irwin Allen, 1978).
5. [following spread] Storyboards for Tim Burton's *Batman* (1989).

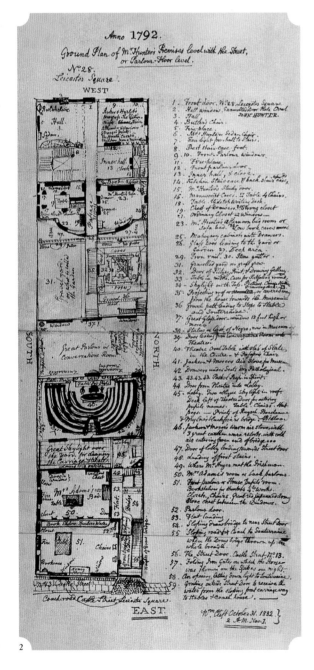

the backstreets of dubious neighbourhoods in Robert Louis Stevenson's *The Strange Case of Dr Jekyll and Mr Hyde* (1886). Stevenson's contemporary Arthur Machen often shuttled between the ancient depths of the Welsh border country, where he grew up, and the choked, alienated streets of late-Victorian and Edwardian London. His search for the occulted truth of the city sometimes produced ecstatic discoveries, as in his short story about a lost arcadia in London's northern suburbs, 'N'. More often, though, Machen's city is a grinding horror: 'I see myself on those wanderings', Machen wrote in *Far Off Things*, 'beating to and fro in the stony wilderness, entangled, as to say, in the endless mazes of unknown streets.'

From the 1980s, a distinct genre of urban fantasy has evolved that slams together the ancient and the modern; mythic, cyclical time and urgent city modernity. It includes writers like Gene Wolfe and Charles de Lint, Neil Gaiman and Emma Bull. The re-imaginings of Gotham City in the Batman comic book *The Dark Knight Returns* (1986) and the subsequent *Batman* trilogy of films by Christopher Nolan were also influential. The Gothic now appears in grimy apartment blocks on the anonymous edges of Tokyo in *Dark Water* (2002) or the shuttered suburban house of Takashi Shimizu's *The Grudge* (2004). It is no longer displaced onto benighted elsewheres, once upon a time in a land far away. Instead, it is up close, here and now.

At the core of the Gothic is a dialectic between the modern and the ancient, often translated as a shuttle between the city and the country. It is from the growing fracture between these spaces – their histories and their cultures – that the Gothic begins to ooze its uneasy dreams.

3

4

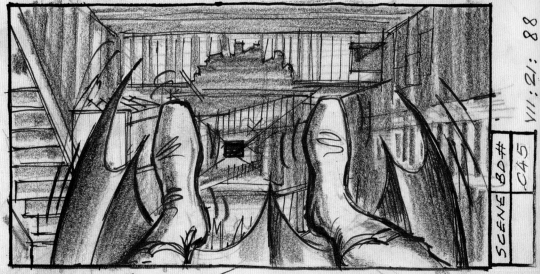

BATMAN'S POV DOWN THE TOWER BENEATH HIS FEET.

SCENE BD # C45 VII: 21: 88

78/MW

78/MW : : 88 PINEWOOD.

BATMAN | SCENE | BD. #

JOKER MOVES DOWN TO
CAMERA (WHICH SEPARATES
HIM FROM THE FLOATS)
HE LOOKS UP AT THE BATWING —

🦇 BATMAN

SCENE	BD.#
220	1

PROCESSION SEQ. BATBOARDS

TB/MW 1:X: 88 PINEWOOD.

THE JOKER PRODUCES HIS
'ANSWER'. & FIRES ONE
SHOT.

🦇 BATMAN

SCENE	BD.#

TB/MW : :88 PINEWOOD.

Shifting Territories

One of the elemental stories told by Gothic romances is that of the city sophisticate arriving in a rural backwater, an apparent pastoral idyll that hides a darker, horrifying truth that will shatter all the protections and pretensions of the civilized modern world. This is the story of Jonathan Harker, an ordinary man unprepared to read the warnings of the Transylvanian peasants along the Borgo Pass. It is a structure repeated in Stephen King's novels and short stories such as *Salem's Lot* (1975), 'Children of the Corn' (1977) or *The Institute* (2019), in which city-slickers confront an evil that bubbles up in small-town settings. The same device is used for a cluster of rural horror films from the 1970s – *Straw Dogs* (1971), *Deliverance* (1972), *The Wicker Man* (1973); for later horrors like *The Evil Dead* (1981), *Kill List* (2011) and *Get Out* (2017); and for the secrets that hide in the bedrooms and backwoods of David Lynch's *Twin Peaks* (1990–91).

Why is the Gothic so wedded to this story arc? The answer lies at the beginnings of the Gothic romance in the eighteenth century, when across Europe the Enlightenment shifted the very ground beneath people's feet, ending traditional modes of living and displacing large populations. In Britain, the lie of the land radically changed. Enclosure, which fenced off commons and wastelands alike, doing away with common land rights, was not just for profit or the domination of the colonized territories of Scotland or Ireland. The Old Testament God ordered his followers to cultivate the wastes – here, uncultivated commons, fenlands and mountain terrain. Thundered the Book of Ezekiel, 'This land that was desolate is become like the Garden of Eden.' Enclosure civilized: it was God's work. This became particularly important to the Puritans and dissenting Protestant sects who travelled to North America as settlers to escape their own persecution. They viewed this 'virgin' territory as a vast wasteland waiting to be tamed by tillage for the glory of God; never mind the savage heathen who inconveniently populated the land.

Under this new organization of the land, the countryside and country folk began to be associated with life stuck in the rural rhythms of a premodern world. What does the urban print culture of the Gothic romance find persisting, out of time, in the countryside?

In the early Gothic of Ann Radcliffe, it is often the overwhelming sublime of the foreign landscapes of the Alps, or the grand vistas of the forests and wild mountains of France and Italy, that can be enough to evoke terror. Although the heroine of *The Mysteries of Udolpho* (1794) is suspicious of the moral corruption that merely the idea of visiting Paris evokes, the mountains seem far worse: lawless, without decent proportions, and an offence to Protestant decorum.

By the mid-nineteenth century, writers clearly felt that Nature could retain restorative, numinous powers – the argument, for instance, of Ralph Waldo Emerson's influential essay 'Nature' (1836). But Nature

> We should ask which particular instances of the past each Gothic tradition is most afraid of seeing return.

was also perceived, to quote Alfred Tennyson's poem 'In Memoriam A. H. H.' (1850), as 'red in tooth and claw'. Tennyson was responding in this section of his poem to the recent discovery of dinosaur fossils, those 'Dragons of the prime/That tare each other in their slime', ancient monsters folded into the rock. Disturbing aeons of time were opened up by these finds and the new geological theories that came with them. They challenged Biblical history, which since the seventeenth century had dated the creation of the world to the year 4004 BC. The traumatic implications of Charles Darwin's biological theory of natural selection famously caused him to delay the publication of *On the Origin of Species by Natural Selection, or the Preservation of Favoured Races in the Struggle for Life* for years; the astonishing cruelty, violence and sheer waste of life in the theory lost him his faith and troubled many of his contemporaries deeply. Nature itself had become a source of Gothic horror.

6. [opposite] *Squirm* (Jeff Lieberman, 1976).

The EcoGothic

The 'EcoGothic' understands Nature as no longer a pristine place outside history, complicating the idea of the natural world as a passive backdrop or useful resource. It hints at troubling ideas of who, or indeed *what*, might have power and agency in the world. A subset of this new kind of fiction, the Botanical Gothic or Plant Horror, starts with the occasional exotic plant, foolishly collected and relocated to a hothouse where its ruthless instinct for survival threatens horrible death, as in Nathaniel Hawthorne's perverse tale of poisonous plants, 'Rappacini's Daughter' (1844). Since an awareness of the ecological damage wrought on the planet by unchecked development has grown, 'Revenge of Nature' narratives have become a strand of the Gothic, with EcoGothic disaster narratives first appearing soon after the first World Earth Day in 1970. These range from blockbusters like James Herbert's *The Rats* (1974) or Peter Benchley's *Jaws* (1974), to a whole succession of films such as *Frogs* (1972), Saul Bass's extraordinary *Phase IV* (1974), about ants outsmarting scientists, *Squirm* (1976) about worms, or *The Swarm* (1978), in which bees attack a host of flustered Hollywood glitterati, ranging from Olivia de Havilland to Michael Caine.

In the EcoGothic, disturbance to the land or the deeps of the sea frequently awakens ancient monsters, a violent, prehistoric Nature returning to wreak havoc on modern civilization. The original Japanese *Gojira* (1954, see pp. 217–21) was followed by a succession of giant monsters, in *Tremors* (1990, with six sequels), *The Relic* (1997), set almost entirely within the confines of the American Natural History Museum in New York, the gloriously sarcastic *Lake Placid* (1999, also with six sequels), or the unhinged, squelchy South Korean horror *The Host* (2006, which has so far managed only one sequel). In the most spectacular instances, these ancient monsters are set on the destruction of modernity's most glittering prize: the city. In *Cloverfield* (2008), chunks of Manhattan and, most memorably, the severed head of the Statue of Liberty, are hurled around by a rarely glimpsed giant invader. In the second American remake of *Godzilla* (2014), it is San Francisco rather than New York that suffers the hit at the crescendo of the film, reflecting the shift of global power to the transpacific.

This strand of films isolates the disjunction in time between nature and culture, the country and the city that is crucial to the Gothic sensibility.

7. *The Relic* (Peter Hyams, 1997).
8. *The Host* (Bong Joon-ho, 2006).

But we don't need such outsized allegorical prehistoric monsters to see this at work. Instead, we should ask which particular instances of the past each Gothic tradition is most afraid of seeing return.

In *Primitive Culture* (1871), Edward Tylor, the first man to hold a university post in the new science of anthropology, called the remaining elements of superseded beliefs 'survivals', defined as 'processes, customs, and opinions…carried on by force of habit'. In his view, 'the doctrine that ghost-souls of the dead hover among the living is indeed rooted in the lowest levels of savage culture'. He had to acknowledge that this belief 'survives largely and deeply in the midst of civilization' – but it was in rural settings that such beliefs persisted most strongly. In the opening pages of *Primitive Culture*, Tylor wrote that there was 'scarce a handbreadth of difference between an English plough-man and a negro of central Africa'. Race is overtly transposed onto class, opening a seam in the Gothic that equates the opposition of country and city to the backward and educated, the savage and civilized, in explicitly racist terms. White city travellers will find Black devils in all those woods and wastes that they will colonize. To travel from the city into the country-side is also to travel back *in time*. What could be more Gothic than that?

Tylor saw his role as documenting superstitions the better to erase them, but some of his contemporaries saw these beliefs as valuable records of a folk history that was fast being forgotten. Several figures across Europe began urgently documenting the customs, songs, annual festivals, folktales and stories handed down for generations in the oral culture of the peasant classes. The French collector Charles Perrault gathered fairy tales and published versions of stories like Cinderella, Little Red Riding Hood and Puss in Boots (with some judicious editing to ensure appropriate moral endings) in the 1690s. In Germany, the Brothers Grimm published their collection of *Children's and Household Tales* in 1812, an anthology of eighty-six stories that they continually expanded, the seventh edition in 1857 carrying over 200 stories. In Britain, figures like Sabine Baring-Gould and Andrew Lang issued multiple volumes of what were now termed *folklore*. Comparative studies began: grand attempts to systematize these primal stories across many cultures into overarching singular narratives. Sir James Frazer's *The Golden Bough* (1890–1902) related many folk rituals and beliefs across the world to survivals of ancient,

9

What if these superstitions turned out to be true? What if these country bumpkins are right?

pre-Christian fertility rites, to secure the return of the harvest each year. In the 1920s, the Russian folklorist Vladimir Propp attempted to synthesize all Russian folktales into a single 'morphology', an analysis that broke down fairy tale quests into standardized narrative units and basic characters. This kind of work has influenced the mythological stories told again and again in superhero comics or Hollywood blockbusters.

In sprawling mythologies like the Marvel Universe, folklore meets fiction and fuses into what has been termed the *folkloresque*, a blurry place between 'true' fictions and 'fake' traditions, real folklore and Gothic fancy. This can stretch from fiction reworking folklore (like Angela Carter's subversive fairy tales, in *The Bloody Chamber*, 1979) to invented yet immersive fantasy worlds.

The shivery effect of Gothic tales comes from the slight hesitation we feel when we confront a story of uncertain status – where we cannot, at first, know if it is a true story, an old legend, a folktale or fiction. So many Gothic romances try to half-persuade the reader that they are reading a faithful record of incredible events in the distant past. An old dog repeats the same trick: in the early days of the internet, some people were taken in by the 'authentic' stories planted online as part of the marketing campaign for *The Blair Witch Project* (1999), and thought it was a real documentary. Successive new platforms repeat the same shivers that overcome the city sophisticate when they enter the superstitious network of beliefs in a village community: *What if these superstitions turned out to be true? What if these country bumpkins are right?* After all, shouldn't Jonathan Harker have listened to the peasants along the road to Dracula's castle?

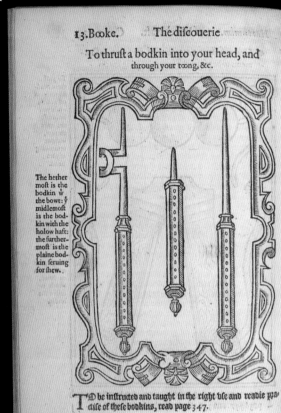

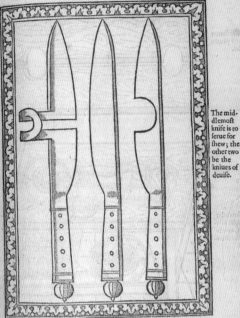

13.Booke.   The difcouerie

To thruft a bodkin into your head, and through your toong, &c.

The hether moft is the bodkin w the bowr: ẏ midlemoft is the bodkin with the holow haft: the furthermoft is the plaine bodkin feruing for fhew.

Tᴐ be inftructed and taught in the right vfe and readie practife of thefe bodkins, read page 347.

Hartumim.   of Witchcraft.   Cap.34.

To thruft a knife through your arme, and to cut halfe your nofe afunder, &c.

The middlemoft knife is to ferue for fhew; the other two be the kniues of deuife.

Tᴐ be readie in the vfe and perfect in the practife of thefe kniues here poſtraied, fee page 347. and 348.

11

12

10. [previous spread] An object presented to the Pitt Rivers Museum, Oxford, UK, in 1911, as a 'Witches' Ladder'. Said to be used by witches to climb over the roof to steal milk, the object's actual purpose remains contested.

11. Plates from Reginald Scot's *The Discoverie of Witchcraft* (1584), depicting stabbing bodkins and knives that were used on people suspected of being witches.

12. Faked museum display including tarot cards and the book *The Blair Witch Cult*, a part of the website built up in anticipation of the release of *The Blair Witch Project* (Daniel Meyrick and Eduardo Sánchez, 1999). The film was one of the first to exploit the internet to suggest that it was part of a larger 'true' story.

13. A bull's heart pierced with iron nails and thorn, found in a chimney at Shutes Hill Farm, Somerset, UK, and likely used as a counter-hex to repel witches.

Witches

What else crawls out of the growing chasm between the country and the city in the Gothic register? Another key co-ordinate of the clash of modern belief and ancient fear in the countryside is the witch trials and executions that spread across seventeenth-century Europe and only came to an end a hundred years later. This historical moment has continued to have a strong influence on the Gothic imagination long after the witch craze receded.

In 1487, the *Malleus Maleficarum* (The Hammer of Witches) was published in Germany. Writing under the name Henricus Institoris, its author, Heinrich Kramer, assumed the power of the Pope to hunt and execute witches discovered to be in league with the devil. His personal investigations resulted in the execution of forty-eight witches in the diocese of Konstanz in the 1480s. A pattern was set: in villages, often far beyond the influence of large cities and centres of learning, a misfortune, a death, the destruction of cattle by disease or crops by wild weather might result in an accusation of witchcraft amongst the peasant population. The accused were typically older women, who often worked as healers, 'cunning folk' who used herbal and other remedies to treat sickness. A priest or magistrate arrived to investigate: a figure of law and authority. Under local jurisdiction, they exercised their own measure of proof. Kramer and his associate Jacob Sprenger, for instance, favoured torture to force confession. The witch craze was further stoked in the seventeenth century when these accusations expanded to fantasies of witches' sabbaths, blasphemous inversions of Christian worship. Women danced in the forests and signed their souls over to the devil, who was held to have manifested in person. There was now an organized demonic conspiracy of witches.

In the centre of Europe, the battleground between Protestant and Catholic states, witchcraft became a way of controlling orthodox belief. Southern Germany, which was reclaimed by Catholic forces, became the worst centre for mass executions of witches. In Trier, over 600 were executed in trials between 1587 and 1593. In Würzburg, in the 1620s, 157 men, women and children

13

were burned at the core trial, with hundreds in the surrounding area caught up in the events. Eight thousand were said to have attended a black mass at night, with the devil himself leading the orgiastic rites. There were mass trials in Fulda and Bamberg. In Germany, Switzerland and the Alsace-Lorraine region, it is estimated that this *épidémie démoniaque* may have killed up to 60,000 people.

In Protestant Britain, the situation was slightly different. The English state was beset with fearful fantasies of Catholic priestcraft and the return of feudal tyranny. England passed its first Act against witchcraft in 1542, but the most famous English document on the subject, Reginald Scot's *The Discoverie of Witchcraft*, first published in 1584, was actually rather sceptical of the whole thing. Historians have come to wonder at the relative lack of successful witch trials in England, ascribing this to Protestant scepticism, the rise of mechanistic philosophy that counted out supernatural interventions into natural law, and the use of judges who travelled from London to preside over cases, rather than leaving it to local justices who might get caught up in the atmosphere of accusations.

This was the problem with the notorious 'witch-finder' Matthew Hopkins, who worked in the rural communities of Essex, Norfolk and other regions in the south. He executed several hundred alleged witches between 1644 and 1646. Hopkins was an anomaly: his own judge and jury, a self-appointed Witchfinder General, in the midst of a civil war. The last execution for witchcraft in England was in 1682, and the last trial under this law was halted by the judge in 1717. In 1736, the English parliament removed the 1604 Act 'Against Conjuration, Witchcraft, and Dealing with Evil and Wicked Spirits' from the statute book. But this abolition took place just as the emergent Gothic was beginning to invest heavily in these premodern beliefs.

The Gothic imagination maintains an obsession with seventeenth-century witchcraft and the village communities that were gripped by these outbreaks. It works partly as a marker of our sceptical modernity, signalling our break from the shackles of the oppressive beliefs of the past. But it exploits our hesitation, too.

What if a witch-cult *does* remain hidden away, conjuring hexes, using the Old Ways that arrogant moderns have failed to remember? What if we are right to fear a fiend in the furrows? Witchcraft might simply be one manifestation of many forms of secret pagan or Dionysian worship, hidden underneath the bland surfaces of village life.

In America, with its early Puritan settlements obsessed with religious conformity in a hostile and godless wilderness, witchcraft belief emerged as a constant shadow, a mocking double of the settlers' fervent piety. The most notorious case was the Salem witch trials of 1692, in which 14 women, 5 men and 2 dogs were executed for the practice of witchcraft. America remains a profoundly religious society, shadowed by the dark others of black magic, Satanism and witchcraft. Covens sometimes hide in plain sight in the cities, as in the films *The Seventh Victim* (1943) or *Rosemary's Baby* (1968), but most often they meet in the woods, at night, for their perverse bacchanals. The return of the paranoid frenzy that accompanies accusations of witchcraft has often been evoked in subsequent moments of socio-political paranoia. Arthur Miller's play *The Crucible* (1953) used the Salem witch trials as a bitter commentary on the hunt for Reds by the House Un-American Activities Committee led by Senator McCarthy in the late 1940s. Nearly every day of his presidency Donald Trump denounced someone for pursuing 'the biggest witch-hunt in history' against him, stoking conspiracy theories about a shadowy Deep State with almost (or perhaps actual) occult powers of influence. QAnon conspiracy theories mutter darkly about Satanist cabals and murderous rituals that hark back to centuries of anti-Semitic fantasies.

In the Gothic, the spatial and temporal dialectic of city and country frequently becomes a dynamic between sceptical, rational, urban modernity and an irrational, superstitious, premodern rural world, the horror often generated when this hierarchy starts to collapse or reverse. The Gothic lifts the veil on prettified conceptions of the countryside by invoking the historical violence of dispossession and the blood soaked into the land.

> **What if a witch-cult does remain hidden away, conjuring hexes, using the Old Ways that arrogant moderns have failed to remember? What if we are right to fear a fiend in the furrows?**

14. [opposite] *Rosemary's Baby* (Roman Polanski, 1968).

Paramount Pictures Presents

Mia Farrow

In a William Castle Production

Rosemary's Baby

co-starring

John Cassavetes

Ruth Gordon / Sidney Blackmer / Maurice Evans / and Ralph Bellamy

Produced by William Castle / Written for the Screen and Directed by Roman Polanski / From the novel by Ira Levin

Technicolor® / Production Designer—Richard Sylbert / A Paramount Picture / Suggested for Mature Audiences

Village

John Landis's film *An American Werewolf in London* (1981) opens with sweeping shots of the Yorkshire moors. Two American backpackers walk down into the village of East Proctor, huddled in a valley. As night falls, the friends have no choice but to enter the pub, The Slaughtered Lamb, its weird sign a severed head of a wolf raised aloft on a sword. Inside, hostility bristles, particularly once the Americans ask about the pentangle scratched on the wall. They are sent out into the dark, under the full moon. The wolf on the moors howls and circles before goring Jack to death but merely scratching David, so passing on the curse.

The energy of Landis's film comes in part from the special effects: we watch David's transformation from man to wolf with no dissolves or cutaways, and see Jack return as a rotting and deeply sarcastic corpse. But it also comes from taking a beast of rural superstition and transporting it to the centre of modern-day London. The final chase scene, through tube tunnels and out into Piccadilly Circus, depends for its effect on the disjoint between folkloric creature and metropolitan modernity. It harks back to a masterpiece of the New York shadows, *Cat People* (1942), only with a slightly higher number of decapitated heads.

In Gothic narratives, the village is the locus of premodern survivals, where the sceptical urban visitor slips out of the present and into another, earlier epoch. Sometimes one encounters the eccentric but essentially harmless customs of local traditions; sometimes, the resentment of the villagers erupts into deadly violence. They might not want you to leave, as in Sam Peckinpah's brutal *Straw Dogs* (1971), or maybe you have been cunningly lured there in the

2

1. [opposite] *The Wicker Man* (Robin Hardy, 1973).
2. *An American Werewolf in London* (John Landis, 1981).

first place, as in *The Wicker Man* (1973) or its imitator *Midsommar* (2019).

This is an old story, taking us back to the origins of the Gothic genre. In the 1730s, just as the statute against witchcraft was repealed in English law, the word 'vampyr' emerged from the remote villages on the Eastern edge of the Austro-Hungarian Empire and travelled to the centres of Western Europe: Vienna, Paris, Amsterdam, London. In the village of Medwegya in Serbia, officers and medics of the imperial army had been called in to restore calm amongst the peasantry. The villagers claimed that a soldier called Arnod Paole, who had returned home from fighting on the Turkish front, had died and been buried, but returned forty days after his death to drain the blood of local livestock and kill four fellow villagers. Paole's body was exhumed and found 'whole and intact with fresh blood flowing from his eyes'. The official report, signed by professional agents of the empire, explained that when the villagers had followed their custom and driven a stake through the heart of the unquiet corpse, the body let out a shriek and gushed (more) fresh blood. In another wave of panic later that year in the same region, thirteen more deaths were ascribed to vampyrs and the suspected corpses were exhumed, decapitated and cremated. Officials had to be sent into the villages to restore order.

Sensational accounts of these outbreaks spread across Europe in 1732, through newspapers, official reports, learned books and treatises. They prompted the great hero of the French Enlightenment, Voltaire, to include an entry on Vampires in his *Philosophical Dictionary* (1764). It opened with a metropolitan sneer: 'What! Is it in our eighteenth century that vampires exist? Is it after the reigns of Locke, Shaftesbury, Trenchard and Collins?', he asked, invoking the eminent rationalist philosophers of his day. 'We never had a word of vampires in London, nor even at Paris. I confess that in both these cities there were stock-jobbers, brokers and men of business who sucked the blood of people in broad daylight; but they were not dead, though corrupted.' Voltaire was already, this early, transposing a real-enough village superstition into a metaphor, a figure of modern satire.

For the critic Jack Halberstam, the Gothic text itself is a kind of machine that generates endless possible interpretations of its monsters, 'a remarkably

Sometimes, the resentment of the villagers erupts into deadly violence.

3. Griffin Dunne being made up as a decaying corpse for *An American Werewolf in London*.
4. Sheila Vand as The Girl, *A Girl Walks Home Alone at Night* (Ana Lily Amirpour, 2014).

mobile, permeable, and infinitely interpretable body'. This might explain the enduring survival of those such as the vampire: an aristocratic bloodsucker in the salons of Europe means something different from the one encountered in a Transylvanian village in 1897, or in New York at the height of the AIDS epidemic in the 1980s and 1990s (Abel Ferrara's *The Addiction*, 1995), in South Korea (Park Chan-wook's *Thirst*, 2009) or Iran (Ana Lily Amirpour's *A Girl Walks Home Alone at Night*, 2014) in the twenty-first century. 'The experience of horror comes from the realization that meaning itself runs riot,' writes Halberstam; the witches, were-wolves and vampires of village belief have all travelled back and forth along the path through popular collections of folklore and into the Gothic repertoire, transforming as they go.

3

4

British Folk Horror

Britain features centrally in mapping this Gothic geography outwards. From 1750, hundreds of villages across Britain either died out because of enclosure or were deliberately depopulated. This displacement was compounded by the steam-powered industrial revolution, which overturned the established lie of the land in Britain and forced landless and starving rural populations to seek jobs in towns and vast cities. Villages became backwaters, silted up and caught in the eddies of old, seasonal time. There is a common nostalgic sentiment about village England, but the village has also become an uncanny place, its populace resentful of the relentless forward thrust of industrial time. It is in these village landscapes that the disjunction of time crucial to the Gothic effect – and specifically to 'folk horror' – is felt most keenly. The term 'folk horror' is usually applied to a core of three British cult films made in the dying days of the 1960s and the early 1970s, all set in remote villages: Michael Reeve's *Witchfinder General* (1969), Piers Haggard's *Blood on Satan's Claw* (1971) and Robin Hardy's *The Wicker Man* (1973). But it has proven to have very flexible boundaries, incorporating music and half-remembered children's television shows as easily as films and horror novels.

Witchfinder General is set in 1645, in the midst of an English witch craze. It follows, with a degree of historical accuracy, the murderous career of Matthew Hopkins and his torturer-in-chief John Stearne, who executed over 200 people as witches in villages amid the chaos of the English Civil Wars. In livid technicolour, *Witchfinder General* shows Hopkins, played with menacing stillness by Vincent Price, directing the 'pricking', torture and burning of innocent villagers as witches. It ends in an extraordinary explosion of violence, frozen on a scream that evokes the complete derangement of order and civil society. The film inevitably also speaks to the bitter harvest of the post-1968 youth movement, and is lent another layer of doom by the fatal overdose of its director, Michael Reeves, who was only twenty-five when he made the film. Alan Bennett called it 'the most persistently sadistic and rotten film I have seen', which of course gives it a kind of trash vitality, anticipating the moral panic induced by the violence of *Straw Dogs* (1971) or *A Clockwork Orange* (1971).

Witchfinder General, with its deliberate smashing of bucolic Englishness, feels like a contribution to a seismic shift as the 1960s dream curdled.

Blood on Satan's Claw is a more fantastical account: a seventeenth-century village is overwhelmed by devil worship, unleashed by something monstrous turned up by a plough. The resultant witch-cult emboldens the young of the village to challenge power, another transparent allegory of youth culture overturning traditional authorities. This genre of folk horror – a term in fact coined by the film's director, Piers Haggard, in 2003 – focuses on the importance of place. In the English landscape, so closely entwined with a certain conception of nationhood, these sites of violence are carefully chosen.

> He should have read Frazer's *The Golden Bough* for clues, especially chapter 64, 'The Burning of Human Beings in Fires'.

Robin Hardy's *The Wicker Man* (1973), the most influential of these three films, creates a total, immersive world of folkloric weirdness. A repressed policeman is called to a remote Scottish island, Summerisle, to investigate the disappearance of a young girl named Rowan – the first clue that we are entering a network of folkloric belief, since rowan berries and bushes have many classical, pagan and occult associations. Sergeant Howie is a severe and appalled Christian, heir to the Scottish Protestant Covenanters who burned hundreds of witches and heretics in the sixteenth and seventeenth centuries. He should have read Frazer's *The Golden Bough* for clues, especially chapter 64, 'The Burning of Human Beings in Fires'. The film's memorable finale has Howie led to the giant wicker man in a ritual pageant, where he is incarcerated and burned alive, a sacrifice for the returning harvest. The scene draws on Roman accounts of the Celts, who their conquerors considered savage beyond imagining. In his *Gallic Wars*, Julius Caesar tells of 'figures of vast size, the limbs of which formed osiers they fill with living men, which being set on fire, the men perish in the flames'. Howie, representative of the mainland, of law and order and Christian orthodoxy, meets the outlandish fate provided by this fantasy of premodern beliefs.

The influence of *The Wicker Man* is well documented, which is impressive given that the film was dismissed, recut and maltreated by its distributors for years.

5

6

5. The Vampire Killing Kit, a fake from the 1970s designed to look like a Victorian antique, in the Royal Armouries Museum collection, London, UK.
6. *Witchfinder General* (Michael Reeves, 1968).

The Mowing - Devil :

Or, Strange *NEWS* out of

Hartford - shire.

Being a True Relation of a Farmer, who Bargaining
with a Poor *Mower*, about the Cutting down Three Half
Acres of *Oats*; upon the *Mower's* asking too much, the *Far-*
mer swore, *That the Devil should Mow it, rather than He*
And so it fell out, that that very Night, the Crop of *Oats*
shew'd as if it had been all of a Flame; but next Morning
appear'd so neatly Mow'd by the Devil, or some Infernal Spirit, that no Mortal Man was able to do the like.

Also, How the said *Oats* ly now in the Field, and the Owner
has not Power to fetch them away.

Licensed, *August* 22th. 1678.

It has been remade, and open homages to the film include M. Night Shyamalan's *The Village* (2004), Ben Wheatley's *Kill List* (2011) and Ari Aster's *Midsommar* (2019). Pilgrimages are made to its locations, seeking to conjure the eerie atmosphere of the film – the best of these is Edward Parnell's book *Ghostland* (2019), which sniffs out *Wicker Man* settings but also journeys through many other 'Gothicized' landscapes. In the late 2010s, as a divided Britain plunged into the Brexit crisis, it was hard to avoid the evocation of eerie landscapes and folk horrors, which seemed to work as subversions of the right wing's appropriation of land-scape and the English Volk as emblems of nationalism.

As the term folk horror has become more familiar, writers like M. R. James have been subsumed into a retrospective English tradition. Historical malice lies in wait for James's unsuspecting antiquaries as they seize old manuscripts in country churches ('Canon Alberic's Scrap Book'), carry off archaeological finds ('O Whistle, and I'll Come to you, my Lad') or hunt for treasure in ancient flint churches on remote, marshy stretches of the East Anglian coast ('A Warning to the Curious'). In 'A View from the Hill', a set of cursed binoculars reveal the lost site of an old abbey destroyed in the dissolution of the monasteries, and the associated Gallows Hill where executions on a gibbet took place.

In the golden age of the English ghost story, those who escape the city for a countryside idyll blunder into weird local survivals and must quickly adjust the parameters of their sceptical modernity if they are not to fall foul of the Old Ways. Edith Nesbit's bohemian Londoners in 'Man-Size in Marble' (1893) retreat from the city to 'a little village set on a hill, over against the southern marshes'. The newlyweds view this set-ting through absurdly rose-tinted spectacles, only to be visited by a malicious form embodied in one of the village church's stone effigies on Halloween, as local legend predicts. E. F. Benson's 1922 tale 'Negotium Perambulans' is set in the Cornish village of Polearn, where the people are 'linked together, so it has always seemed to me, by some mysterious comprehension: it is as if they had all been initiated into some ancient rite'. The narrator, brought up in the village but now a lawyer in London, is pulled back into its orbit against his will. Something monstrous and abject returns to the village in a cycle of revenge that operates in a time outside modernity. The creeping paranoia of the lone urban incomer encountering a closed community whose occulted ties seem to linger from another age

7. [opposite] Title page of *The Mowing Devil*, an account of a sighting of the devil in 1678. This woodcut is sometimes regarded as the first representation of a crop circle.
8. *Kill List* (Ben Wheatley, 2011).
9. *The Village* (M. Night Shyamalan, 2004).

also powers the bleak post-1945 stories of Robert Aickman, all the way up to the grotesque comic world of the village in *The League of Gentlemen* (1999).

But there are also sly subversions of this 'folk horror' trope, using the village setting in a different way. Sylvia Townsend Warner's novel *Lolly Willowes* (1926) features a spinster aunt who late in life abandons her tedious, passive existence in her brother's home in London and moves to a Buckinghamshire village. Frustrated by the closed village mentality, she soon joins a community of witches. This turns out to involve a lot of benign, politely joyous dancing in the woods at night. The book ends with an amicable discussion with the devil himself about the state of respectable but thunderously bored women 'all over Europe, women living and growing old, as common as blackberries, and as unregarded'. It is possible to see a direct line of influence from Warner's feminist witchcraft to Angela Carter's reworkings of European fairy tales in *The Bloody Chamber* (1979).

Another subversion is the extraordinary BBC-commissioned film *Penda's Fen* (1974), set in the village of Pinvin in Worcestershire. It is a dense, hallucinatory work in which a confused schoolboy, educated to adhere to a militaristic, patriotic, heterosexual and Protestant identity, is slowly undone by realizing that 'Pinvin' is a corruption of 'Penda's Fen', named after the last pagan king in England in AD 655. Stephen is visited by angels and demons, the ghost of the composer Edward Elgar (who lived in the area and whose music is often elided with nationalist sentiment), daydreams of same-sex desires and, in the last, memorable scene, by King Penda himself, who commands the boy: 'Stephen be secret, child be strange: dark, true, impure and dissonant. Cherish our flame. Our dawn shall come.' Mixing folktales of sleeping kings under English earth, paganism, Manichean heresies and Gothic tropes of angelic and demonic visitations, *Penda's Fen* does everything to undo the idea that the English village can simply be mobilized as a bucolic idyll for English nationalism. Its past is violent and riven, its soil soaked in blood.

Folk horror and the rural Gothic explore spaces that seethe with specific, local histories. Modernity is unevenly distributed. This is why, in such a small island, there is a distinct Cornish Gothic (from Daphne Du Maurier's *Rebecca* in 1938 to Mark Jenkin's film *Bait*, 2019), a Gothic of the Welsh borders (where Arthur Machen's writings still preside, and to which Iain Sinclair's writings often return), a post-industrial Northern Gothic (in contemporary writers like Jenn Ashworth, Benjamin Myers, Andrew Michael Hurley and Fiona Mozley), a Gothic of the Fens (in books by Sarah Perry, Daisy Johnson and Michelle Paver, stretching back to Sabine Baring-Gould) and a Gothic of occupied territories in Scotland, Ireland and Wales. This regional specificity, the distinctness of particular locales, generates a Gothic grounded in the dark ecologies of *place* that resist the abstraction and homogenization of modern urban *space*.

> Stephen be secret, child be strange: dark, true, impure and dissonant. Cherish our flame. Our dawn shall come.

10. Cornish horrors in *Bait* (Mark Jenkin, 2019).
11. Ancient tremors in the Malvern Hills: *Penda's Fen* (Alan Clarke, 1974).

10

11

The Global Village

The Hammer horror film *The Witches* (1966), written by Nigel Kneale, opens with the white teacher (Joan Fontaine) under attack from African witch-doctors in her missionary school. The scene then cuts to the English village idyll of Heddaby, where she is to teach in bucolic calm following her recovery from a mental collapse. But the village hides its own 'savage' superstitions, from the benign magic of the traditional 'cunning-woman' Granny Rigg to the coven run by the lady squire of the village, who hopes for a suitably nubile young virgin sacrifice to renew her own life on Lammas Night. If this film is folk horror, its strong implication is that there is a global network of superstitions that connects local eruptions together. Folk horror not only collapses time, but global space too.

However local it might seem, dark global energies thrum under the hood of the Gothic. William Beckford's Fonthill Abbey (see pp. 58–62), built on the hills outside Bath, depended on money generated by slave plantations in the Caribbean. The notorious author of *The Monk*, Matthew Lewis, also inherited and ran slave plantations in Jamaica. In the later imperialist era, the supernatural was used as a mode of exchange at the very edges of empire, turning unaccountable experiences into familiar Gothic tropes. The ethnographer and explorer Mary Kingsley documented the 'Black Ghosts' of West Africa, and believed she had telepathic sympathy with the natives. Among the British community in colonial India, writers like Rudyard Kipling, B. M. Croker and Alice Perrin transposed the haunted house, the vengeful spectre or the uncanny village onto their encounters with the complex, varied cultures of India. Just as colonists built Gothic churches across the world to impose the centre on the margin, so the travelling tropes of the Gothic romance worked their magic. The village can journey from the bucolic landscapes of England to become a frontier fortress or a fragile camp planted on the edge of vast and terrifying unknown lands.

Local superstitions might have been officially condemned by colonizing authorities as primitive or backward, but the Gothic in fact subsumed these local versions of the supernatural. The vampire came from far-flung villages on the eastern edge of Europe. The zombie stumbled out of the forced labour and violent oppression of the plantations of Haiti into North America through New Orleans, that cosmopolitan

12

13

centre of swirling supernatural beliefs, freely borrowing from the syncretic religions of Haitian Voodoo, Santería from Cuba or Obeah from Jamaica. The flesh-eating wendigo came from Native American beliefs in North America and Canada, while the weird, amphibious bunyip was seen in billabongs in the outback of Australia, the term borrowed from the Aboriginal Wemba-Wemba language.

The travelling fragments of Gothic story have become a means of exchange. In the post-colonial years, beliefs in witchcraft and malign supernatural powers have persisted in very different regions of the African continent, where the occult erupts in the fissures of modernity and tradition, or along physically imposed borders – as in the subtle presence of migrants-turned-spectres in Mati Diop's French-Senegalese film *Atlantique* (2019). Zombies and witches harass populations in the border-zones between Zimbabwe and South Africa, a region under constant pressure from refugees and migration. In Rungano Nyoni's *I Am Not A Witch* (2017), inspired by stories of witchcraft accusations in Zambia, the nine-year-old outsider Shula is sent to a 'witch camp', where (predominantly older) women accused of witchcraft lead tethered lives.

Looking back towards the old, colonial West, the oblique intercutting between an elite French public school and the life of a zombified Haitian man in Bertrand Bonello's film *Zombi Child* (2019) works the horror trope hard to put colonial traffic in the supernatural back into the foreground, while France's colonial violence in Algeria haunts the comfortable, bourgeois lives of a Parisian couple in Michael Haneke's spooky, unnerving film *Caché* (2005).

Dark global energies thrum under the hood of the Gothic.

If we are to map the lie of the Gothic land, we have to keep up with tropes that travel and mutate as they move. There are specific and localized versions of the Gothic that are rooted in particular places and regions, like the quintessential English village. But they often hide the global inside the local, and this constant translation keeps the genre in continuous transition.

12. *Zombi Child* (Bertrand Bonello, 2019), partly based on the real-life case of the Haitian man Clairvius Narcisse, who, having been pronounced dead eighteen years earlier, returned home in 1980 with the tale of having been turned into a zombi.

13. New York vampires in *The Addiction* (Abel Ferrara, 1995).

14. [following spread] *The Village of the Damned* (Wolf Rilla, 1960).

Forest

If you leave the city, never go into the trees.

One of the most important tropes of the Gothic romance is the fateful decision to enter the forest – that absolute outside where the outlaw, the wolf and the Wild Man meet. In Ann Radcliffe's *The Romance of the Forest* (1791), the villain La Motte retreats to a mouldering ruin hidden by 'the gloomy grandeur of the woods'. For the menaced heroine, Adeline, the forest represents lawlessness, a place of banditry and potential violence that can only 'perplex, with its labyrinths'. The dark, trackless woods figure her moral confusion. Her rescue is symbolized by a return to the clear lines and rational order of the cultivated and contained picturesque, where the trees are subservient to the gaze once more.

All the stories and stories-within-stories in Carl Grosse's *Horrid Mysteries* (1796) – one of the German 'shudder novels' devoured by the naïve heroine of Jane Austen's *Northanger Abbey* (1803) – unfold in the 'mazy labyrinths' of the forest. But at its heart is a secret clearing, a 'spacious grove' where an awful secret society meets for its evil convocations and from where its assassins will pursue the protagonist to the ends of the earth.

'The woods enclose and then enclose again, like a system of Chinese boxes opening one into another,' the narrator in Angela Carter's story 'The Erl-King' (1979) says. 'The intimate perspectives of the wood changed endlessly around the interloper.' A multitude of writers evoke the eerie moment in the wilds when history seems to fall away and the millennia start to whisper through the leaves. Trees often outlive us; the tendrils of the forest network outflank us; they can manipulate and change us.

Even Francis Pryor, a no-nonsense archaeologist excavating material history, repeatedly admits in *Paths to the Past* (2018) to 'being very alone and a little frightened' amid the ancient monuments and landscapes of Britain.

The shiver seems to come from a succession of layered associations, the sense of falling out of history and into a mindset of prehistoric or 'primitive' belief. The way we reconstruct these beliefs is always tricky, of course, but we still associate many early religions

The woods enclose and then enclose again.

with animism, with spirits that occupy every river, rock, distinctive landscape or tree, whether spirits of place, local gods or ancestors. The worship of the tree, an emblem of life, seasonal death and return, is found in the symbols of many early religions, whether the palm tree of the Assyrians and Egyptians or the immense ash tree Yggdrasil, the world-tree, that holds the cosmos together in Norse mythology. J. G. Frazer's rather over-coherent *The Golden Bough* (1890–1915) sees 'survivals' of tree worship everywhere, from maypole dances to Christian Palm Sunday festivals.

There is a reason why Count Dracula arrives from Transylvania, the place *beyond the trees*. In the woods, what comes back is a sense of the pagan world. Although pagan and 'Celtic' beliefs are often latter-day reconstructions by fearful Romans or Christians, their associations are with the worship of fecund Nature, and the annual rituals associated with the beginning of summer ('Beltane', 1 May, taken over by May Day), the harvest and the beginning of winter ('Samhain', 1 November, taken over by Halloween). Darker suggestions of animal and human ritual sacrifices, the storing of ancestral

1. [opposite] *Troll Hunter* (André Øvredal, 2011).

bones in barrows for ritual use and the display of severed heads on defensive walls are amply supported by the archaeological record, even if their significance remains unclear.

Just as Julius Caesar projected his worst imaginings of those beyond the civilized empire of Rome onto the Gauls and Celts, so Gothic fiction remains oddly Christian in its pagan nightmares. In *The Blair Witch Project* (1999), the student filmmakers are confounded by a pathless forest that leaves their map and compass useless while the unseen 'witch' picks them off one by one; in *The Ritual* (2017), Sweden's unmapped northern forests hide a primitive tribe who worship some incomprehensible woodland deity with the sacrifice of yet another group of unlucky backpackers. In *Wake Wood* (2009), the dead are conjured back to life but bound to the limits of the village and its trees; *Troll Hunter* (2010) offers found footage of the bad-tempered forest and the mountain trolls who need constant government-led containment lest they break out from a dying folklore and into the modern world. The woods make their way indoors and into the family in *Little Otik* (2000), as Gothic tropes blend with the Czech fairy tale of a childless couple who adopt a tree stump. In all of these works, the edge of the forest marks the beginning of a fall into a prehistoric, pagan world.

To step outside this Western tradition is to find the forest inevitably changing meaning again, from Shintō to Buddhist to Christian belief. The localized animistic tradition in Japan, which allows for thousands of gods, monsters and 'spirits of place', suggests that certain trees are occupied by *kodama*, spirits that live in mountainous areas, their voices responsible for mountain valley echoes. The insistence on sites that hang heavy with demonic presences also picks up a deeply Gothic thread running through the Japanese forest. Aokigahara, also known as Jukai (Sea of Trees), an ancient, twisting forest at the foot of sacred Mount Fuji, has a reputation as a home to *yurei*, the tormented spirits of the dead, who can lure unwise adventurers deeper into the dark. More recently, it has become popularly known as the 'Suicide Forest', the origins of which are often attributed to Seichō Matsumoto's novel *Tower of Waves* (1960), which ends among the trees, with the heroine dying by suicide.

The 'spirit of place', the *genius locii* of sea and mountain, woodland and water, also animated the polytheistic religions of Greece and Rome. The most relevant god in this endlessly malleable panoply is Pan,

2. Algernon Blackwood's classic 1912 collection *Pan's Garden*, illustrated by W. Graham Robertson.
3. Arthur Machen, *The Great God Pan*, illustrated by the scandalous Aubrey Beardsley for Allen Lane in 1894.
4. [opposite] Twelfth-century carving of Yggdrasil, the world-tree, the only surviving element of the wooden Urnes Stavkirke in Norway.

the half-god, half-goat spirit of Arcadia, of woods and sacred groves and Nature as a whole. He is the benign god of shepherds and sportive delight, but also a protective god for the warrior, a figure who can strike terror into the hearts of foes, the root of the word 'panic'. In the Roman panoply, Pan becomes the gods Faunus and Silvanus (the latter meaning 'of the woods'). Faunus is an earthy, rutting beast, a celebrant of goatish, lusty revels who later fuses with the Christian devil. Silvanus is the tutelary god of the woods and fields, who polices the boundaries between cultivated land and the wild, uncivilized world beyond. On the very edges of the Roman Empire, on the islands of Britain, then thick with dark forests, dedications and shrines to Faunus and Silvanus have been found.

Pan is crucial in the Christian imagination because he marks another boundary. Plutarch's 'Oracles in Decline' tells the story of a traveller on a boat hearing a disembodied voice command, 'When you reach Palodes, announce that Great Pan is dead!' Early Christian commentary suggested that this event took place at around the same time as the birth of Christ; the death of Pan thus marked the passage from a pagan to a Christian world, the driving-out of the heathen gods and demons. At a time of heightened religious anxiety in the nineteenth century, Pan made an unlikely return in English literature. The poet and novelist Algernon Swinburne regularly evoked Pan as a figure deliciously balanced between ecstasy and terror, the sweet spot of his own sado-masochism, while the late-Victorian Gothic revival also went through a notable Pan phase, generating terror from the uncanny return of pagan gods thought to have been superseded.

The most notorious of these Gothic stories is Arthur Machen's 'The Great God Pan' (1894), told in fragments that suggest an amoral scientist has opened the neural gateways of a young girl to see into the beyond and couple with Pan. She produces a half-human, half-demonic child, Helen. As an apparently orphaned girl, this child proves to have a penchant for 'expeditions to the forest' near the village where she is raised, causing a boy who comes across her in the groves 'great terror'. His 'violent hysteria' is renewed when he sees the face of a Roman statue of a faun dug up near the woods. Helen's dread career goes on to cause sexual ruin, despair and suicide among the wealthy gentlemen of bohemian London.

No wonder one reviewer denounced the book as 'a nightmare incoherence of sex and the supposed mysteries that lie behind it': through the fragments, the reader glimpses the face of Pan.

The god returns in other tales of this era. Saki's 'The Music of the Hill' (1911) is a short, nasty story that sees a young city bride (ironically called Sylvia) defy an altar to Pan in a woodland terrain of 'almost savage wildness', only to be gored to death by an antlered stag to the insistent sound of Pan pipes. E. F. Benson's 'The Man Who Went Too Far' (1912) is told by a staid, worried man visiting a long-lost friend in his country retreat close to the New Forest, where 'the inhabitants will not willingly venture into the forest after dark'. The friend has become an unapologetic pantheist, tuning into the distant melodies of Pan's pipes. He awaits, he says, the 'final revelation': 'on this day, so I take it, I shall see Pan. It may mean death, the death of my body that is, but I don't care.' This is the Christian rendition of pagan panic: 'To see Pan meant death, did it not?', Benson's narrator asks. But a different sensibility and less orthodox belief can depict this same encounter in a very different emotional register.

Algernon Blackwood's novella 'The Man Whom the Trees Loved' (1912), is centred on an artist, Brittacy, who also lives at the edge of the New Forest and has devoted himself to the painting of trees. His guest, Sanderson, gathers that there is something awry when Brittacy talks dreamily of the Forest Personality, a collective consciousness that has somehow noticed

The edge of the forest marks the beginning of a fall into a prehistoric, pagan world.

him and his service, and wants to 'amalgamate' him into its network. The Gothic horror is located with Brittacy's conventional, Christian wife, as her attempts to retrieve her husband for the human world breed malice: the trees '*saw her*. In some unkind, resentful, hostile way they watched her.' Her unease is matched by her husband's ecstatic calm, and in the end Brittacy simply disperses into the trees, redistributed into the forest, his voice joining the rustle of the leaves. If there is less terror here, it is because Blackwood was an avowed seeker in other, often heterodox religious traditions. In his case, the paganism is deeply considered, and Pan an emblem of a coherent philosophical stance rather than cheap trick horror.

5. [opposite above] *Little Otik*, or *Greedy Guts*, stop-animation based on a Czech folktale (Jan Švankmajer, 2000).

6. [opposite below] Paul Nash, *Monster Field*, 1938.

7. [previous spread] The looming forest of
   The Witch (Robert Eggers, 2015).
8. The malevolent forest of *The Evil Dead*
   (Sam Raimi, 1981).

8

Some of Blackwood's earliest writings were for the occult journal of the Theosophical Society, *Lucifer*, in which he wrote of instances in Nature where 'the beholding spirit seems to leave its own plane of consciousness and to enter that of the surrounding nature-life, to commune, indeed, with the potentials...above and behind all natural phenomena'.

This kind of approach also feeds directly into the work of the English landscape artist Paul Nash. Nash was reading Blackwood and E. F. Benson early in his career, and stated that 'I sincerely love and worship trees and know they are people' and 'I quite believe in Pan'. As a response to his shattering

experiences of war he became obsessed in the 1920s with what he called the 'natural magic' of Neolithic standing stones at Avebury and the gigantic earthwork of Silbury Hill. He travelled restlessly across the south of England, drawing the rolling hills and ancient woodlands of the south Downs and the strange forms of Wittenham Clumps, hills topped with beechwoods that had survived since the Neolithic and been used by the Romans as a refuge from attack. In the deeply troubled era between the wars, Nash was unapologetic

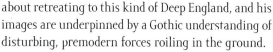

Lifted up in ecstasy by the Devil's promise to 'live deliciously.'

about retreating to this kind of Deep England, and his images are underpinned by a Gothic understanding of disturbing, premodern forces roiling in the ground.

In fantasy fiction, the influence of Blackwood's promissory tone of occult revelation and the salving of psychic wounds in the woods is evident in novels such as Robert Holdstock's *Mythago Wood* series (started in 1984) or Charles de Lint's *Wild Wood* (1994). De Lint's novel, although set in the Canadian woods, invokes the spirit of the magical forest Brocéliande, found in medieval European romances such as those by Chrétien de Troyes. The forest changes shape and meaning again in these romances, even as it retains its potency as a symbolic site capable of holding opposing ideas in tension. It is a place of chaos, of untamed Nature in a state of flux, still the place of the gods, spirits, magical transformations and supernatural intervention. From Virgil's *Aeneid* to Dante's opening lines in the *Inferno*, the forest blurs into the entrance to the Underworld:

> I came around and found myself now searching
> through a dark wood, the right way blurred and lost,
>
> How hard it is to say what that wood was,
> a wilderness, savage, brute, harsh and wild.
> Only to think of it renews my fear!

In Christian Europe, the forest becomes the equivalent of the Biblical wilderness, where the paths of error and temptation multiply and the devil tempts Christ. Yet precisely because of this, the forest is at the same time the place where error and labyrinthine deceit can strengthen faith – and also where redemption might be finally secured. Hence the allegorical quests of Arthurian romances, in which the questing knight enters a dark forest that becomes a place of spiritual crisis, of Merlin's weird magic, a test of chivalric codes and Christian virtue. At the end of this tradition, the Renaissance poet Edmund Spenser's self-conscious echo of the romance form in *The Faerie Queene* (subtitled *The Legend of the Knight of the Red Crosse, or, Of Holinesse*) begins with the Gentle Knight escorting his lady through a 'shadie grove', only to find a 'labyrinth' of paths through 'the wandring wood, this *Errours den*', where a 'monster vile', representative of the Antichrist, is found coiled at the entrance of a cave.

The shape of this narrative even persists behind Sam Raimi's primal 'cabin in the woods' horror film, *The Evil Dead* (1981). In this glorious shocker, the emblematically named Ash, played with manic energy by Bruce Campbell, undergoes awful torments, a pitiless Passion driven by the demons that have been unleashed to possess and malignly animate every element of the dark wood. By the third film in the series, *Army of Darkness* (1993), Ash has been dumped back in time into a medieval mash-up of shotguns and chivalry.

The strong Christian association of the untamed woods with devilry continues in the enduring connection of the forest and its secret clearings with the practice of witchcraft. This became an essential part of the Puritan imagination that drove the witch trials to their height in the seventeenth century. An account of the Pendle Forest witch trial in Lancashire, in 1612, was published by the legal clerk Thomas Potts as *The Wonderfull Discoverie of Witches in the Countie of Lancashire*. Later, in the Puritan settlements of New England, witches were believed to gather beyond the stockades of civilization, first in the forests that crowded Hartford, Connecticut, where the first executions took place in 1647, and then in the town of Salem, where the notorious trials took place in 1692. In Robert Eggers's reconstruction of these phantasmal terrors, *The Witch* (2015), the uncultivated wood looms at the edge of the family farm throughout, but the film ends with the girl Thomasin welcomed to a coven deep in the forest, lifted up in ecstasy by the Devil's promise to 'live deliciously'. *The Witch* hints at the complex knot of terror and desire that the forest might deliver to women who rebel against restrictive roles, the sort of dark desires explored in the woods in Angela Carter's subversive retellings of folktales in *The Bloody Chamber* (1979). Many of these ancient resonances persist into modern conceptions of eco-friendly Wiccan worship and contemporary horror films, even as the old sigils of devil worship largely fall away.

Just as we begin to comprehend the distributed networks of individual trees and their collective and collaborative work, the Gothic changes shape again. What exactly happens to human scientists inside the complex networks of flora and fauna in the forest of Martin MacInnes's novel *Gathering Evidence* (2020)? Can flowers use pollen to re-programme and control the humans who tend them, insidiously weaving them into their extended networks, as in Jessica Hausner's clinical horror *Little Joe* (2019)? These are the dense layers of association that have mulched down into the unnerving terrain of the forest floor over the millennia.

9. [opposite] 'I found myself within a forest dark...': One of French artist Gustave Doré's celebrated illustrations for Dante's *Inferno*, 1857.

OLD FAITHFUL

Wilderness

Derived from the Old English *wild-dēor*, the place of wild animals, the wilderness is defined by its negation of everything civilized: *un*known, *in*human, *un*ruly, *un*tamed, *un*cultivated. It is the place of the savage other, populated by unimaginable beasts. It offends the eye by being so vast and ungovernable; it offends morality by being so unproductive; and it can be used interchangeably with 'wasteland', territory that is useless and unused. It is not a fixed place, but a judgment: it can be the desert, the plains, the mountains, the swamp, the fen, the sea. What links these places is their indifference to humanity. It is a place of terror, where you lose your way, get turned around, become lost and be*wild*ered.

The wilderness is not just a place of monsters. The first translation of the Bible into English, organized by John Wycliffe in the 1380s, used the term many times, a usage fixed in place by the King James Version of 1611. The exodus from Egypt takes God's chosen people into the Sinai Peninsula for forty years, 'in a desert land, And in the wasteland, a howling wilderness' (Deuteronomy 32:10). Eden is a watered garden; Adam and Eve are cast out into the wilderness. God's blessing means 'I will even make a way in the wilderness, And rivers in the desert' (Isaiah 43:19), while His punishment is exile to the stony wastes. Christ's forty days in the wilderness, tempted by the devil, have been a crucial influence on Christian practice. It is why many early Christians sought the eremitical life, living alone as hermits or in remote monastic communities. Later, the wilderness came to represent the bewilderment of earthly, fallen existence. The opening line of John Bunyan's allegorical Puritan tract, *The Pilgrim's Progress* (1678), reads: 'As I walk'd through the wilderness of this world, I lighted on a

2

1. [opposite] William Henry Jackson, photograph of Old Faithful, a geyser in Yellowstone National Park in Wyoming, USA, taken in 1870.
2. On the road in *Wendy and Lucy* (Kelly Reichardt, 2009).

certain place, where was a Denn...'. Faith must forge the righteous path through the thorny wastes.

The Gothic emerged just as wilderness was being rethought by discourses of the sublime. The violence, darkness and obscurity of Titanic mountains and thunderous seas or endless forests could, in Edmund Burke's view, lead terror away from the threat of human failure or annihilation and towards the greatest pinnacles of aesthetic response. Frankenstein's creature, for instance, is continually associated with wildernesses, reflecting his outcast status. He hides in the forests, picks his way across vertiginous mountain peaks and is pursued into the blinding whiteness of the Arctic wastes, yet remains – at least in Mary Shelley's subversive original – a self-fashioned, Promethean man, rendered monstrous only by his creator's wild-eyed revulsion. The lawless Heathcliff of *Wuthering Heights* is always connected to the blasted moors, but remains alluring to readers because his exorbitant passions seem to defy death itself. The recasting of wild landscapes by Romantic poets and painters – Percy Shelley at Mont Blanc, the dizzying vistas of Caspar David Friedrich in the Alps or Thomas Cole in the Catskill Mountains or at Niagara Falls – piles further pressure on the meaning of the wilderness in the Gothic.

For the wave of Puritan settlements that began in North America after 1609, the encounter with the New World was strongly filtered through Biblical understandings of wilderness. William Bradford's *Of Plymouth Plantation* (eventually published in 1657) spoke of arriving in a wild, uncultivated land, an offence to God, 'devoid of all civil inhabitants, where there are only savage and brutal men'. If the indigenous population were considered at all, it was as servants of Satan: their religion, Cotton Mather of Salem later wrote, 'was the most explicit sort of devil-worship'. There was also a strong association of the people of the wilderness with cannibalism, that terrible taboo. The American Gothic is suffused with the secret shame of starvation cannibalism to survive the first winters, as if the wilderness had got inside some of the earliest settlers. Being in the wilderness too long makes you become it; white settlers feared 'going native'.

Just as often, though, the wilderness was regarded as simply 'unpeopled'. The Europeans seldom understood that they had settled on land that had often already been carefully managed by native systems of cultivation,

3

A ghost wilderness hovers around the entire planet.

3. Frederick McCubbin, *Lost*, 1886, a painting inspired by the case of a young girl, Clara Crosbie, who was found alive after three weeks lost in the Australian bush.

4. Top Withens, Yorkshire, UK, the house that Emily Brontë used as the model for *Wuthering Heights*, photographed by Fay Godwin in 1977.

5. *Picnic at Hanging Rock* (Peter Weir, 1975), an enigmatic tale of the disappearance of schoolgirls in the Australian outback.

4

5

6

7

though some early settlements only survived their first years by being shown how to grow local crops by indigenous people. In Virginia, the Powhatans had a complex economic, political and social system underpinned by farming and woodland management; like many indigenous people, they had their own distinctions between cultivated and uncultivated land. But soon, the introduction of European diseases began to obliterate the indigenous inhabitants. This population collapse was often viewed with serenity by settlers, who read it as an affirmation that they were God's chosen people. 'Manifest Destiny' would later legitimize active, genocidal clearances of Native Americans, as the wilderness was transformed first by dispossession and then by development.

In 1799, in the preface to *Edgar Huntly; or, Memoirs of a Sleep-Walker*, Charles Brockden Brown dismissed the European devices of 'puerile superstition' or 'Gothic castles and chimeras' and instead suggested that for America 'incidents of Indian hostility and the perils of the Western wilderness are far more suitable'. *Edgar Huntly* was the first Gothic novel of the new republic. In Brown's fractured, nightmare narrative, the protagonist Huntly pursues the mystery of a small-town murder 'into the heart of the wilderness', only to be hypnotized by its dark energies and become a wild man himself. In his symbolic journey, Huntly enters the wilds, discovers a cave (a hellmouth), and plummets into an abyss in the darkness. In a daze, no longer in control of his actions, he is gnawed by hunger, kills a wild beast and devours its raw flesh, then sets about a frenzied massacre of the Indian camp he stumbles across. The eruption of the savage wilderness within him is immediate. Huntly might return to civilization, but he carries violence within him.

In modern visions of the wilderness, there has been a return to this Gothic rendition of the frontier life as a 'war of all against all', as Thomas Hobbes had it. Cormac McCarthy's *Blood Meridian; or, The Evening Redness in the West* (1985), set in the borderland between the United States and Mexico in the 1840s, is filled with relentless slaughter, rendered in stately Biblical cadences. McCarthy's later novel, *The Road* (2006), is a trek through a post-apocalyptic wilderness of ash, dead towns and forests, where the last marker of civilization is refusal to eat human flesh. More recently, in the extraordinary vision of the 1820s American wilderness

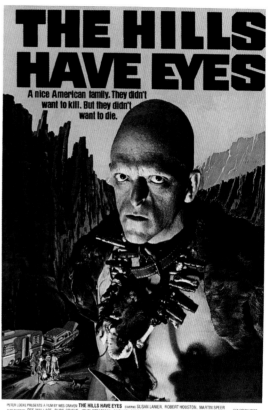

PETER LOCKE PRESENTS A FILM BY WES CRAVEN **THE HILLS HAVE EYES** STARRING SUSAN LANIER, ROBERT HOUSTON, MARTIN SPEER ALSO STARRING DEE WALLACE, RUSS GRIEVE, JOHN STEADMAN, MICHAEL BERRYMAN & VIRGINIA VINCENT AS ETHEL CARTER COLOR BY MGM JAMES WHITWORTH AS JUPITER DIRECTOR OF PHOTOGRAPHY ERIC SAARINEN EDITED BY DON PEAKE WRITTEN AND DIRECTED BY WES CRAVEN (WRITER & DIRECTOR OF LAST HOUSE ON THE LEFT) PRODUCED BY PETER LOCKE A VANGUARD RELEASE

8

Where the earth and its community of life are untrammelled by man, where man himself is a visitor who does not remain.

6. Thomas Cole, *A View of the Two Lakes and Mountain House, Catskill Mountains, Morning*, 1844.
7. Boris Karloff as the monster in *Frankenstein* (James Whale, 1932).
8. *The Hills Have Eyes* (Wes Craven, 1977).

in Alejandro González Iñárritu's film *The Revenant* (2015), the war of all against all involves English settlers, American soldiers and mercenaries, French fur-traders, Pawnee and Sioux, wild animals, the wilderness and the extremes of the winter weather, in long, drifting, hallucinatory sequences of pitiless slaughter. It is based on the much-mythologized story of Hugh Glass, the tracker who existed in an ambiguous terrain between mountain settlers and the Pawnee, and who survived betrayal, bear attacks and bewilderment in the depths of the Missouri winter. While in this film the white settlers are the true degenerates, in Craig Zahler's *Bone Tomahawk* (2015), a film that glories in all the stereotypes of pulp Westerns, the Gothic horrors are ascribed to an utterly demonic Native people. But settler terror sometimes needs no natives at all: Robert Eggers's *The Witch* (2016) and Emma Tammi's *The Wind* (2019) explore the psychic projections of isolated people onto the wilderness itself.

One of the most famous depictions of the North American wilderness in the Gothic is more sensitive to native culture. Algernon Blackwood's 'The Wendigo' (1910) centres around an Algonquin mythical belief to create a Gothic suited to the new territory. 'The Wendigo' evokes the sublime terror of the Canadian wilderness, in which a small hunting party is 'planted...so audaciously in the jaws of the wilderness', on the fringes of 'uninhabited regions as vast as Europe itself'. Those of Scottish descent in the party have flinty, Protestant reserves to combat 'the strange fever of the wilderness', 'the seduction of the uninhabited wastes'. But the dreamy Frenchman Défago is clearly terrified by something there, an invisible presence that manifests horribly at night, just beyond the thin canvas of the tent or the dying embers of the fire. Défago is snatched by this gigantic thing, traced only by its foul odour and its incomprehensible tracks in the snow. This is the windigo: a monster that embodies the wild itself.

Many versions of the *wintiko* or *wīḫtikō* (for the Ojibwa or Cree) speak of this monster as a former member of the tribe who has fallen outside its social bonds and reverted to the savagery of devouring raw human flesh in the wilds. A more controversial debate surrounds whether an Algonquin-specific 'windigo psychosis' can be identified, in which anxiety about becoming such a monster induces the very condition it pathologizes. Either way, the windigo shows a very familiar anxiety about the borders of the human and animal, civilized and uncivilized, out there in the wilds, comparable to the Bigfoot or sasquatch of the northwest American wilderness or to the distribution of werewolf folklore in Europe, particularly in the Black Forest or the vast wilds of the Eastern Steppes. Ideas of the windigo have stalked through the American Gothic into the present day, most prominently in the Wolverine comics (from 1974) and *X-Men* films (from 2009), and in Stephen King's *Pet Sematary* (1983), but also in native American re-appropriations from the Gothic such as Gerald Vizenor's *Darkness in St. Louis Bearheart* (1978) or Louise Erdrich's *The Antelope Wife* (1998).

The wilderness is to be feared because it causes men to degenerate into savagery – a fear never clearer than in the sub-genre of 'backwoods horror', a distinctly American spin on folk horror. The backwoods cut

The American Gothic is suffused with the secret shame of starvation cannibalism.

families or communities off from modernity, leaving them out of time, sunk in poverty, the absence of social ties producing inbreeding, outlandish physical disfigurement and mental disability, used in this mode to embody transgressions of civilized behaviour. It is often, if not always, a form that abjects the poor as responsible for their own conditions.

In cinema, backwoods horror has been traced back to Herschell Gordon Lewis's Z-list shocker *Two Thousand Maniacs!* (1964), and can be tracked through horror films made outside the Hollywood system, including Tobe Hooper's *The Texas Chainsaw Massacre* (1974) or Wes Craven's *The Hills Have Eyes* (1977), the latter strikingly shot in the Mojave Desert. Both toy with the wilderness trope of cannibalism. The final shot of Craven's brutal film is a freeze frame of one of the lost campers reduced to the condition of the mutant family that hounds them, as he hacks at a body in an unrestrained frenzy of violence.

10

11

9. The Agassiz Column, Yosemite, photographed by Carleton Watkins, 1878.
10. Invisible forces threaten Lizzy Macklin in the Gothic Western *The Wind* (Emma Tammi, 2019).
11. William Henry Jackson, *Grand Canyon of the Colorado River*, photographed in 1883.

12

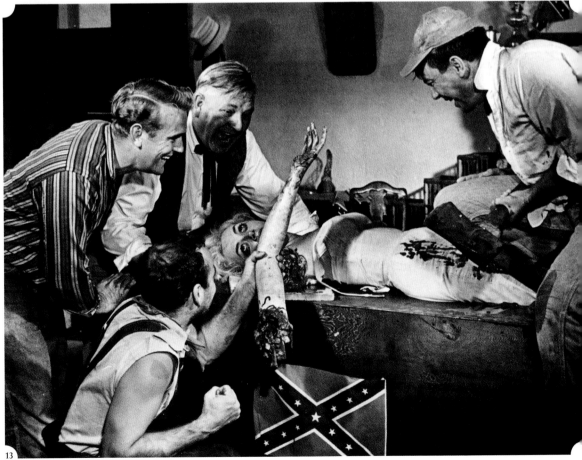

13

Hooper's vision of the lunatic inner world of Leatherface's remote house created an enduring vision of backwoods insanity that directly influenced the baroque horrors of Thomas Harris's *The Silence of the Lambs* (1988; filmed in 1991) or the later television series based on the same character, *Hannibal* (2013–15). That something bug-out weird still hankers for slaughter out in the wilderness continues to drive fiction such as Benjamin Percy's novella 'The Uncharted' (2019).

The seduction of the uninhabited wastes.

14.

The backwoods went mainstream with Martin Boorman's *Deliverance* (1972), about a group of Atlanta city boys on a kayaking weekend through the last uncharted stretches of a river in the South. Burt Reynolds plays the survivalist alpha male of the group, mourning the corrupting softness that has crept into modern man. 'There's something in the woods and the water we lost,' he tells his feminized fellows. They enter a remote world of crumbling roads and inbred mountain men, and soon receive their violent, humiliating comeuppance. Rugged models of hypermasculine survivalism in the wilderness were not far off: cue *Rambo: First Blood* (1982) or the first *Predator* film (1987), set in the forests of Central America. These later additions feel like swaggering ripostes to the unmanning of macho domination of nature in the 1970s. In the rueful era after the 2008 financial crash, we have seen a return to thoughtful interrogations of abandoned backwoods populations and landscapes, from Kelly Reichardt's *Wendy and Lucy* (2008) or *Meek's Cutoff* (2010) to Jeff Nichols's *Mud* (2012), Debra Granik's *Leave No Trace* (2018), and the uneasy post-apocalyptic horrors of Trey Edward Shults's *It Comes At Night* (2017).

Every industrialized culture creates its own backwoods folk, its own wilderness. This can range from the remote Sweden of *Midsommar* (2019), to the moors and fenland Gothic of England, to Australia's outback, with its own syncretic folklore that Gothicizes Aboriginal myths: where the Canadian woods has the wendigo, the Australian outback has the bunyip, a monstrous creature of creeks and billabongs. Early settlers in the 1840s remained unsure about whether it existed; in 1891, Rosa Campbell Praed's Gothic story 'The Bunyip' centred around the creature. It has since featured, de-fanged, in a number of Australian children's books and films, alongside its career in horrors such as *Red Billabong* (2016). The outback has continued to be a place of horror: it is where girls disappear in *Picnic at Hanging Rock* (1975); where violent animals

12. The lawless backroads of *Mad Max* (George Miller, 1979).
13. *Two Thousand Maniacs* (Herschell Gordon Lewis, 1964).
14. *Wake in Fright* (Ted Kotcheff, 1971), titled *Outback* in Australia.

terrorize in *The Long Weekend* (1975) or *Razorback* (1984); where remote communities develop murderous rituals for ill-advised visitors, in *Wake in Fright* (1971), *The Cars that Ate Paris* (1974) or the deadly backroads of *Mad Max* (1979); and where lone killers prey on backpackers, from *The Inn of the Damned* (1975) to *Wolf Creek* (2005). As in America, colonization has often been justified by settlers finally putting 'empty' or 'wasted' wilderness to godly, productive use. The colonial Gothic fills this emptiness with ominous signs of vengeful return of the displaced or dispossessed.

Cultural attitudes to the wilderness have profoundly changed in the era of raised ecological awareness. In America, the Wilderness Act of 1964 defined wilderness as 'an area where the earth and its community of life are untrammelled by man, where man himself is a visitor who does not remain'. As William Cronon has noted, this definition leaves the wilderness idealized and entirely dispeopled, erasing a whole history of displacement. Ecologists have begun to understand that much of the devastation of these habitats in the twentieth and twenty-first centuries could have been avoided by learning from indigenous populations.

The nascent ecological movement of the 1960s revived the nature writing of the eccentric Transcendentalist thinker Henry Thoreau, who embraced the spiritual virtues of the wilderness. 'I fear not spirits, ghosts, of which I am one', Thoreau said, in his account of a mountain climb in 1846, 'but I fear bodies, I tremble to meet them.' This anti-Gothic relation to the wild has been picked up by the post-1960s generation. The poet Gary Snyder, in *The Call of the Wild* (1990), suggests that the legal definition of wilderness might locate it in a pristine state, but that has come at the end of its life, when there is no 'Nature' left untouched by human actions. But, he adds, 'a ghost wilderness hovers around the entire planet', in overlooked backwoods, in explosions of fungi, moss, mould, spiders, mice – 'exquisite complex beings... inhabiting the fertile corners of the urban world in accord with the rules of wild systems'.

Elements of the Gothic have undoubtedly shared some of the worst aspects of 'ecophobic' modernity, where Nature is represented as an intrusive, vengeful alien other. But the lie of the land has radically changed, and fictions have emerged – particularly from the 'New Weird' school of writing since 2000 – that have set about reformulating the old Gothic tropes of antithetical Nature, and imagining an embrace of the possibilities of resituating humanity as Nature, in perpetual transformation, as humans-become-animal, become-fungus, become-hybrid, ecstatic-exploded-distributed beings permeable to the ecologies in which we are immersed. A wholly different, hybrid Gothic is beginning to emerge in fiction such as Jeff VanderMeer's *Southern Reach* trilogy (2014) or Aliya Whiteley or Martin MacInnes's post-human novels. These books signal that the wilderness need not be a space of fear.

> # The possibilities of resituating humanity as Nature, in perpetual transformation, as humans-become-animal, become-fungus, become-hybrid, ecstatic-exploded-distributed beings.

15. [opposite] The poisoned pastoral of Takashi Miike's delirious musical comedy-horror *The Happiness of the Katakuris* (2001).

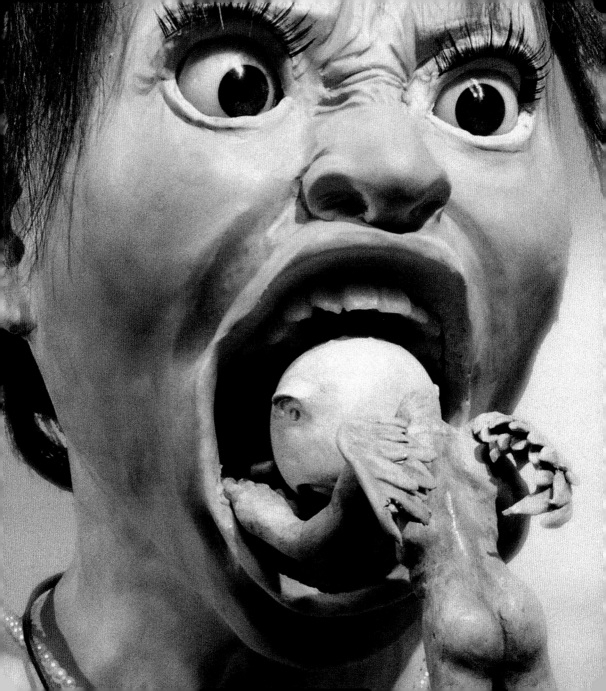

Edgelands

Most human lives do not happen in the extremes of the wilds or the thick of the city. Instead, we occupy messy, ill-defined spaces in between: suburbs, satellite towns, ribbon developments, transport corridors, out-of-town shopping malls, all bordered by even more liminal zones, parcels of undeveloped land, industrial buildings left to ruin, overlooked patches of wildness in railway sidings, canal paths or marooned between traffic interchanges, scrubby fields that become informal playgrounds or rubbish tips. In 2002, the geographer Marion Shoard called these places *edgelands*, a 'mysterious no-man's land' that appears in temporary and provisional forms. The poets Paul Farley and Michael Symmons Roberts followed this in the fragmentary *Edgelands: Journeys into England's True Wilderness* (2012). 'Somewhere in the hollows and spaces between carefully managed wilderness areas and the creeping, flattening effects of global competition, there are places where an overlooked England still exists,' they proclaimed. This is the territory of the paintings of George Shaw, who specializes in uncannily precise renditions of housing estates, garages and lock-ups, bus shelters and playing fields, and the ambient terrain of the music of Karl Hyde, who produced the album *Edgelands* in 2013, about the outskirts of London. For Shoard, edgelands are 'a vaguely menacing frontier land', and indeed these places have proved to be rich terrains for a distinctly modern, interstitial Gothic to emerge.

14

Looked through the window of
a commonplace, brand-new house,
and seen hell open before me.

1. [opposite] Little boxes: Levittown, built from kit-houses, on Long Island, New York, 1951.
2. Scenes of the M1 Motorway, UK, Martin Parr, *Boring Postcards*, 2019.

3

It is an identifiable trend across the world: in Japan, the anonymous suburbs of *The Grudge* or *Ring*; in South Korea, the blighted spaces of Bong Joon-ho's serial killer film *Memories of Murder* (2003), or the ultra-wealthy suburbs of *Parasite*; in Mexico, the urban terrain of Guillermo del Toro's vampire movie, *Cronos* (1993), or the alien invasion of Amat Escalante's *The Untamed* (2016); in Brazil, the gated suburban community of Kleber Mendonça Filho's *Neighbouring Sounds* (*O som ao redor*, 2012) under threat from intruders and shadowed by a legacy of colonial violence.

In England, the city began extending its grubby fingers into the countryside in the nineteenth century. Arthur Machen's 'The Inmost Light' (1894) is all the more appalling for taking place in the London suburb of Harlesden, 'a city of the dead'. In a row of houses that cut callously into the fields, the narrator sees a face, female yet not quite human, in one of the windows: 'I knew I had looked into another world – looked through the window of a commonplace, brand-new house, and seen hell open before me.' Richard Marsh used the London suburbs to the same horrifying effect in *The Beetle* (1897), when the homeless narrator Robert Holt makes the mistake of illicitly creeping over an open window sill into an apparently empty surburban house. His transgression proves deadly: he finds himself at the mesmeric mercy of a monstrous hybrid foreign Thing lurking there, mustering its strength to take on the capital.

These sites seem haunted in a new way: precisely because of their bland absence of history. This continued into the 1920s and 1930s, with Elizabeth Bowen's sequence of horror stories about women trapped on housing estates at the very edge of suburban civilization. The most unnerving of Bowen's sequence is 'Attractive Modern Homes' (1941), in which a couple move to a new-build on 'the far edge of the estate, facing a row of elms along a lane that used to be called Nut Lane'. There, the lonely wife, cut off from any form of organic community, sinks into depression and seeks relief in the pitiless fields up the lane 'which, unknown, edged the estate with savageness'. The husband, on his first venture up Nut Lane, finds his wife lying unmoving in a scrubby field, pole-axed by despair, spiritually if not physically dead. The edgelands can be occupied only by the undead, forced to persist in a limbo embodied by soulless housing developments.

After the Second World War, the German philosopher Martin Heidegger wrote in 'Building Dwelling Thinking' (1951) of the 'plight of dwelling' in the modern world,

3. *Memories of Murder* (Bong Joon-ho, 2003).
4. George Shaw, *The National Game*, 2017, from a series of hyperrealist paintings of anonymous suburban spaces made using Humbrol enamel paints.
5. Ominous threats hover around a gated community in Recife, Brazil, in *Neighbouring Sounds* (Kleber Mendonça Filho, 2012).

4

5

6

7

where the vast new housing developments built at pace to replace bombed-out housing stock no longer approached authentic dwelling-places. Instead, they represented a condition of existential *homelessness*. This condition prompts a new kind of haunting. Hilary Mantel's novel *Beyond Black* (2005) features a Spiritualist medium who exists in bland edgeland spaces around London in the forlorn hope of escaping the dead that continually drag around after her, barracking her every move:

> Alison kept out of London when she could. She would fight her way in as far as Hammersmith, or work the further reaches of the North Circular... But the hubs of their business were the conurbations that clustered around the junctions of the M25, and the corridors of the M3 and M4. It was their fate to pass their evenings in crumbling civic buildings from the sixties and seventies, their exoskeletons in constant need of patching: tiles raining from their roofs, murals stickily ungluing from their walls.

The medium's affectless assistant Colette grows up in another suburb, Uxbridge, and even after she reaches for something to re-enchant her – the New Age worlds of crystals, Tarot and mediumship – she finds only evidence of this same cheerless existence in the afterlife, a pointless, disenchanted enchantment. The drosscape spreads through every sphere.

The Welsh writer and filmmaker Iain Sinclair, in *London Orbital* (2002), sets out not to drive the motorway that circles the city, but perversely to walk the 'rage-inducing asteroid belt, debris bumping and farting and belching around a sealed-off city. The orbital motorway is a security collar fixed to the neck of a convicted criminal.' In his earlier works, Sinclair uses eccentric forms of occult ritual to conjure ghosts and vanished histories from a cityscape burnished to a vacant shine by property speculators and estate agents. *London Orbital* recovers a subversive sense of place from these abstracted edgelands, ordinarily smeared into an indifferent blur through a car window.

What erupts along these edgelands is not always supernatural, but a grindingly material violence. In the film *Eden Lake* (2008), a young middle-class couple

Suburbs, satellite towns, ribbon developments, transport corridors, out-of-town shopping malls, undeveloped land, industrial buildings left to ruin, overlooked patches of wildness in railway sidings, canal paths or marooned between traffic interchanges.

6. Michael Myers's first return to the suburbs in *Halloween* (John Carpenter, 1978).
7. Director John Carpenter and star Jamie Lee Curtis on the set of *Halloween*.
8. The Double R Diner, home of cherry pie and coffee, in the television series *Twin Peaks* (David Lynch, 1990–91).

head for a weekend at a disused quarry, which in childhood memory was a rewilded realm of woodland and lake, a bike ride away from suburban civilization. They find it in the process of being fenced off and rebranded as a luxury retreat, renamed 'Eden Lake'. The local community is portrayed as feral and lawless, brimming with violent resentment at incomers and intent on revenge. This same territory of chain hotels and suburbs, car parks and lock-ups is used in the first hour of Ben Wheatley's film *Kill List* (2011), a shiftless terrain full of indefinable dread and meaningless violence. On its release, *Eden Lake* was taken as social commentary on gentrification and its discontents – but it is rarely far from demonizing the poor. The debate at the time of the film's release was over the social fears embodied in the 'feral youth' that hound the young urban professional protagonists. Edgeland Gothic often marks out the terrors that bump against the insecure boundaries of the middle classes.

A distinct Gothic of the American suburbs has also developed since 1945, when planned suburbs began to drain urban centres of tens of millions of people. The most famous of these were the Levittowns constructed using assembly-line methods by William Levitt and Sons. A whole system of highways and shopping centres emerged that further hollowed out any notion of a central city hub: we arrive at the journalist Joel Garreau's notion of the 'edge city'. The rise of 'post-urban' America was fuelled by a system of federal loans to returning soldiers, but also by 'white flight' from urban centres. Levittowns were segregated. A violent riot occurred among hundreds of neighbours when an African American family moved into the Pennsylvania suburb in 1957, an instance echoed in Matt Ruff's horror novel about race and racism, *Lovecraft Country* (2016). There were also ominous national security reasons behind the encouragement of suburbanization: it dispersed the population in the event of nuclear war. Some of the sliproads in the new highway system were built with nuclear shelters huddled underneath the concrete, giving another new turn to the American Gothic.

In the suburbs, the somehow invisible-yet-rigid policing of normative values resulted in a stream of paranoid horrors that stretch from Jack Finney's *The Body Snatchers* (1954; filmed as *The Invasion of the Body Snatchers* in 1956), to Ira Levin's *The Stepford Wives* (1972; filmed in 1975) and Brian Yuzna's gross-out

9

A kid begins to suspect his model suburban mom and pop are secretly cannibals.

9. The undertow of racism in middle-class white America menaces Jordan Peele's *Get Out* (2017).

10. [opposite above] The robotic women of *The Stepford Wives* (Bryan Forbes, 1972).

11. [opposite below] *Dawn of the Dead* (George A. Romero, 1978) was filmed in one of America's first out-of-town shopping malls, in Monroeville, Pennsylvania.

12

13

14

satirical horror film about Beverly Hills, *Society* (1989), and on to Jordan Peele's exploration of the racial politics of middle-class liberal suburbia in *Get Out* (2017). Bob Balaban's earlier film *Parents* (1989), set in 1958, in which a kid begins to suspect his model suburban mom and pop are secretly cannibals, links the terrors lurking under benign Eisenhowerian conformity with Ronald Reagan's self-conscious evocation of that period.

Even the undead have moved to the suburbs. George Romero filmed *Dawn of the Dead* (1978) in one of the first out-of-town shopping malls in America. The success of the film, in which zombies shuffle through a consumer dreamland, was partly down to the mall cinemas that showed it, reflecting deadhead consumption back to its own suburban audiences. Meanwhile, part of the comic premise of the television series *Buffy The Vampire Slayer* (1997–2003) was the acceptance that a pretty suburb like Sunnydale was more than likely to hide a Hellmouth beneath the asphalt.

Violence can erupt from anywhere into the un-historied dream-worlds of suburban life. The American slasher horror subgenre typically plays out its slaughter of teens in the faceless, interchangeable tract houses of the suburbs. John Carpenter located the action of *Halloween* (1978) in the fictional town of Haddonfield in Illinois, but in fact used the interchangeable suburban streets of Pasadena. The protagonist Laurie Strode (played over and over in many sequels by Jamie Lee Curtis) is tracked by the inhuman glide of the camera along undifferentiated streets, the killer glimpsed through neat hedgerows or on trimmed lawns. It is a location and device that have been recycled many times; Carpenter isolates a specific suburban dread punctuated by sudden eruptions of psychotic violence. In the *Scream* franchise (1996–2011) or in David Robert Mitchell's smart revisionist rewrite of the slasher genre, *It Follows* (2015), the suburbs, mysteriously emptied of parents and populated by affectless teens, remain the crucial backdrop for this kind of murderous intrusion.

As always, alongside these sweaty serial nightmares, the Gothic is open to gentler, more insidious moods of suburban unease. Don DeLillo offered a strangely ecstatic embrace of apocalyptic dread in his suburban comedy *White Noise* (1984). In A. M. Homes's *Music for Torching* (1999), a bored couple with the ideal life break ranks, smoke crack and set fire to their lovely suburban house. An ineffable sadness settles over the doom-laden anti-hero of Richard Kelly's film *Donnie Darko* (2001),

12. *Buffy the Vampire Slayer* (Joss Whedon, 1997–2003), set in Sunnydale, a California suburb unfortunately built over a hellmouth.

13. The miseries of suburban teenagerhood in *Donnie Darko* (Richard Kelly, 2001).

14. The village lynch mob in *The Invasion of the Body Snatchers* (Don Siegel, 1956).

as time-loops tighten around his neck in the bland suburb of Middlesex, Virginia, resting on the edge of the wild woods beyond.

The edgelands described here evoke feelings ranging from utter paranoia that intensifies into abject horror, to quieter forms of unease. But in a recent turn, there are also works that begin to embrace the spectres of these territories. Gareth Rees's *Marshland: Dreams and Nightmares on the Edge of London* (2013) explores the shifting worlds of Hackney Marshes and the Lea Valley, East London, a once-overlooked zone that was targeted for major redevelopment in the run-up to the 2012 Olympic Games. 'Here you straddle a paper-thin border between London's future and that dark, primal memory which flows beneath the city and bubbles, occasionally, to the surface in the Old River Lea.' Rees does not suffer the untreatable melancholia that afflicts Iain Sinclair in his rages against the steady erasure of the old London. He is more attuned to the provisionality – and therefore the creative possibilities – of these edgelands: 'This place was a living hub for those excluded from the city.' They might be haunted, but the nightmare of history does not weigh heavily upon them.

The writer Gary Budden has used the term 'landscape punk' for his attempts to wrestle the landscape of Kent, one of the main recruiting grounds of racist groups and fringe parties, away from English nationalist ideology, by emphasizing the hybrid cultures and spectres that haunt its fragile, shifting shoreline. For Budden, home is an intrinsically 'bastard place, multi-cultural and multi-layered, mixed, impure'. Edgeland Gothic does not promise a re-wilding, but a re-weirding of our sensibility, finding new enchantment in the unlikeliest terrains. As we enter the so-called Anthropocene, an epoch where human development has definitively changed the planet, often for the worse, there is no way to separate 'nature' and 'culture' anymore. The Gothic speaks to this sense that we are all entangled in a messy middle, living in weird borderless biomes whose complex networks we can barely fathom. Edgeland Gothic comes to the fore as we teeter on the cusp of something terrible, something species ending. This is the truth the lie of the land presents to us: we all live in edgelands now.

> Home is an intrinsically 'bastard place, multi-cultural and multi-layered, mixed, impure.'

15. Class inequalities, explored in the South Korean black comedy *Parasite* (Bong Joon-ho, 2019).

III

THE
GOTHIC
COMPASS

North

The Goths

Where does the Gothic come from? Although the genre was named for a vague, all-encompassing medieval period, underlying that is the name of the Goths, that northern tribe who swept south, sacked Rome in AD 410, ended the Empire and plunged Europe into the so-called Dark Ages. While the Greeks demonized the Scythians from the Russian steppes as brutal warriors who devoured their own children, the ruthless efficiency of the Goths in conquest led some late Roman writers to depict them as an inexorable, supernatural force. They identified two branches – the Visigoths (from the west) and the Ostrogoths (from the east) – as they moved down the Danube towards Rome. Claudian's *The Gothic War* (AD 402–3), talks of a 'fatal horde' who 'poured pell-mell over remote lands, over every obstacle, like a storm of hail or a pestilence'. The Goths came with terrible portents: he tells of comets, severed human hands found still writhing in the bellies of slaughtered wolves (the emblem of Rome) and repeated solar eclipses that some Romans believed were directed by 'Thessalian witches, accompanying the barbarians'. Alaric's Gothic army could not be stopped by the riven and exhausted Roman Empire.

The most significant text after the Ostrogoths sacked Rome and occupied Italy, Jordanes's *The Origins and Deeds of the Goths*, was written in Constantinople in AD 551. It intended to redress the Goths' reputation, giving them a noble lineage and history; the geographical introduction locates their beginnings in the north, possibly on the island of Britain, which Jordanes finds difficult to describe because 'the whole of their disagreeable sort of day'

2

A 'fatal horde' who 'poured pell-mell over remote lands, over every obstacle, like a storm of hail or a pestilence.'

1. [opposite] Myths of the North: Franz Betz magnificently outfitted as Wotan in Richard Wagner's *Die Walküre*, 1876.

2. The *Flateyjarbók*, a fourteenth-century Icelandic illustrated manuscript containing the sagas of the Norse kings.

3

4

is always shrouded in mist 'and so is hidden in sight'. Eventually, he plumps for the island of Scandza (perhaps Scandinavia), hooking the Goths into the plethora of rich mythologies that hailed from the icy north.

Norse mythology was shared by the seafarers known as Vikings, whose diaspora stretched from Greenland through Scandinavia to settlements in northern Europe, a body of lore only written down in the Icelandic sagas composed in the thirteenth century. The sagas told stories of vengeful gods, menacing giants and dwarves, and bellicose humans battling for their place in Valhalla. Traces of this cycle have saturated the Gothic imagination ever since, from revivals and translations in the nineteenth century, in William Morris's poetry or Richard Wagner's *Ring Cycle* operas (1857), all the way up to Marvel comic rewrites of Thor, the trickster Loki and the Norse apocalypse, Ragnarök.

The intrinsic northernness of the genre remained essential to the Gothic Revival, posed in opposition to the south. This is the insistent message of John Ruskin's 'On the Nature of the Gothic', the most famous chapter of his *Stones of Venice* (1851–53). He speaks of the 'fellowship' between the Gothic spirit 'and our Northern hearts', and in a tortuous single sentence, fills out this structural opposition:

> Strength of will, independence of character, resoluteness of purpose, impatience of undue control, and that general tendency to set the individual reason against authority, and the individual deed against destiny, which, in the Northern tribes, has opposed itself throughout all ages to the languid submission, in the Southern of thought to tradition, and purpose to fatality, are all more or less traceable in the rigid lines, vigorous and various masses, and daringly projecting and independent structure of the Northern Gothic ornament: while the opposite feelings are in like manner legible in the graceful and softly guided waves and wreathed bands, in which Southern decoration is constantly disposed; in its tendency to lose its independence, and fuse itself into the surface of the masses upon which it is traced; and in the expression seen so often, in the arrangement of masses themselves, of an abandonment of their strength to an inevitable necessity, or a listless repose.

3. Depiction of a battle between Romans and Goths on the Grand Ludovisi sarcophagus, *c.* AD 260, which was rediscovered in Rome in 1621.
4. Lilli Lehmann as Woglinde in Richard Wagner's *Das Rheingold*, 1876.
5. Fragment of the Visigothic Code, proclaimed under King Chindasuinth in AD 642.

This line, as craggy and eccentric as any of the Gothic buildings Ruskin admired, also develops a racial profile of the sceptical, independent, Protestant northern character against a slothful, indolent Catholic south. In a later passage, Ruskin maps the Gothic from the bird's-eye view of the cartographer, moving northwards from the 'peacefulness of light' that bathes Syria, Greece, Italy and Spain, towards the mountains of Switzerland and France, the 'dark forests of the Danube and Carpathians' and further to 'irregular and grisly islands amidst the northern seas, beaten by storm, and chilled by ice'. Landscape here elides with both architecture and race, speaking of 'this wildness of thought, and roughness of work; this look of mountain brotherhood between the cathedral and the Alp'.

The return of the Gothic romance in the late Victorian period was also explicitly theorized as the revival of healthy northern romance forms against the effete styles of Realism and Naturalism. Robert Louis Stevenson was championed in the 1880s by his fellow Scot Andrew Lang, an influential critic, folklorist and anthropologist who tied the primal energy of the romance form to its origins in old Icelandic sagas, Scottish folk- and fairy-lore and the *Kalevala*, a Finnish epic. Lang also got the colonial administrator and adventure writer H. Rider Haggard into print. Haggard's first big hit, *King Solomon's Mines* (1885), idolizes manly bloodletting in battles on the colonial frontier. One of the central characters, Sir Henry Curtis, is repeatedly compared to 'an ancient Dane', a noble lineage of northern warriors; Haggard himself went to Denmark to trace his northern ancestry. 'Not for nothing did Nature leave us savages under our white skins,' Lang wrote in his essay 'Realism and Romance'.

In *The Supernatural Horror in Literature* (1927), the American writer H. P. Lovecraft made explicit his belief that the Gothic belonged to the northern tribes: 'Wherever the mystic Northern blood was strongest, the atmosphere of the popular tales became most intense.' In a letter to a friend, he talked of his favourite Gothic writers, such as Poe and Machen, as exhibiting 'a purely *Teutonick* quality' in which he found 'plain evidences of *Nordick* superiority' in its 'natural...race-stock'. Lovecraft's terms were taken from the avowedly racist theories of ideologues such as the eugenicist Madison Grant, who regarded unchecked immigration to America as a threat to the supremacy of a 'purely European type' from the countries of the Protestant north. Lovecraft adhered to this Nativist view, and his horror of grotesque, slobbering, hybrid monsters was all too often driven by an adherence to racist ideals of the northern Gothic.

There are, of course, more sympathetic ways of conceiving of a pan-northern European culture. Seamus Heaney's poetry collection *North*, which appeared in 1975, at the height of the sectarian war in Northern Ireland, deploys the terse rhythms and harsh, clashing consonants of Old Norse, language of the ancient North – the language that underpins *Beowulf*, the Icelandic sagas and Scandinavian poetry – in order to escape narrow national boundaries. Heaney connects the preserved bodies of human sacrifices, then recently rediscovered in the peat bogs of Jutland, Denmark, to the rituals of violence in the contemporary Irish conflict, as though these acts are imprinted in the deep past of northern tribes. Both Heaney and his contemporary Ted Hughes strongly influenced the emergence of a distinctly northern Gothic in Britain, associated with writers like Benjamin Myers.

This wildness of thought, and roughness of work; this look of mountain brotherhood between the cathedral and the Alp.

6. The disappearance of Sir John Franklin's expedition to find the North-West passage in 1845 left only enigmatic traces, such as this pocket chronometer. The wrecks of the ships were finally located in 2014 and 2016.

7. *Midsommar* (Ari Aster, 2019).

6

Far North

The idea of 'far north' persists in the Gothic imagination, derived from a much wider set of cultural mythologies, projections and fantasies of what lies in the unknown icy wastes beyond the edges of the known world. Greek and Roman geographers spoke of *Ultima Thule*, the furthest land in the far north – sometimes situated very precisely six days' sailing north of the British Isles, sometimes identified as present-day Iceland or Greenland. Even to northern cultures there is always a *further* north that terrifies: Norsemen feared the Sámi for their weird magic; Saxons feared the seafaring Vikings for their violence; the Danes feared the Norwegians; the Finns brooded on a dark Northland full of man-eating savages. Christian geo-theology sometimes placed hell in the icy north; sometimes it was the terrestrial location of Lucifer, the fallen angel. The unbaptised and those who died by suicide were buried on the north side of Christian churches, and some have a 'devil's door' on the north side. In Japan, it is ill-advised to sleep with your head pointing to the north, as this is the direction the souls of the dead depart. Margaret Atwood has argued that Canadian settler literature has been haunted by the idea of a malevolent north from its very beginnings: 'The North was uncanny, awe-inspiring in an almost religious way, hostile to white men, but alluring; it would lead you on and do you in.' The monsters that swim in the icy seas of the north are giant leviathans or narwhals (derived from the Norse *nar-hvalr*, meaning 'corpse-whale'), with tusks that, when taken south, were valued as proof of unicorns' existence. It is in the darkness and cold of the far north that one encounters the transcultural figure of the revenant, the returning dead, where the shamans of tribes across Siberia and into Canada conjure ghosts or icy blasts of wind, while the Northern Lights, traditionally believed by the Sámi to be the souls of the dead, dance in the sky. As the Polish journalist Mariusz Wilk put it in his *Journals of a White Sea Wolf* (2003), 'reality in the North is thinner than anywhere else, like a jumper worn out at the elbows, and the other world shines through it'.

Perhaps this explains why so many cultures have built walls to keep out what lies in the north. The Great Wall of China protected from northern incursions, either from Tartars or a mythical kingdom of deformed ghosts. The Gates of Alexander, built by Alexander the Great,

> **Reality in the North is thinner than anywhere else, like a jumper worn out at the elbows, and the other world shines through it.**

7

8

9

were said to block the entry of uncivilized barbarians from the north, keeping southern climes safe as long as they stood fast. Hadrian's Wall in England was a kind of northern limit to the Roman imperial imagination; the Byzantine scholar Procopius wrote that beyond its border 'it is actually impossible for a man to survive there even a half-hour, but countless snakes and serpents and every other kind of wild creature occupy this area as their own. And strangest of all the inhabitants say that if a man crosses this wall and goes to the other side he dies straightaway. They say, then, that the souls of men who die are always conveyed to this place.'

This mythology of the far north still feeds directly into the contemporary Gothic imagination. It is a zone that features Nazi zombies in the Norwegian film *Dead Snow* (2009), vampires who exploit a month without sun to slaughter a whole northern outpost in *Thirty Days of Night* (2007) and the bizarre sacrificial cults of northern Sweden in *The Ritual* (2017) or *Midsommar* (2019). In the television version of *Game of Thrones* (2011–19), the northern Wall is manned by the Night's Watch, who keep the 'wildlings' at bay. Feared by those savage tribes are the mythical White Walkers, whose Night King commands an army of the undead.

Yet what shadows these developments of the Gothic is not just the mythologies of the north, but very real explorations of the planet's northern reaches. Mary Shelley's *Frankenstein* (1818) begins and ends in the Arctic ice, where the explorer Robert Walton, trapped, listens to Victor Frankenstein unfold his awful tale. Shelley scholars have speculated that Walton, the mirror image of Frankenstein's obsessive hunt to transgress known limits, is based on Arctic explorers like Sir William Scoresby or the young John Franklin, who would publish his account, *Journey to the Shores of the Polar Seas*, in 1823. Shelley herself had visited the 'Sea of Ice' glacier in the French Alps in 1816, and responded to it with the mix of terror and delight described in the philosopher Edmund Burke's account of the sublime. Frankenstein's monstrous creation, a cold construct of dead body parts, is itself constantly associated with icy wastes, first cast out onto the Alpine glacier and finally pursued into the polar snows.

The British history of polar exploration is integral to a national mythology of heroic failure. The awful fate of John Franklin's expedition in 1845, with the loss of 128 men on his two ships, the *Erebus* and the *Terror*, and the death of Robert Falcon Scott and his team in the failed attempt to be the first to reach

8. 'A strange animal was bounding along within a cable's length from the ship': Illustration from Jules Verne's *At the North Pole, or, The Adventures of Captain Hatteras* (1874).

9. The disappearance of Franklin obsessed the Victorians. Several spiritualists claimed to have received the answer direct from the departed spirits of the crew, as in this 1889 text.

10. In the snowy wastes: *Frankenstein* (Kenneth Branagh, 1994).

11. The 'Victory Point' note, found in 1859, confirmed the fate of the Franklin Expedition. The first handwritten note is Franklin declaring 'All well' in May 1847. The additional note, scrawled nine months later, announces that Franklin and twenty-three others are dead.

12. Medicine chest from the Franklin Expedition.

10

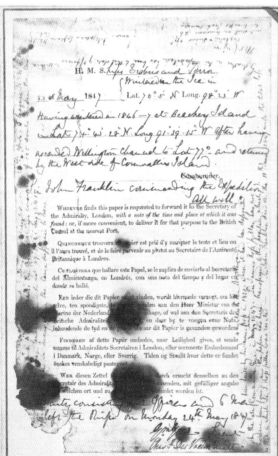

11

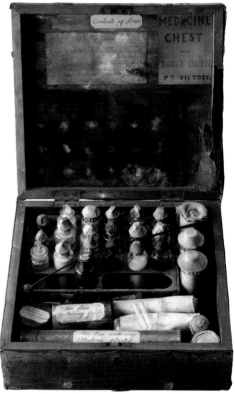

12

the South Pole in 1912, are both thoroughly ingrained into national myth. 'These rough notes and our dead bodies must tell the tale,' Scott wrote when he knew death was inevitable.

The disappearance of Franklin haunted the transatlantic imagination for decades. Last seen in Baffin Bay in July 1845, rumours that the seamen, trapped in the ice, had resorted to cannibalism – a tale that proved true – incensed many invested in Franklin's heroic masculinity. The true cause of the mass death of his crew remained a mystery for over a century; it is now assumed to have resulted from lead poisoning from the tinned food on the ships, a slow death that would have caused weakness, disorientation, impaired judgment and likely states of paranoia. The whole affair has continued to leave space for Gothic fantasy: Dan Simmons's novel *The Terror* (2007; serialized on television in 2018–19) follows the timeline of the last desperate year of the expedition, with the surviving crew menaced by a vengeful monster that emanates from indigenous supernatural beliefs, somewhat like a flesh-eating windigo.

In *The Spectral Arctic* (2018), Shane McCorristine tracks the ways that strange hallucinations, uncanny presences, weird dreams and visions and a blend of the superstitions of seamen and the beliefs of indigenous populations crowd in at the edges of the extensive scientific and topographic literature in the field. The bluff accounts of explorers and sea captains alike are doubled by 'alternative voices, sometimes dissenting, gothic or ghostly', he says. The Victorian writer and doctor Arthur Conan Doyle, who as a poor medical student in 1880 took a job as ship's surgeon on the Arctic whaler *Hope*, wrote in his *Memories and Adventures* (1924) that 'the peculiar other-world feeling of the Arctic regions [was] a feeling so singular that if you have once been there the thought of it haunts you all your life'. In an early tale, 'The Captain of the "Polestar"' (1883), the Scottish captain of a whaler is led to his death by a spectral image of his lost lover, who haunts the ship with keening cries – an image perhaps based on the legends of alluring sirens or mermaids, glimpsed as a vague shape through the icy hoar frosts that surround them. When the search party finds the Captain dead on the ice, 'his hands were still outstretched as though grasping at the strange visitor which had summoned him away into the dim world that lies beyond the grave'.

Conan Doyle was a Spiritualist, a believer in contact between the living and the dead. The movement arrived in England from America in the early 1850s, and was inevitably caught up in the drama of the search for John Franklin. Emma, 'The Seeress of Bolton', fell into trance states and made 'distant excursions' to people; shown a sample of Franklin's handwriting, she claimed to have contacted the still-living Franklin (he had actually died in 1847). Other clairvoyants and crystal gazers drew maps of his location, but the weirdest case was of the spirit of a four-year-old girl from Liverpool, Little 'Weezy' Coppin, who became a guide to her older sister, the conduit for messages that purported to come from Franklin's ghost. Weezy's story was told nearly fifty years later in Henry Skewes's book *Sir John Franklin, The Discovery of his Fate: A 'Revelation'* (1889), perpetuating the spooky atmosphere surrounding Franklin's disappearance.

'The white north has thy bones....' Thus begin the poet Alfred Lord Tennyson's words on Franklin's memorial in Westminster Abbey: a neat summation of the hooded intent the Gothic imagination has long ascribed to the icy climes of the north.

13. [opposite] 'Lost on the Ice Cap', illustration from Albert Operti's *The White World: Life and Adventures within the Arctic Circle* (1902).

LOST ON THE ICE-CAP

South

Ancient geographers knew that the planet was a sphere, but the fierce climate in the deserts of Africa and the Middle East meant that, to most of the western world, the south was considered almost entirely inaccessible. Fantasy projections about it went into overdrive. Pliny's *Natural History* recorded such fabulous southern races as the Sciapodes (men who hopped on one giant foot) and the Blemmys (men with no heads, their eyes being on their shoulders and their mouths in their chests). On medieval *mappa mundi*, the south seas teem with sea monsters. The far south is still frequently referred to as the *Antipodes*, deriving from the name of a place where the feet are turned backward – a mark of its antithesis to everything about the known world. Hence, also, the Antarctic: the opposite of the primary, northern pole.

2

1. [opposite] Ice grotto, photographed during the Terra Nova Expedition to the Antarctic led by Robert Falcon Scott. Scott died attempting to reach the pole in March 1912.
2. Post Office safe from the 'Little America' exploration base established on the Ross Ice Shelf, Antarctica, 1934.

Antarctic Gothic

The journey into the remote, unpopulated and yet long-imagined Antarctic has produced a fascinating interchange between exploration and the Gothic imagination. Samuel Taylor Coleridge's *The Rime of the Ancient Mariner* (1797), a hypnotic ballad of supernatural guilt and horror in the South Atlantic, is thought to have been partly inspired by the poet's tutor, William Wales, who had served with Captain Cook on his second voyage south in 1772–75. Yarns of ghost ships are transformed into Coleridge's hallucinatory vision of 'The Night-Mare, LIFE-IN-DEATH', who seems to be a nemesis for the Mariner's dreadful transgression. Extreme latitudes and mental states merge into a distinct psychotopology of the far south:

> The ship drove fast, loud roared the blast
> And southward aye we fled.
>
> And now there came both mist and snow,
> And it grew wondrous cold:
> And ice, mast-high, came floating by
> As green as emerald.

The same propulsion south is evident in Edgar Allan Poe's enigmatic *The Narrative of Arthur Gordon Pym of Nantucket* (1838). Poe had been fascinated early on by the exploration of the Antarctic; his first published story was the Gothic sea adventure 'MS Found in a Bottle' (1833). Both of Poe's Antarctic tales explore the American army officer John Cleve Symmes's theory that the Earth was hollow and open at both poles. Symmes's advocates wrote utopian fictions about the societies that might blossom at the South Pole in the 1820s,

The ultimate in alien terror.

THE THING

3

3. *The Thing* (John Carpenter, 1982).
4. *Alien vs. Predator* (Paul W. S. Anderson, 2004).
5. Portraits of members of Scott's fateful
   Terra Nova Expedition, 1910–13.
6. The site of the second 'Little America' station,
   Antarctica, 1935–36.

eventually proving influential enough to foster an official American expedition south in the 1830s to test the theory. The three-part *Pym* takes Poe's antagonist progressively further south, through torture, shipwreck and starvation cannibalism, until an escape from a cannibal island in a canoe leaves Pym drifting into the 'wide and desolate' Antarctic ocean, 'a region of novelty and wonder' that seems to pass through the latitude of ice and into warmer waters, in accordance with Symmes's theory. In its famously abrupt ending, Pym enters the luminous white glare around the chasm at the end of the world, and 'a shrouded human figure, very far larger in its proportions than any dweller among men' leaps up as if to meet him, with a skin the colour of 'the perfect whiteness of the snow'. What allegorical intent is shrouded in this puzzling end?

The incompleteness of the tale places it firmly among those torn fragments typical of the Gothic form. But the fade into blank whiteness also accords well with the scholar Eric Wilson's observation that the Antarctic 'has spawned a history of negative discovery, a hermeneutics of despair'. The hollow end of the tale has prompted several writers to try to 'finish' it. Jules Verne wrote a breathless sequel, *An Antarctic Mystery*, in 1897, set eleven years after Poe's account and retracing its steps. More enduringly, H. P. Lovecraft's 'At the Mountains of Madness' (1936), one of his most sustained evocations of creeping dread, takes elements of Poe's whited-out ending to advance the exploration into the cold heart of Antarctica. For Lovecraft, devoted to the Nordic Gothic, it is logical that his worst nightmares should be located at the opposite, Southern pole. His story is saturated in references to the literature of Antarctic exploration, including the American expedition from 1928 to 1930 that established the 'Little America' base station on Antarctica.

The Antarctic 'has spawned a history of negative discovery, a hermeneutics of despair.'

Lovecraft's expedition team uses an aircraft to fly over the unknown peaks in the interior of Antarctica, where they find a 'nameless stone labyrinth', a city built in non-Euclidean geometric shapes by an alien race. With typical Lovecraftian revulsion, these mighty gods have been brought low by their own creation, the Shoggoths, 'shapeless entities composed of a viscous jelly...constantly shifting shape and volume'. What the expedition encounters, still alive in those frozen wastes, drives all but the narrator to irreparable madness or death.

Petty Officer P. Keohan

B. C. Day.

C. H. Mearos

C. S. Wright

'A shrouded human figure, very far larger in its proportions than any dweller among men' leaps up as if to meet them, with a skin the colour of 'the perfect whiteness of the snow.'

We can be sure that the writer John W. Campbell Jr. read Lovecraft. In his polar terror tale 'Who Goes There?' (1937), an idealized crew of American engineers, clearly modelled on Richard Byrd's 'Little America' station, discover an alien ship and a visitor that, unthawed, wreaks havoc until the pragmatic-minded crew resolves how to kill it. It was moved to the Arctic for its first cinematic outing as *The Thing from Another World* (1951), an early contribution to the 1950s science-fiction B-movie craze. In John Carpenter's unexpectedly grisly remake *The Thing* (1982), which returns the setting to the Antarctic, the heroic age of American exploration and engineering is very much over. The shape-shifting creature that explodes from within the lifeforms it colonizes and mimics, including the men at the station, can never be defeated. The film ends, rather like Poe's *Pym*, without closure.

Since Carpenter, alien lifeforms breaking out of suspended animation in the polar icecaps have proliferated: *The X-Files Movie* (1998), Charles Stross's novella 'A Colder War' (2002) and the decidedly silly *Alien vs. Predator* (2004) have all been set in the Antarctic. This terrain has also continued to haunt the scientific imagination. The measure of the polar ice sheet is not only the bellwether for registering the runaway logic of the climate crisis. In 2016, it was in the Antarctic that scientists discovered a high-energy particle so completely anomalous that it has led some physicists to suggest that they emanate from an anti-universe symmetrically opposite to ours, made of anti-matter, where time goes backwards. That this hypothesis emerges in the blank void of the Antarctic seems somehow perfectly apposite: this antithetical space continues to be the opposite of everything in the known world.

7

7 'Monstrous Races' as depicted in the Nuremberg Chronicle, 1493.
8. [opposite] Alien costume design for *Alien vs. Predator*, based on H. R. Giger's original drawings.

The Other Deep South

In a dismissive review of new writing by Erskine Caldwell and William Faulkner, the novelist Ellen Glasgow first described Southern Gothic as a 'Raw-Head-and-Bloody-Bones' branch of American fiction, filled with a parade of 'half-wits', 'whole idiots', 'nymphomaniacs' and 'paranoiacs'. This may sound pretty good – but it was intended to smother this new Gothic of the American South at birth.

As so often, this attempt to bury a trend instead crystallized it. It became a self-conscious tradition from the 1920s and 1930s, marked by the use of a heightened grotesque that ran first through Caldwell and Faulkner, and then after 1945 into the work of Tennessee Williams, Flannery O'Connor and Carson McCullers, through the 'Rough South' school that included Cormac McCarthy in the 1960s and into the present with books such as Jesmyn Ward's *Sing, Unburied Sing* (2017). In 'Some Aspects of the Grotesque in Southern Fiction' (1960), Flannery O'Connor described 'Christ-haunted' stories with 'strange skips and gaps', sudden conjunctions of the 'violent and comic' and deliberate 'distortion', remarking that, in the South, 'ghosts can be very fierce and instructive'.

The Gothic offers a language of guilt, dread and horror in which to communicate the inescapable nightmare of history that clings to the American South. In Toni Morrison's *Beloved* (1987), the keening ghosts of the South's slave history are routine, innumerable and everywhere: 'Not a house in the country ain't packed to its rafters with some dead Negro's grief.' Jesmyn Ward's characters are latched onto by ghosts needy for acknowledgment, unable to pass on until their story is told. The landscapes of the American South, from its bayous and swamps, to its moss-choked plantation houses fallen into ruin and its segregated cities, are haunted; the unappeasable ghost of the baby Beloved is an emblem of the imperative, impossible mourning for the victims of slavery, 'sixty million and more', as Morrison's dedication page starkly has it.

But these more celebrated literary works are shadowed by a parallel, earlier tradition of Gothic genre fiction written in the South. Thomas Moore's 1802 ballad, 'The Lake of the Dismal Swamp', already uses the language of haunting in the swamps and bayous. Early transpositions of European Gothic began to transform the castle ruin into the isolated or abandoned plantation, romanticized in novels

9

9. Clarence John Laughlin, *Elegy for Moss Land,* double exposure photograph
    used for the cover of his book *Ghost Along the Mississippi* (1940).

10

11

like John Pendleton Kennedy's *Swallow Barn* (1835) or William Gilmore Simms's German-influenced *Martin Faber* (1833). Thomas Nelson Page's short story 'No Haid Pawn' (1887), about an abandoned plantation house, built on a 'primeval swamp' by slaves, is characteristic of such transpositions. It contains the requisite 'mysterious rooms and underground passages', with rumours of dungeons for the torture of those enslaved there. But its true horror concerns No Haid Pawn's association with the 'underground railway' – the secret network of contacts that helped slaves escape north to freedom in the years before the Civil War. Page was an apologist for slavery and the lynchings that lasted long into the twentieth century. In his tale, a monstrous man, 'the most brutal negro I ever knew', portends the threat of free slaves to 'the foundations of the whole social fabric' of the South. The man's murderous revenge on the planters is repeated again and again, in a headless haunting that only comes to an end when a lightning strike burns the accursed ruin to the ground, and all traces of this past sink below the 'dark waters'. Page helped establish a formula repeated onscreen in D. W. Griffiths's *The Birth of a Nation*, with its racist, melodramatic tropes of Black 'bucks' menacing white women and a reinvented Ku Klux Klan riding in as the white knights of medieval romance to preserve the purity of the race.

Still more influential was Edgar Allan Poe, educated at the University of Virginia and often claimed as a Southern Gothic writer. To read Poe in this context turns exercises in horror such as 'The Black Cat' (1843) into allegories of phobic racism. The decaying mansion at the centre of 'The Fall of the House of Usher' (1839) underlies many Southern Gothic fictions, from the doomed plantation house of Sutpen's Hundred in Faulkner's *Absalom, Absalom!* (1936), to the dark secrets of sex, violence and murder in the grand house at the centre of Gillian Flynn's Missouri-set novel, *Sharp Objects* (2006), or, moving into Gothic crime fiction, the tangle of violent white supremacy that reaches from the deep past into the present in Greg Iles's *Natchez Burning* trilogy (*Natchez Burning*, 2014; *The Bone Tree*, 2015; *Mississippi Blood*, 2017).

One of the most evocative accounts of the tangled family histories of the South is the memoir with photographs *Hold Still* (2016) by the artist Sally Mann, which explores 'a payload of Southern Gothic'

12

Death owns these fields entirely. It sculpted this ravishing landscape and will hold the title to it for all time.

10. Sally Mann, *Deep South, Untitled (Checkmark Windsor)*, 1998.

11. Sally Mann, *Untitled (Swamp Bones)*, 1996.

12. Poster for *The Birth of a Nation* (D. W. Griffith, 1915). The film's depiction of the Ku Klux Klan played a part in reviving the group among white supremacists.

running for over a century through the history of Mann's family: 'deceit and scandal, alcoholism, domestic abuse, car crashes, bogeymen, clandestine affairs...maybe even bloody murder'. The defeat of the South in the Civil War in 1865 produced a deeply complex and divided culture, ravaged by still unhealed wounds. Mann locates her account in this 'lingering aftermath of defeat', asserting: 'pain is a dimension of old civilizations. The South has it. The rest of the United States does not.' For many years she photographed that pain-filled South, finding in Mississippi and Louisiana, 'the gracious splendour of its lost world founded on a monstrous crime.'

William Faulkner's combination of daunting, high-Modernist narrative experimentation with all the apparatus of genre horror makes him the unavoidable central figure of any account of the Southern Gothic, his work a potent hybrid, rancid with the stench of unquiet history. 'A Rose for Emily' (1930) finds an elderly woman sharing her bed with the mummified corpse of her husband; *As I Lay Dying* (also 1930), its narrative fractured between increasingly unhinged members of the same impoverished white family, involves a repeatedly cursed attempt to drag the rotting

13

corpse of the mother to proper burial, a situation so extreme it ends with one son committed to the local asylum. The juxtaposition of farce with physical and mental torture clearly influenced writers like Flannery O'Connor, who breezily slaughters a whole family as the strange, unmotivated twist of her funny story 'Good Country People' (1955). Sally Mann shares these preoccupations, exploring the obsession with death that she inherited from her father, who was a country doctor, in her remarkable series *What Remains* (2003), for which she photographed corpses in various states of decay at a research facility called (somewhat farcically) the 'Body Farm'. The series also includes large-format photographs of Antietam, the site of the battlefield that, on 17 September 1862, during the American Civil War, had the worst death toll of any single day in American history. Mann had asked herself: 'Does the earth remember?', and at Antietam found that 'death owns these fields entirely. It sculpted this ravishing

landscape and will hold the title to it for all time.' By using the nineteenth-century technique of brushing wet collodion onto glass plates to expose them, she also constructs a material link to the Civil War, when collodion was used to dress soldiers' injuries. Her images bloom out of the traumatic wound itself.

Faulkner's later novella 'The Bear' (1942) uses the pursuit of a fabled bear through 'the immemorial darkness of the woods' by a rag-tag group of hunters to form an elegiac account of the South as a landscape tamed, ruined and living in the aftermath of defeat. Down the generations, long after the Civil War, the South remains 'their ravaged patrimony, the dark and ravaged fatherland still prone and panting from its etherless operation'. In *Sanctuary* (1930) and *Light in August* (1931), Faulkner had begun to use Gothic armature to address the abiding legacy of slavery and racism in the South. Segregation was obsessively policed long after slavery was abolished, and after the First World War the economic, political and violent social containment of the Black population of the South intensified. The Ku Klux Klan, reimagined in *The Birth of a Nation* (1915), reached its largest membership in the 1920s, and used institutional corruption, violent summary justice and lynchings to uphold white supremacy. The South became the abject, Gothicized other of the supposedly liberal northern states. But in Faulkner's novels, sexual violence bleeds across races to produce secret family histories, children tortured by an inheritance of mixed blood that they have been raised to loathe. A white man can become Black, and thus subject to the communal rage of the South, in a single revelation.

The Southern Gothic also has a distinct presence in American cinema, divided between mainstream studio productions and low-budget shock horror. The early, sustained presence of African American filmmakers such as Oscar Micheaux, Richard Maurice and James and Eloyse Gist tends to be swept aside by the huge impression made by D. W. Griffiths. Micheaux in fact directed a riposte to Griffiths, *The Symbol of the Unconquered* (1920), advertised with the line 'See the Ku Klux Klan in action – and their annihilation'.

14

15

13. A zombie head prop from the George A. Romero Collection.
14. Swamp Gothic: *Two Thousand Maniacs* (Herschell Gordon Lewis, 1964).
15. 'Going native' in *Deliverance* (John Boorman, 1972).
16. [following spread] *Night of the Living Dead* (George A. Romero, 1968).

17

17. At a creepy old plantation house in Donald Glover's television series *Atlanta* (2018).
18. *Southern Comfort* (Walter Hill, 1981).
19. Photograph of Felicia Felix-Mentor, introduced to Zora Neale Hurston as a real zombie, from Hurston's book on Haiti, *Tell My Horse* (1938).
20. Ritual artefacts from the Voodoo Museum, New Orleans, Louisiana.

18

Faulkner was lured to Hollywood in the 1930s, largely to drink himself into stupor, but the adaptation of his novel *Intruder in the Dust* (1949) was part of a line of liberal protest films about the South that most famously included *To Kill a Mockingbird* (1960) and Roger Corman's daring *The Intruder* (1962), on which the film crew and actors were nearly lynched during location shoots in Missouri and Charleston. Norman Jewison's *In the Heat of the Night* (1967), with its incendiary performance by Sidney Poitier as a Black policeman from the north who strikes an old, racist planter aristocrat in the face, was a distinct sign that the representation of race on film, controlled in Hollywood for fifty years by the 'Hays Code', was coming to an end. At the same time, low-budget horrors from entirely outside the studio system, such as *Two Thousand Maniacs* (1964), the overt racial politics of George Romero's inaugural mass zombie film *Night of the Living Dead* (1968) or the backwoods lunacy of *The Texas Chainsaw Massacre* (1974), could speak even more openly about the remains of genocidal legacies.

Southern Gothic need not be the crazed Cajuns of *Southern Comfort* (1981) or murderous, inbred hillbillies of *Deliverance* (1972), where the tangled backwoods of the South swallow northern liberals alive; recent films by Jeff Nichols interrogate the complexities of the South from within, touching on Southern Gothic conventions in *Shotgun Stories* (2007) and exploring apocalyptic visions in *Take Shelter* (2011) and *Midnight Special* (2016). African American filmmakers with Southern heritage, such as Barry Jenkins and Ava DuVernay, have also incorporated echoes of the Southern Gothic into their work, including Jenkins's *Moonlight* (2016), adapted from Tarell Alvin McCraney's previously unpublished play *In Moonlight Black Boys Look Blue*, and the DuVernay-created television show *Queen Sugar*, which premiered in 2016, based on Natalie Baszile's novel of the same name.

Plantation imagery is put to haunting use in Beyoncé's music video 'Formation' (2016) and across her visual album of the same year, *Lemonade*, and adds to the surrealistic unease of Black life in Donald Glover's television series *Atlanta* (2016–18). Meanwhile, the rapper–artist–director M. Lamar declares himself a 'NEGRO-GOTHIC devil worshipping free black man in the blues tradition', and since 2016, the African American clothing brand Gothic Lamb has been selling AFRO-GOTH T-shirts, promising to 'Make America Goth Again'.

New Orleans is always the exception, the Other to the furious, white, 'Christ-haunted' slave states. This is in part to do with the intrinsic mixing of cultures in Louisiana, a French settlement from 1718, home to the French Acadians – hence 'Cajuns' – expelled from Canada; a Spanish colony from 1762; then handed back to the French and sold to America in 1803. New Orleans was a port and a place of refuge for freed slaves, its rich heritage of indigenous traditions, associated with the Mardi Gras tribes, mingling with the diverse cultures of the Caribbean. If the city is now associated with magic, Gothic excess and of course Louisiana voodoo, a syncretic religion forged on slave plantations that fuses elements of West African and Catholic belief, that was largely generated by Gothic writers from the late nineteenth century onwards.

In the 1880s, the journalist, Gothic novelist and sometime-explorer Lafcadio Hearn told a friend that he had 'pledged [himself] to the worship of the Odd, the Queer, the Strange, the Exotic, the Monstrous'. In New Orleans in 1881, he documented the lavish funeral of the 'Queen of the Voudous', Marie Laveau. An anthology of his journalism, *Inventing New Orleans* (2001), perhaps claimed too much for him, but he was certainly one of the first to tinge the city's cultural life with the Gothic. In the 1920s, the Harlem Renaissance novelist Zora Neale Hurston undertook her anthropological training in New Orleans and Louisiana, where she reported on 'conjure' and 'hoodoo' traditions and studied under a Catholic hoodoo doctor. Her mostly dry report, published in the *Journal of American Folklore* in 1931, occasionally lets true fear peek out: 'It was very dark and eerie there at the fork in the road in the wood, and I was genuinely frightened. It was a very long hour. I hope never to meet its brother.' It sounds like the same road where the legendary bluesman Robert Johnson was said to have met the devil. Hurston went on to explore voodoo in its most developed form in Haiti, where she met – and photographed – a person she believed to be a zombie, her account of which was published in *Tell My Horse* (1938).

> It was very dark and eerie there at the fork in the road in the wood, and I was genuinely frightened. It was a very long hour. I hope never to meet its brother.

New Orleans, and Louisiana more broadly, has also become the chosen home of a succession of extremely famous fictional vampires. Anne Rice's *Vampire Chronicles*, beginning with *Interview with a Vampire* in 1976, sees the cultural mixing and outlaw status of the city as a natural home for an old-world aristocracy of the undead. Charlaine Harris's *Sookie Stackhouse* books, the basis for the television series *True Blood* (2008–14), more overtly explore the contemporary sexual and racial politics of the South through the vampire premise. In a universe where vampires have emerged as uneasily tolerated fellow citizens, there are those, like the Fellowship of the New Sun, who demand racial purity and seek to exterminate vampires. An endlessly malleable metaphor, the vampire has evolved into another useful tool by which to continue to explore what one early reviewer of Faulkner called the 'Horrible South'.

21. [opposite] The first gesture of the greeting ritual, performed by Haitian Voodoo priest Louis Romain, photographed by Rex Hardy Jr., 1937.

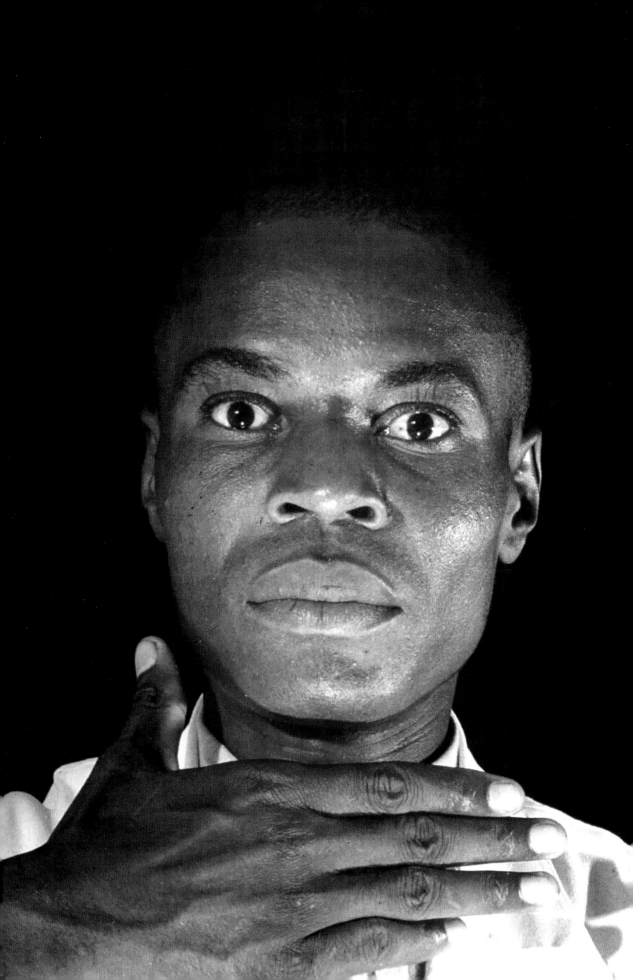

1

East

On medieval *mappa mundi*, east was at the top of the map, with the Garden of Eden at the very top, at once inside and outside the frame. This positioning follows many other 'solar mythologies', where east was the sacred direction; Ancient Egyptian theology, for instance, was premised on this east–west axis, where the sun rose and set. But if the spiritual east can appear to be paradisiacal, European thought has often cast the geographical east as a locus of the unknown, the barbaric, the threatening horde. Christian Europe became more cohesive as a religious and cultural formation by defining itself *against* the east: first the Arabs and Jews of the Levant (another name derived from the sunrise,denoting a region that included Syria, Jordan, Lebanon and Palestine), then later against the 'Near East' of the Ottoman Empire, ruled from Constantinople. The Goths themselves have, as part of this same discourse, long been claimed for the virile and superior races of the north, but they were also once an eastern horde, the ominous migrants who became the wreckers of Rome's empire. 'Near', 'Middle' and 'Far' East are relative terms; they define an other in relation to the west, a project we now call 'Orientalism'.

In the eighteenth and nineteenth centuries, scientific racism re-ordered this world again, placing the fictive Caucasians of the west above the Semites or Asiatics of the east, while anxiety about the rise of China or Japan later in the nineteenth century began the anti-Asian discourse of the 'Yellow Peril'. After 1945, Cold War blocs shifted the meaning and shape of east and west again, as, in the twenty-first century, has the United States and Britain's 'War on Terror'. In Gothic fiction, various modulations of the east have been used to constitute different kinds of threats to Western identity and integrity. In an epigraph to their documentary history of the 'yellow peril', John Kuo Wei Tchen and Dylan Yeats use a particularly telling quote attributed to American President George W. Bush on the eve of the invasion of Iraq in 2003: 'Gog and Magog are at work in the Middle East. Biblical prophecies are being fulfilled.'

L'OGRE D'ORIENT

Il rend le jaune pour avaler le blanc. Collection T. Bianco.

2

1. *The Mask of Fu Manchu* (Charles Brabin, 1932).
2. *The Ogre of the Orient*, hand-tinted lithograph, 1904.

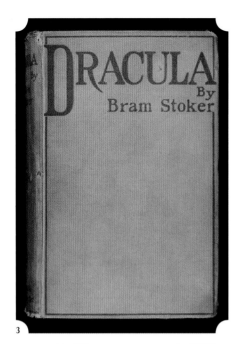

3

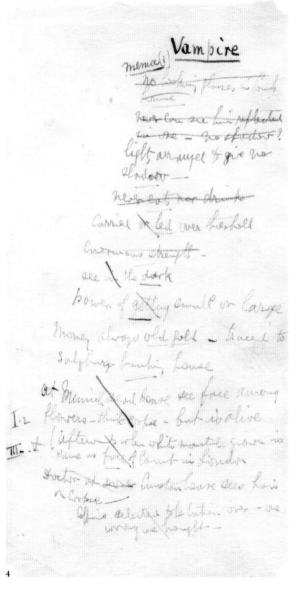

4

Eastern Questions

The fuzzy eastern edges of Europe caused constant anxiety in the imperial metropoles of the late eighteenth century – a confusion of blurred lines that is echoed in Bram Stoker's *Dracula* (1897). The titular vampire, as though he had been reading the British press closely, calls Transylvania a 'whirlpool of European races'. Many critics have explored the possibility that Stoker's monster exploited fears of a Jewish 'invasion' of London's East End in the 1890s; one letter in the *East London Observer* in 1902 reported: 'We in East End London know only too well what blood suckers the Jews are. Here they drive the worker from his home through their rapacity; they verily suck the life blood of the nation.' The monster of *Dracula*, which is rife with anti-Semitic tropes, is also a product of the 'Eastern Question' that haunted European geopolitics throughout the nineteenth century.

Bram Stoker had immediate knowledge of these liminal eastern zones from his brother George Stoker, who had volunteered as a surgeon during the Bulgarian wars in the 1870s. *Dracula* also builds on a long history of Eastern European or Slavic superstitions used in the Gothic; vampire belief was widespread in the villages of the Balkans and across Greece. A Greek island saturated in vampire myths is the location for Mark Robson's evocative horror film *Isle of the Dead* (1945); the undead soldier who returns from war to his lover in Gottfried Bürger's 'Lenore' (1773) is coming back from the far reaches of Hungary; Paul Féval's *La Ville Vampire* (1867) locates the vampires near Belgrade, Serbia; and Sheridan Le Fanu set his vampire tale 'Carmilla' (1872) in Styria, a location also used for Stoker's short story 'Dracula's Guest'. Recently, the writer Vesna Goldsworthy has identified a 'Balkan Gothic' that makes the territory a space of horrified projection for Western Europe, reinforced by the war that erupted in the former Yugoslavia in the 1990s.

Shifting into the Arab world, Edward Said's epochal study *Orientalism* (1978) argued that stereotypes about the 'Middle East' were systematically fixed in a colonial discourse propounded through different avenues: politics, war, administration, philology, anthropology, theology, tourism and cultural representation. In 1885, the scholar and traveller Sir Richard Burton, who had previously disguised himself as an Arab to reach Mecca, published an unexpurgated edition of *The Arabian Nights*, so risqué

it was available to wealthy subscribers only, and with an appended 'Terminal Essay' that explored the supposed sexual vices of Arabia, calling it a 'Sotadic Zone' where pederasty was culturally sanctioned. Such fantasies of sexual possibility are also glimpsed in the paintings of John Frederick Lewis or the lascivious Egyptian diaries of Gustave Flaubert.

After the British occupation of Egypt in 1882 and the consequent entrenchment of language about 'untrustworthy' Arabs, a particular, British Gothic of Egypt developed, full of tales of vengeful mummies, conniving Arabs and stolen artefacts that cursed their owners, a clear register of displaced anxiety about the colonial violence behind such acquisitions. By 1923, when the fifth Earl of Carnarvon died just six weeks after attending the formal opening of the tomb of the boy pharaoh Tutankhamun, the stage for 'Tutankhamun's curse' had been prepared by over forty years of mummy curse narratives, from Conan Doyle's 'Lot No. 249' (1894), through Bram Stoker's *Jewel of Seven Stars* (1902) to Sax Rohmer's *Tales of Secret Egypt* (1918). Rather like *Dracula*, some of the most insidious and unnerving Gothic narratives feature the arrival in London of an avenging force from the east. Richard Marsh's *The Beetle* (1897) is an effectively nasty narrative of a weird and powerful man-woman-beetle-Thing exacting revenge in the city, while Guy Boothby's *Pharos, the Egyptian* (1899) presents an even more exorbitant story of revenge, a strange Egyptian figure who brings a devastating plague across Europe and into every district of London as a punishment of Biblical proportions. Boothby begins to imagine, in this invisible wave of plague, a kind of horde arriving from the east, reviving that Roman Gothic sense of an irrepressible mass hurtling towards complacent western powers.

We need to provincialize Europe, to tell plural stories of the modern world.

The cinema has sputtered with versions of *The Mummy* since Boris Karloff played the revived Imhotep in 1932. The Hammer House of Horror version in 1959 speaks powerfully to the then-recent failed attempt by the British to seize the Suez Canal back from the Egyptians, an episode of post-war decline often considered to mark the end of empire. The defiance of Mehemet Bey in the face of British meddling burns with a very modern kind of anti-colonial rage.

These Orientalist narratives render the Middle East a voiceless object, pinned in place by the discourse of the other. But a distinct Gothic has also emerged from

3. Bram Stoker, *Dracula* (1897).
4. Bram Stoker's working notes on vampire characteristics, 1890.
5. *A Girl Walks Home Alone at Night* (Ana Lily Amirpour, 2014).

10

9

6

11

8

7

these ancient cultures, transposed and transformed by context. The Egyptian film industry has been rewriting the 'mummy's curse' since it entered the language of colonial Gothic in the late nineteenth century, whether in *The Night of Counting the Years* (Shadi Abdel Salam, 1969), set among Arab tomb-raiders in 1881, the television series *Zodiac* (2019), about a group of Egyptian university students killed off one by one by a curse, or *Paranormal* (2020), in which the lugubrious medic Refaat deals with hauntings, mummy curses and malicious jinni.

Arabic folklore around ghouls and jinns has provided a place for local belief to fuse with the travelling Gothic, producing key horror fictions such as Mohamed Radi's *The Humans and the Jinns* (1985) and Babak Anvari's *Under the Shadow* (2016), in which a malign jinn hounds an Iranian family during the Iran–Iraq War. Jinni have now translated to other parts of the Gothic, as in the American soldiers harassed during the Afghan War in *Red Sands* (2009), or the exuberant cultural transmutations of the international collection *The Djinn Falls in Love* (2017), edited by Mahvesh Murad and Jared Shurin. *A Girl Walks Home Alone at Night* (Ana Lily Amirpour, 2014), set in the fictional Iranian 'Bad City', reworks vampire and Western movie tropes, while Ahmed Saadawi's *Frankenstein in Baghdad* (2018) offers a rewriting of Shelley's monster, this one assembled from bombing victims during the height of the American occupation of Baghdad in the early 2000s. Known as the Whatsisname, he has his own ideas of monstrosity: 'what they don't understand is that I'm the only justice in this country...the impossible mix that never was achieved in the past. I'm the first true Iraqi citizen.'

What they don't understand is that I'm the only justice in this country...the impossible mix that never was achieved in the past.

Further east lies India, where from the 1600s the British East India Company ran relations with the population in brutal, cynically commercial terms, exerting increasing control. By the 1830s, 'Thuggees' or 'Thugs', a secret society of assassins said to ritualistically strangle their targets in the name of the Hindu goddess of death, time and doom, Kali, were haunting the British colonial imagination. In 1857, the Indian Rebellion resulted in mass slaughter of both settlers and locals, an eruption of anti-British violence and chilling, murderous suppression by the British Army. Direct rule under the British state was formalized, and imperial ideology hardened; racial science insisted on Western European superiority over all other races, and the consequent right to rule.

6–8. Posters for Universal Studios' *The Mummy* (Karl Freund, 1932), from Sweden, Argentina and the USA.

9–11.Posters for Hammer House of Horror's *The Mummy* (Terence Fisher, 1959), from Italy, France and the USA.

12. *Under the Shadow* (Babak Anvari, 2016), set in Iran, reworks beliefs about malevolent jinni.

13

The colony was defined as the margin to the imperial centre; culture and civilization flowed in one direction, outwards, from that centre. Indians themselves featured in the colonial Gothic as exoticized or menacing, vengeful figures, as in Wilkie Collins's melodrama *The Moonstone* (1868) or Rudyard Kipling's debut, *Plain Tales from the Hills* (1889), which promised to take readers 'Beyond the Pale', 'where the last drop of White blood ends [and] the full tide of Black sets in'. Similar ghost stories were published by the Irish writer B. M. Croker, the wife of a British army officer serving in India, in the 1880s, and by Alice Perrin in *East of Suez* (1901).

In the most disturbing of Kipling's tales, terror lies in the breakdown of the Imperialists' sure divide of east and west. 'The Mark of the Beast' is about a foolish newcomer in India who insults a local temple while drunk and is promptly cursed by the leprous holy man who guards it. The British transgressor begins to degenerate into animal form, as though suffering an awful biological regression. The policeman and intelligence officer Strickland can only reverse this curse by actively accepting that something supernatural has occurred; he and the narrator save their foolish friend by horribly torturing the holy man, and realize in the process that 'we had disgraced ourselves as Englishmen forever'. The encounter hybridizes everyone involved.

At the same time as Kipling was starting out, the Hindu writer Rabindranath Tagore wrote several Gothic short stories narrated by Western-educated Bengali men. The female spectres of 'Kankal' (Skeleton) and 'Nishite' (In the Night) seem to emanate from pre-colonial settings, and slyly undercut the narrators' assimilation into the administrative rationality of colonial rule. Tagore's short stories neatly illustrate the hybridization of the European Gothic in contact with, in this case, traditional Bengali folktales.

13. A traditional depiction of the Hindu goddess Kali, wearing a necklace of slaughtered demons, her bloodlust halted by her husband, Lord Shiva, under her feet, 1890s.

14. Shyamal Dutta Ray's illustration for a staging of Rabindranath Tagore's 1890 play *Bisarjan*, which centres around a ban on ritual sacrifice.

15. Thuggees or 'Thugs' were alleged by the British to be a secret sect of assassins in India, and were ruthlessly suppressed by colonial authorities from the 1830s.

14

15

16

17

Yellow Perils

To many European civilizations, the Far East meant Asia, and the terror of those near-mythical leaders that rose up from the central plains: Attila the Hun in the fifth century; Genghis Khan, the Mongol Emperor who slaughtered millions and pushed at the far edges of Europe in the thirteenth century; and Timur, or Tamerlane, the Turco-Mongol conqueror of Islamic Central Asia in the fourteenth century. Whispers of their pitiless armies contributed to an idea of the Far East as seething with hordes forever threatening to march on the west. The racist trope of Yellow Peril figured these hordes as insects or vermin; today, it has been reimagined by those such as Donald Trump as the source of contagion that slips through all western defences.

The closed societies of the Chinese and Japanese Empires made them opaque to Europeans, the subject of fantasies masquerading as travel narratives. This began to change in the eighteenth and nineteenth centuries, with the forcible extension of trade into the east culminating in the Opium Wars (1839–42 and 1856–60), in which the British violently imposed the export of opium on a Chinese government that had outlawed the drug and tried to stop the spread of addiction for a century. The peace treaty that followed forced the opening of Chinese ports and the Yangtze River to world trade. This was never intended to be reciprocal: indeed, the United States passed the first Chinese Exclusion Act in 1882, to prevent a 'yellow tide' arriving on American shores. The act was renewed in various forms down to 1968. Yellow Perilism intensified in the twentieth century during the Second World War, when Allied propaganda caricatured Japanese forces as vermin, again during the Cold War era, when Mao Tse-Tung's Chinese Communism was demonized, and yet again when American fears of a 'domino effect' in the east sucked them into a series of proxy wars against Communists in Vietnam, Laos and Cambodia, starting in the late 1950s and ending in defeat in 1975.

As the discourse of Yellow Perilism hardened in the 1890s, the Gothic was central to its cultural circulation. M. P. Shiel wrote a stream of horrors, starting with *The Yellow Danger* (1898), that dealt with the dastardly plots of the Chinese supervillain Dr Yen How, a criminal genius driven by bitter hatred of the white west. Shiel set *The Yellow Wave: A Romance of the Asiatic Invasion of Australia* (1905) in the white settler nation he perceived

18

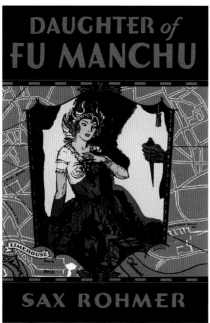

19

as most threatened by the east, and returned to his theme again and again, in near-pathological repetition. Born on the Caribbean island of Montserrat to a Methodist missionary father who decided to crown his son the King of Redonda, a tiny island barely a mile long, Shiel's books spoke to increasing numbers of racial pessimists, who believed that the white race was on a path of self-destruction, to be overwhelmed unless the 'Far Eastern Question' was addressed.

Shiel also prepared the ground for the most famous of this strand of master-criminals, Sax Rohmer's Dr Fu Manchu, who appeared in 1911, just as the Manchu dynasty ended and a new nationalist republic formed in China. Fu Manchu is a Gothic condensation of the east, variously described as having the face of Buddha, the features of the Egyptian pharaoh Seti I, or the brow of a genius like Shakespeare. He commands a global network of anti-western assassins: secret Chinese societies, Indian Thuggees, anti-colonial agitators in Cairo and the sorcerers of Dahomey. 'Fu Manchu is omnipresent; his tentacles embrace everything,' we are warned in *The Mystery of Fu Manchu* (1913), in a standard, tentacular metaphor for the Asiatic enemy. The same plot recurs in each book: the evil genius makes a brilliant advance in his plans to overthrow western governments, only for the plucky Brits, Nayland Smith and Dr Petrie, to defeat him, an outcome made inevitable given their inherent racial superiority. It is a toxic cycle of pulp horror that spewed into the lurid genre magazines of the 1920s and 1930s, built on a century of scientific and philosophical racism. Fu Manchu films began to be made in the early 1920s. The Hollywood production of the *Mask of Fu Manchu*, made in 1932 and starring Boris Karloff as the moustachioed fiend, was so extreme that it prompted a formal complaint from the Chinese government.

In 1890, amid this Yellow Perilism, the journalist and writer Lafcadio Hearn travelled to Japan on a newspaper commission. He was charmed by 'this tiny, artificial, fictitious world', he wrote in *Japan: An Attempt at Interpretation* (1904), 'which I felt I knew from the paintings of lacquer and porcelain.' This purely aesthetic appreciation was typically Orientalist, but Hearn remained in Japan for the rest of his life, marrying the daughter of a samurai family, adopting Japanese citizenship and going by the name Koizumi Yakumo. His publications about Japan were predominantly collections of folklore and classic supernatural tales, with titles like *Japanese Fairy Tales* (1898) and *In Ghostly Japan* (1899).

16. Sax Rohmer, *The Hand of Fu Manchu* (1917).
17. Sax Rohmer, *The Insidious Fu Manchu* (1913).
18. Sax Rohmer, *Yellow Shadows* (1924).
19. Sax Rohmer, *Daughter of Fu Manchu* (1931).

He had already published *Some Chinese Ghosts* in 1886, with a fey introduction commending the 'weird beauty' and subtlety of their invocations of the supernatural. Hearn believed that western literature needed renewing through an encounter with 'Eastern Literary growths', which he hoped would create a 'universal literature'. Perhaps something like this has been achieved with the cross-pollination of Gothic and ghostly tropes throughout world literature.

An annual feast to welcome back the dead each year – but also guide them home at the end of the day.

Hearn's legacy has been a complex, cross-cultural one. His renditions of the tales he collected can seem shorn from their specific cultural and religious contexts in China or Japan, but his collection *Kwaidan: Stories and Studies of Strange Things* (1904) was imported back into Japan, and became the basis for the pivotal ghost story anthology film *Kwaidan* (1964), directed by Masaki Kobayashi and an international hit when screened at the Cannes film festival. The first segment, 'Black Hair', fixes the trope of the returning, vengeful female ghost, her presence signalled by her menacing, abundant hair, which recurs in probably the most successful Japanese horror film, *Ringu* (1998), and its endless cycle of sequels, remakes and reboots. This chain of influences suggests a complex transcultural switching between very different traditions of the supernatural, another sign of the restlessly travelling and mutating tropes of the Gothic.

It has become increasingly important to give space to the rich and distinct traditions of the specific countries that tend to be subsumed under the category of the 'Far East', an elision made by an imperious, Eurocentric worldview. We must start to displace Europe from the presumed centre of global narratives. As the historian Dipesh Chakrabarty has argued, we need to provincialize Europe, to tell plural stories of the modern world and listen to voices from multiple places. Modernity should not be a single account of development, but must comprehend the world in decentred, plural, sometimes overlapping, sometimes divergent narratives. The Gothic might have emerged from a particular moment of modern development in Britain, Germany and France in the eighteenth century, but it has since met and been transformed by local traditions, creating hybrid forms that are in turn transformed as they travel.

In Japan, both the older Shintō religion and later Buddhist beliefs offer a panoply of spirits and supernatural forces. *Yōkai*, the general term for supernatural creatures, contains many subdivisions – water sprites, foxes,

20

21

20. The vengeful Sadako, *The Ring* (Hideo Nakata, 1998).
21. In the 'Hoichi the Earless' episode of the anthology Japanese ghost-story film *Kwaidan* (Masaki Kobayashi, 1965), a sacred text is written on Hoichi's skin to render him invisible to vengeful ghosts.
22. [opposite] Tsukioka Yoshitoshi, *The Old Woman Retrieves Her Arm*, woodblock print from the series *New Forms of Thirty-Six Ghosts*, 1889.

23

cats, trickster raccoon-dogs, shapeshifters, ghosts – catalogued and depicted in illustrated books such as Toriyama Sekien's *Night Procession of the Hundred Demons* (1776). These taxonomies of terrors have fed directly into the weird and wonderful worlds of manga comics and Studio Ghibli animations.

Rituals of mourning and respects paid to the dead create a complex culture of *yūrei*, ghosts or 'dim spirits', centred on an annual feast to welcome back the dead each year – but also guide them home at the end of the day. When things go wrong, buildings can be burdened with lingering spirits (*jiko bukken* translates literally as 'stigmatized property', and is written into law), while Buddhist *gaki*, 'hungry ghosts', demand recompense for unfulfilled hungers. There is a geography of this spiritual journey within the islands of Japan; the dead are said to pause at Mount Osore (Mount Doom or Dread), an extinguished volcano in the far north identified in Japanese mythology as an entrance to the underworld, before leaving the world completely. The terrain is crowded with temples and priests vying to give comfort to the mourners who visit, a culture explored in Marie Mutsuki Mockett's *Where the Dead Pause, and the Japanese Say Goodbye* (2015), which deals with mourning her own father in the context of the aftermath of the devastating tsunami that killed thousands in 2011.

In Japanese drama and poetry, the encounter with the supernatural has been a consistent theme for centuries, but the rise of 'Gothic' literature and film after 1945 has been linked by some critics to exposure to the European Gothic in the context of national defeat, a lingering culture of denial and silence, and, of course, the traumatic effect of the destruction of Hiroshima and Nagasaki by nuclear bombs in August 1945. Globally successful films such as Hideo Nakata's *Ringu* (1998) and Takashi Shimizu's *Jo-On: The Grudge* (2002) have undergone bewilderingly rapid translations between their originals and American remakes. Along with Takashi Miike's extraordinary *Audition* (1999), they were packaged in Britain under the label 'Asia Extreme', risking Orientalist stereotype; but Japanese horror film has also had a discernible effect on how European and American horror films have sought their horrors, from the representation of vengeful or 'hungry' ghosts down to the shock rhythm of editing.

In parallel, Japanese computer game design has led in the development of video games, which shifted from science fiction scenarios to 'survival horror',

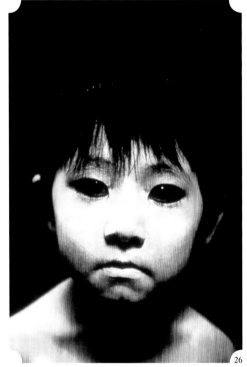

23. Toyohara Kunichika, *The Actor Onoe Kikugoro as the Ghost of Okiku*, woodblock print, 1892.

24. Spirits travel by train in the Studio Ghibli animation *Spirited Away* (Hayao Miyazaki, 2001).

25. Confronting the monster in *The Host* (Bong Joon-ho, 2006).

26. The *onryō*, or 'vengeful spirit' of *The Grudge* (Takashi Shimizu, 2002).

27

a term coined by designer Shinji Mikami for his 1996 game *Biohazard*. This starts in a haunted house, which soon reveals an entrance to a secret military-industrial complex, where a weaponized virus has started to infect everyone and turn them into ravenous hordes of zombies. The game travelled around the world as *Resident Evil*, now a gigantic franchise that has spawned over twenty sequels and seven films, made in America and retaining (often stereotypical) elements of the Japanese original in the use of martial arts and highly stylized violence.

Such international translations of the Gothic can be tracked across the distinct cultures of the 'Far East'. There has been an incredible flowering of terrifying ghost stories in South Korean cinema from the 1990s onwards, following the relaxation of censorship laws. The vampire tradition is transformed yet again by Park Chan-wook's *Thirst* (2009), in which Sang-hyun, a Catholic priest, is turned into a deeply conflicted vampire by a failed medical experiment; Chan-wook also directed *The Handmaiden* (2016), an adaptation of the Welsh writer Sarah Waters's novel *Fingersmith* (2002) translated from Victorian Britain to early twentieth-century Japanese-occupied Korea. Bong Joon Ho's similarly noirish *The Host* (2006), meanwhile, satirizes the very specific circumstances of heightened anxiety and repressive regimes on the Korean peninsula since the Second World War.

The one-way traffic of Orientalizing the east has long been exploded by the globalization of the Gothic. As it travels back and forth across continents, the genre continues to be reshaped and reinvigorated.

28

27. Gameplay in *Resident Evil Survivor* (2000), a video game series first developed by Shinji Mikami, who coined the term 'Survival Horror'.
28. *Thirst* (Park Chan-wook, 2009).
29. [opposite] Pages from *Night Procession of the Hundred Demons,* by Toriyama Sekien (1776).

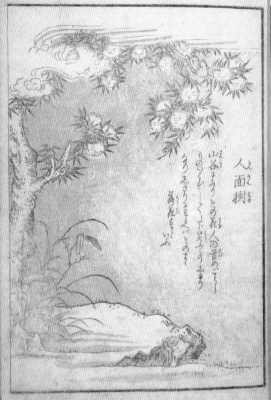

燭陰

怪
山海経に曰
鐘山の神を
燭陰と云
燭陰と云
そのひらく
目は千里を
てらすなり

人面樹

山谷まゝ人面の花
ものつくして笑いすゝ

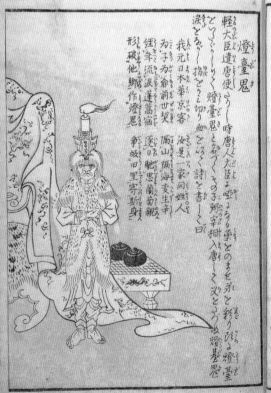

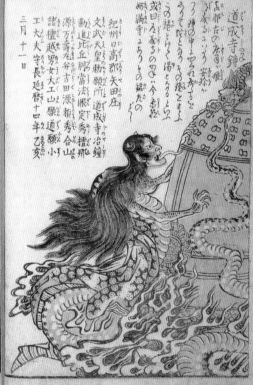

道成寺鐘

三月
十一日

West

Opposite *oriens*, the rising sun, lies *occidens*, the place of the setting sun. The Egyptians split the sun god Ra into different aspects: Atum was the setting sun, the name associated with finishing or completing, sometimes figured as an old man with a staff, wise in the twilight of his long years. The 'lord to the limit of the sky' protected devotees in the passage through the night. In the twilight, in the gloaming, we all know that the rind of the world thins and the other world peeks out. How many Gothic tales start with the hero misjudging the time and being overtaken by the sun setting in the west, the darkness pooling around them?

On ancient maps, the west marked the limit of the known world. Greek knowledge ran out at the pillars of Hercules, which guarded the entrance to the Mediterranean; the Romans got a little further, but called Ireland the 'terminus Europa'. When medieval *mappa mundi* were arranged with the east at the top and the west at the bottom, the trajectory of the eye down the page followed the path of the soul, heading towards the Last Judgment. But beginning in the fifteenth century, European exploration reoriented the shape of the world map. Western expansion into the Americas, first by the Spanish and the Portuguese and then by northern European empires, began to consolidate a conception of the geopolitical 'West'. The persistent ideology of 'Manifest Destiny' was first expressed by John O'Sullivan in 1845 in an essay called 'Annexation', in which he wrote of 'our manifest destiny to overspread the continent allotted by Providence for the free development of our yearly multiplying millions'. O'Sullivan ascribed this divine right to the vigorous 'Anglo-Saxon' races of northern Europe; the frontier

writer Joaquin Miller, in his poem 'Westward Ho!', praised instead 'O bearded stalwart, westmost man,/ So tower-like, so Gothic built!'

Most accounts of the American frontier begin, curiously enough, with a lecture that announced that it had finally come to an end. At the Chicago World's Fair in 1893, Frederick Jackson Turner, a young university lecturer at the University of Wisconsin, delivered a talk called 'The Significance of the Frontier in American History'. For three centuries, he argued, the frontier had been a constantly self-renewing sharp edge, where America had carved out a distinctive, vital identity. He ended his lecture with a paean – 'to the frontier the American intellect owes its striking characteristics' – and yet he had opened in a very different tone, announcing that the 1890 Census had declared the frontier

The Western World ends on a shore devoid of all signification, like a journey that loses all meaning when it reaches its end.

formally closed. The journey westward had demonstrably run its course. Lurking here was a fear of stasis, of ossification, of decline and fall, and the tone of the lecture is actually not so much triumphalist as tolling a mourning bell.

The concerted push westwards had moved steadily beyond daunting physical boundaries: the Mississippi River, the Allegheny Mountains, the Great Plains and the Rockies. If Turner's west seems suspiciously emptied of people, the new states formed in the vanguard openly acknowledged their violent displacement of Native American cultures. In the southwest, the uncertain borderline between the new American states and Mexico had yet to determine its final lines in the sand.

1. [opposite] *Bubba Ho-Tep* (Don Coscarelli, 2004).

2. Stereoscopic photograph of the Crow
   Nation performing the Ghost Dance
   in Plateau City, Colorado, c. 1890.
3. *Westworld* (Michael Crichton, 1973).
4. Head-ring from Ghost Dance
   ceremony of the Kakuiti, donated to
   the Smithsonian by the American
   anthropologist Franz Boas in 1895.
5. Memorabilia (c. 1890s) from *Buffalo
   Bill's Wild West and Congress of Rough
   Riders of the World*, which toured the
   world, imprinting a myth of 'how the
   west was won'.

The movement west had bloody footprints, and white American manhood, as Dana Nelson has it, has ever since been 'haunted within...by its own violences towards its others' – a foundational violence articulated especially, Leslie Fiedler has argued, by the 'cheapjack machinery of the Gothic'.

Although Turner did not mention it, 1890 was also the culmination of Native American resistance to white settlement through the Ghost Dance Movement, an apocalyptic theology that spread among the indigenous nations of the Great Plains in the 1880s. The Ghost Dance was meant to conjure the ghosts of dead warriors for a last fight. The Lakota Sioux Nation, devastated in 1889 by influenza and the tearing up of the land agreement that protected the Great Sioux Reserve, turned the Ghost Dance into a vision in which the settlers were to be eliminated by supernatural intervention, while they themselves would be protected from harm by clothes and talismans that would make them invulnerable to bullets. In 1890, their warriors were massacred at the Battle of Wounded Knee.

Turner fixed the mythology of the frontier at exactly the moment it died, and the Westerns that dominated twentieth-century popular culture in America were always, therefore, fundamentally *undead*. The Native American becomes a spectral presence. This shift to an undead afterlife happened very quickly. The 1893 Chicago Fair, where Turner spoke of the end of the frontier, also hosted Buffalo Bill's 'Wild West' Show, where twice a day Bill Cody staged a spectacular fabulation of the West, using 'real' cowboys and Native Americans who had become circus performers. His show restaged the Battle of Little Big Horn, Custer's Last Stand and a ceaseless repetition of Cody's own killing and scalping of the Cheyenne warrior Hay-o-Wei, or Yellow Hand. In these shows, the West was already a simulation of itself, fake-real or real-fake, anticipating the immersive, 'hyperreal' dioramas of American history that so bewildered the European intellectuals Umberto Eco and Jean Baudrillard when they travelled across the post-modern United States a century later. The Wild West is always already a theme park, just as Michael Crichton's film *Westworld* (1973) and the reimagined television series *Westworld* (premiered 2016) dramatize.

It is a curious element of the ethos of the west that while it celebrates its status at the apex of every hierarchy it invents, it also broods anxiously on its own collapse.

5

ORIGINAL NEGATIVE

EFFECT NO. 33

FL

FILM CLIP TO LEFT - EFFECT 33- WAS MADE AS A TEST OF THE THEN
"OLD" MIRROR SHOT. A METHOD THAT I HAD SEEN MELEIS DO AND ALSO
THE LUMIERES. MATT HANDSCHEIGL ALMOST INSISTED ON ME DOING IT
AND AFTER WE FINISHED, HE HAD TO ADMIT IT WAS A CUMBERSOME AND
LONG WAY AROUND OF DOING THE EFFECT.(Consisted of putting an
actor in doorway of minaret tower.) (

My first experience with these mirror illusions occured when I
was a boy and visited Paris. Many men have toyed with the idea
and it is surprising how many keep thinking they found somethin
new. Many years later a German named Schufftan, got a patent o
the idea. HE SHOULD NEVER HAVE HAD IT. In 1935, Mr. Laemmle tol
me he paid $5000. for rights to use it. When I tried to explain
how old it was he was chagrined. Universal abandoned any use of
it. IT WAS THE LONG HARD WAY TO GET AN EFFECT.

EFFECT NO. 34 Jan. 1912
Just in order to keep the record
straight- I make this brief explanation of something we did in
this era. It shows that men were
busy thinking about the wide-
screen idea long before it was
made practical.
One of these men was Bill Alder,
in some ways quite a thinker who
never got anywhere near where he
deserved. He made one picture
for Universal

EFFECT NO. 34.

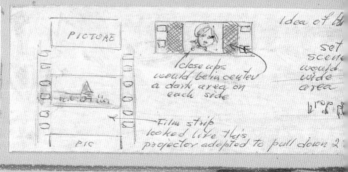

PICTURE

PIC

close ups
would be in center
a dark area on
each side

Film strip
looked like this
projector adopted to pull down 2

Idea of b

set
scene
would
wide
area

EFFECT NO. 35

EFFECT NO. 35- May 1912. THE PRELIMINARY IDEA OIL SKETCH TO THE RIGHT-----
was for a contemplated scenic opener shot. It was for a two reel, black and
white silent picture, a western titled "MAN OF THE WEST" produced by the
IMP. Co. (Independent Motion Picture Company which eventually became the
Universal co.)
All of my lifetime I have made my preliminary sketches in color, since they
were more attractive and helped to sell the idea or sequence in the film.
It must be remembered at this early stage in the business, these particular
kind of effects were more or less mysterious with most of the people.
I often had difficulty influencing early producers that I had a little some
thing that could enhance the pictorial and dramatic qualities of the production and lend it a little extra distinction, even just pictorially-- and
pictures were what we were selling.
For this particular effect I did not receive any money. Besides I used my
own camera and film. Only the wagon and players were contributed by the pro-
ducer. (Later he was well pleased)
But I was so interested in advancing this kind of effect work that I was
glad to get the practice and to keep advancing my own skill and knowledge of
what could be very baffling if it did not work out right.

"MAN OF THE WEST"
IMP.
Typical still of
the period gives
idea of photogra
phy of that era.
Director, Walter
Wright, players
Warren Kerrigan
Louise Fazenda,
Eagle Eye, Jack
Gavin, Wheeler
Oakman, etc etc
was made in hills
in San Fernando
Valley.
Studio was just
an old shack and
corral along the
Edendale road.

30×40 BLACK PASTEL OF MINARET UNDER LIGHTS
IN STUDIO

ALL MIRROR
PE OF DOOR
MINARET-
RROR SET
5° ANGLE

ACTOR OUT IN SUNLIGHT

BLACK FLAT

ACTOR REFLECTED ON MIRROR

de picture

*4

At about this time Bill Alder, a well known cam-era man, wanted me to join him in a wide screen idea. He would split the frame with two sprokett holes and make pictures which were a forerunner of the present wide screen. But I thought it was ahead of its time.

TWO SPROCKETTS

UPPER HALF OF ONE FRAME

WIDER SCREEN

THIS PORTION WAS SECOND EXPOSURE

ELIMINARY IDEA - OIL SKETCH

6. One of Norman O. Dawn's display cards for the special effects in the classic Western *Man of the West* (Anthony Mann, 1958).

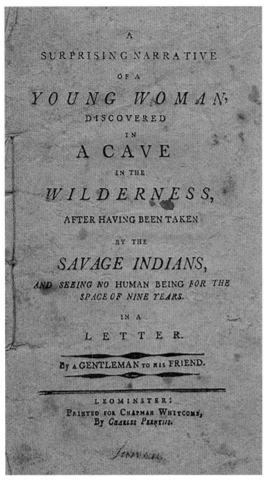

7

8

7. Abraham Panther, *A Surprising Narrative of a Young Woman Discovered in a Cave, after having been taken by the Savage Indians, and Seeing no Human Being for the Space of Nine Years* (1787).

8. George Catlin was a painter who developed an ambition to visit and record every Native tribe in America. In the 1830s, he travelled to the Great Plains. *Mandan Scalping an Enemy, c.* 1835–37.

9. George Catlin, *The Scalp Dance*, n.d.

10. The cut trees in this image mark the site of the fateful 1846 winter camp of the Donner Party, who, snowbound in Summit Valley, California, resorted to starvation cannibalism to survive.

11. *The Revenant* (Alejandro González Iñárritu, 2015), based on the true story of frontiersman Hugh Glass.

Standing on the beach at Santa Monica, Baudrillard proclaimed: 'The Western World ends on a shore devoid of all signification, like a journey that loses all meaning when it reaches its end.' That the logic of western expansion might secretly carry this intrinsic deathliness coiled inside it is something the Frontier Gothic has always been unafraid to speak.

The Frontier Gothic's origins lie in early 'Indian Captivity Narratives', which transpose the tropes of the European Gothic onto the distinct conditions encountered at the bleeding edge of colonization. An early Spanish account, *The Florida of the Inca* (1605), told of the capture and prolonged torture of the Spaniard Juan Ortiz; Mary Rowlandson's tale of kidnap in 1676 by Narragansett Indians was published in 1682 as *The Sovereignty and Goodness of God*. These set the tone. Rowlandson describes the trial of faith that followed in her three months of capture: to enter into the condition of the heathen, coded by the eating of raw meat simply to survive. Hannah Dustan's story of capture two decades later, in 1697, formed part of the Puritan Cotton Mather's influential book *Magnalia Christi Americana* (1702). Unlike Rowlandson, Dustan aided in her own escape, taking up a hatchet to slaughter and scalp the ten sleeping Abenaki Indians – including children – who guarded her party, though Mather assures the reader that this is a legal and godly act: 'she was not forbidden by any Law to take away the life of the Murderers'.

Among the first American Gothic bestsellers was another such narrative told by 'Abraham Panther' in 1787, *A Surprising Narrative of a Young Woman Discovered in a Cave, after having been taken by the Savage Indians, and Seeing no Human Being for the Space of Nine Years*, which rehearsed the arc of traumatic capture, torture and escape by violence. The pamphlet was reissued many times in the following decades, becoming part of the founding mythology of the frontier.

In these narratives, the frontier becomes a *contact zone*: not an exterior encounter between self and other, good and evil, but a hybrid place where in order to survive the westerner must in some crucial sense become the savage. 'Going native' is the risk of lighting out just ahead of wherever the frontier falls. What waits there, out west, as it did for the Donner Party, who were reduced to starvation cannibalism in the Sierra Nevadas in 1846, is the terror of losing all markers of civility and being subsumed into the savage other. This has come down even into the myth of the gunslinger,

9

CENTRAL PACIFIC RAILROAD.
By Thomas Houseworth & Co.

Entered according to Act of Congress, in the year 1868, by THOMAS
HOUSEWORTH & CO., in the Clerk's Office of the District Court of the
United States, for the Northern District of California.

778. "Starvation Camp." Stumps of Trees cut by the Donner Party in Summit Valley, Placer Co., in 1846.

10

11

who forges his essential identity in the violence of ritualized murder. If the Gothic has often been deployed to affirm the Manifest Destiny of the movement west by monstering all others that lie in the way, it has also been a mode in which those who shaped the mythology of the west can find themselves hopelessly and terrifyingly undone.

The explicit fusion of the Western and the Gothic began to take place in the early twentieth century, as tales by the likes of Robert E. Howard melded Westerns with the 'shudder pulps' published *en masse* in magazines in the 1920s and 1930s. Howard is better known for his *Conan the Barbarian* stories, which were as saturated with hypermasculine, racial hierarchies as one might expect from a close ally of H. P. Lovecraft. His horror Westerns 'The Horror of the Mound' (1932) and 'Old Garfield's Heart' (1933) are set in his home state of Texas: 'of all the continent of North America there is no section so haunted'. The contrast of the two stories is instructive: 'The Horror of the Mound' appears set to deploy the trope of the haunted Indian burial ground, but instead turns on the long history of Spanish colonial activity in the area. The titular 'mound' was used to wall up a 'mysterious nobleman' from Castile, infected with vampirism by the Moors. Disturbing it unleashes 'a grisly lurking horror', in a perfect illustration of the awkward transposition of the European Gothic into the frontier landscape. 'Old Garfield's Heart' is much more attuned to the possibilities of the American context. It relies for its shivers on the supernatural powers of Native American medicine: the 'Ghost Man' of the Lipan Apaches lends a wounded white man a 'posthumous' life that must be returned on his deathbed. In this tale, the Gothic has adjusted to the American frontier, overdetermined with the transgressed borderlines of Indian and settler, life and death.

Native American writers have since occupied and subverted the imported tropes of this tradition, taking it through a process of transculturation. Early Indigenous Gothic works include Leslie Marmon Silko's *Ceremony* (1977), which uses Laguna Pueblo ritual to explore the healing of a traumatized war veteran, and Gerald Vizenor's *Darkness in Saint Louis Bearheart* (1978), which inverts the 'Frontier Gothic' to depict the horror of natives forced from their reservation land. Later, Alexie Sherman's *Indian Killer* (1996) confronts the stereotype of the savage scalp-hunter – a key trope in the popular fusion of the Western and the Gothic – head-on, and Vizenor's *Chancers* (2000),

12

13

12. *Curse of the Undead* (Edward Dein, 1959).
13. *Billy the Kid vs. Dracula* (William Beaudine, 1966).

about a series of murders associated with a display of native remains in Berkeley's anthropology museum, evokes the Ghost Dance. Vizenor has allied indigenous fiction with that movement of counter-narrative and resistance to erasure: 'Many native stories and novels are visionary,' he told an interviewer, 'a literary dance of ghosts.'

Other Native American writers have reoriented narratives of Indian capture for a contemporary setting, as in Stephen Graham Jones's short story, 'Captivity Narrative 109', in which ancient assumptions by white settlers twist the interpretation of the Native protagonist's actions. Jones has long used the horror genre to approach the monstering of Native Americans, as in *Growing up Dead in Texas* (2012) and *Mongrels* (2016). The myth of the windigo, meanwhile, is recast by Louise Erdrich in *The Antelope Wife* (1998), and by Tomson Highway in *Kiss of the Fur Queen* (1998). Native American conceptions of ancestral spirits transform the alarming supernatural intrusion of the ghost in the European Gothic into something entirely different, infused with a sense of awe. The annihilating, hungry ghost of the dead father has to be defeated in Stephen Graham Jones's novella 'Mapping the Interior' (2017), a narrative explored more gently in Eden Robinson's *Monkey Beach* (2000). Jones has also explored and undercut the trope of the supernatural curse, casting his on four Native hunting friends in *The Only Good Indians* (2020), the title an echo of the chilling motto of the nineteenth-century U.S. Army General Sheridan: 'the only good Indian is a dead Indian'.

It is regularly argued that the Western film, already a posthumous mythology of the West, has long died and ceased to be the defining cultural myth of America. Its afterlife is so potentially large that I'll just concentrate on the explicit figuring of this 'undead Western', in films that both continue the tradition and iconography of the classic Western and also throw into doubt its investment in the 'frontier thesis'. In Anthony Mann's *Man of the West* (1958), an anxious, late-middle-aged Gary Cooper, bent on escaping his outlaw past – and his own association with the iconic Western hero – is drawn back into the dysfunctional family of Doc Tobin's murderous gang. The final scenes make clear that the elderly outlaw has fallen behind the times: the railroad has made the frontier a ghost town,

and the shoot-out among the ruined houses ends with Cooper trading shots with an untimely ghost. This is true of many of Mann's 1950s Westerns, where the protagonists fall oddly outside the landscapes they occupy, becoming, as Jacques Rancière puts it, 'no longer a figure of the Western', but an uneasy presence that can only foreground 'the gestures and the codes' of the genre while emptying them of meaning. The same could be said of Sam Peckinpah's run of bitter Westerns, starting with *Ride the High Country* (1961) and reaching its crescendo with a notorious hail of balletic bullets in *The Wild Bunch* (1969), in which nineteenth-century rough-riders with six-shooters and horses must face the murderous modernity of Maxim guns, anticipating the mechanized slaughter of the First World War. The extreme stylization of the Italian 'spaghetti Western' cycle, most commonly associated with the films of Sergio Leone, also reduces the Western to a hollowed-out, undead repetition of the genre's iconic symbols.

> The movement west had bloody footprints, and white American manhood, as Dana Nelson has it, has ever since been 'haunted within… by its own violences towards its others.'

Whenever John Wayne's character introduces himself in *Big Jake* (1971), the response is, 'I thought you were dead.' The iconic Western hero's last films are saturated with this undead melancholy; meanwhile, Clint Eastwood was literally playing undead. *High Plains Drifter* (1973) slides gently out of one genre and into another, as Eastwood's nameless gunfighter paints the town red, renames it Hell and exacts revenge on a cowardly populace that has allowed the sheriff to be horse-whipped to death. Early in its narrative, *Pale Rider* (1985) shows the fatal pattern of bullet wounds on Eastwood's back that will recur in the final shootout. There is a perfect equivocation about his persona in these films, borrowed from the already-pastiched mythic landscape where his 'Man with No Name' first appeared. Eastwood's Western hero is a depthless man, the brim of a hat and a cigarillo, the frontier main street he strides through mere house-fronts made of plyboard and plaster.

This internal subversion has some notable late additions. Very early in Jim Jarmusch's soporific *Dead Man* (1995), Johnny Depp's character William Blake

WARNER BROS-SEVEN ARTS PRESENTS
A PHIL FELDMAN PRODUCTION

"THE WILD BUNCH" (X)
starring

WILLIAM HOLDEN   ERNEST BORGNINE
ROBERT RYAN   EDMOND O'BRIEN
WARREN OATES   JAIME SANCHEZ
BEN JOHNSON

PANAVISION^   TECHNICOLOR^
RELEASED BY WARNER-PATHE DISTRIBUTORS LTD.

14

15

is shot through the chest; he spends the next two hours becoming ever more inert, supine and corpse-like as he travels through a hallucinatory Western landscape of ruined settlements and abandoned Indian villages, ending at the blank ocean. Meanwhile, Tommy Lee Jones's *The Three Burials of Melquiades Estrada* (2005) is a plain tale of a man fulfilling a promise to a dying Mexican man that his body be returned to his family over the border. As he carries the body back through the southwestern desert, the corpse slowly rots and his quest becomes ever more difficult, the journey a way of figuring the impossible burden of guilt for the millions of unhoused and unmourned people who have lost their lives in this border territory. By the time it ends, any surety of 'home' has been undone.

The more explicit hybridizing of the Western and horror genres stretches back to B-movie double *Billy the Kid vs. Dracula* and *Jesse James Meets Frankenstein's Daughter* (both 1966). The contemporary pulp writer Joe Lansdale has been associated with the 'weird west' in his hybrid comics and novels, including *Dead in the West* (1986) and another unclassifiable gem, *Bubba Ho-Tep* (1994; filmed in 2002), a Western/mummy-curse tale featuring the duo of Elvis Presley and John F. Kennedy, still inexplicably alive in an old people's home and ready for one last fight against cosmic forces. But it is Kathryn Bigelow's *Near Dark* (1987) that really brings the horror Western into the mainstream, as the vampire outlaws, long circling the west for cheap kicks and human blood, are finally caught in the sunrise. Bigelow's film was a low-key commercial success, and helped foster a niche for horror Westerns, from the pastiche of the *Tremors* films (1990, with six sequels), through the cannibal horror of *Ravenous* (1999) to the more conventional monsters found out beyond the Western frontier in *The Burrowers* (2009), *Deadwalkers* (2009) or *Priest* (2011). *Priest*, a super-hybrid science-fiction, post-apocalyptic, vampire Western set in scorched desert badlands, offers a stylized version of the west based on the Korean comics by Hyung Min-woo. It just about keeps a semblance of coherence by placing an old-fashioned captivity narrative at its core – but with fangs.

A wholly different order of Western/Gothic fusion is envisaged in Cormac McCarthy's novel *Blood Meridian, or The Evening Redness in the West* (1985). In sonorous Biblical tones, it turns the wars to determine the border between America and Mexico in the 1840s into a hallucinatory nightmare in 'the bloodlands of the west'.

14. Lobby card for Sam Peckinpah's bloody elegy for the Western, *The Wild Bunch* (1969).
15. *Priest* (Scott Stewart, 2011), the hybrid Western based on Hyung Min-woo's comic of the same name (1998–2007).
16. Tommy Lee Jones directed and starred in the melancholic border Western *The Three Burials of Melquiades Estrada* (2005).
17. *No Country for Old Men* (Coen Brothers, 2007).

The exorbitant, genocidal violence of the mercenary Glanton Gang is focalized through the gaze of 'the kid', for whom one Indian massacre is a single sentence that accumulates horrific details:

>...riding down the unhorsed Saxons and spearing and clubbing them and leaping from their mounts with knives and running about on the ground with a peculiar bandy-legged trot like creatures driven to alien forms of locomotion and stripping the clothes from the dead and seizing them up by the hair and passing their blades about the skulls of the living and the dead alike and snatching aloft the bloody wigs and hacking and chopping at the naked bodies, ripping off limbs, heads, gutting the strange white torsos and holding up great handfuls of viscera, genitals....

The enigmatic and terrifying Judge Holden, the monstrous Gothic father to the kid, expounds a philosophy that equates culture with violence, and defines history as merely a succession of slaughtered peoples who become the geological layers of dust and bone that they traverse: 'The old ones are gone like phantoms and the savages wander these canyons to the sound of an ancient laughter.' History is indistinguishable from the Gothic itself, where the height of civilization, the sun's meridian at noon, 'is at once his darkening and the evening of his day'.

McCarthy's austere vision is found everywhere in the undead Westerns that came in its wake, whether in the battle scenes of *The Revenant* (2015) or the Coen brothers' adaptation of McCarthy's later novel *No Country for Old Men* (2007), again set on the Texas/Mexico border. Here, all the ideals have finally bled out of the wounds of the west, and what is left is much like the philosopher Giorgio Agamben's 'state of exception', in which people are reduced to the condition of 'bare life', stripped of all protections. The frontier is now the blood-soaked, deathly end of the day, no longer the proud birthplace of the American Republic. It is, as McCarthy subtitles his apocalyptic vision, 'the evening redness in the west': the last gasps of the dead sun.

I thought you were dead.

18. [opposite] Map of the western and northwestern frontier in 1837, suggesting defences against the territories of the Native tribes beyond the borders of white settlement.

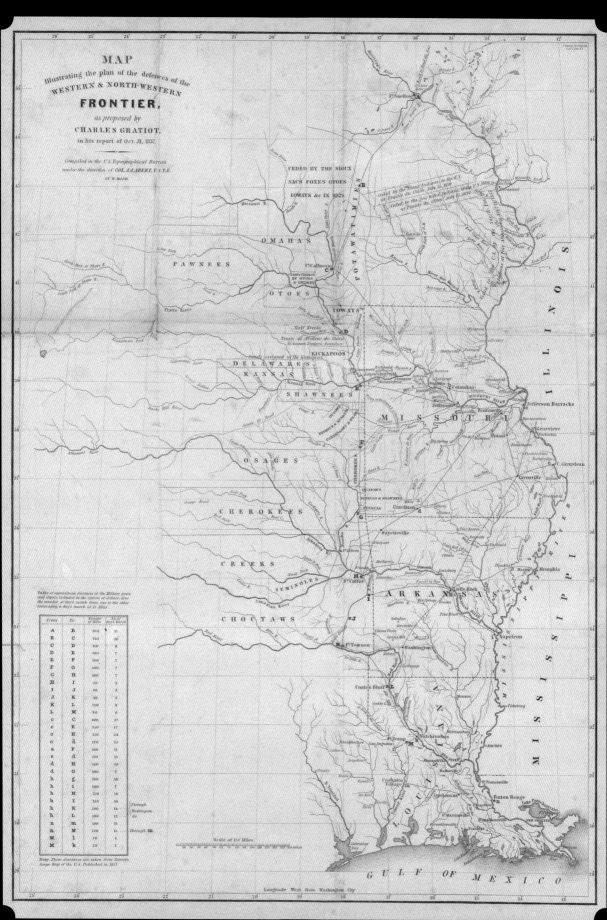

MAP

Illustrating the plan of the defences of the

WESTERN & NORTH-WESTERN

FRONTIER,

as proposed by

CHARLES GRATIOT,

in his report of Oct. 31, 1837.

Compiled in the U.S.Topographical Bureau
under the direction of COL. J.J. ABERT, U.S.T.E.
BY W. HOOD.

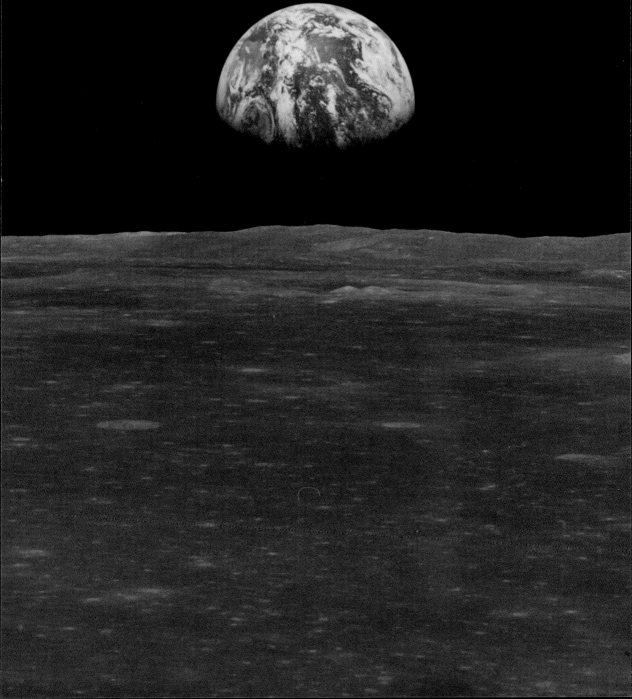

Planetary & Cosmic Horror

We are used to the melodramatic image of monstrous villains astride the globe. The Gothic can conjure catastrophes that far exceed the Bad Place, the ruined castle or abandoned city; calamities so vast that they encompass the world. From about 1750 onwards, Enlightenment thinkers had begun to theorize the development of world history, while explorers extended the mapping of previously unknown territories and armies led the colonization of the planet. 'I would annex the planets if I could; I often think of that,' the imperialist Cecil Rhodes once reflected. Less than a century later, when the Americans did reach the moon, the famous photograph taken by astronaut William Anders on 24 December 1968, now known as 'Earthrise', triggered not so much triumphalism as an agonized new awareness of the fragility of the planet. Perhaps it no longer matters from which compass point the disease spreads when we watch a zombie infection track across the Earth, as in World War Z (2013). The COVID-19 pandemic brought home the realities of a virus that can ride on the intricate networks and interconnections of the global village, the microbe turning modern globalization against itself. The Gothic thrives on this doubled or split consciousness.

In 1805, Jean-Baptiste Cousin de Grainville published Le Dernier Homme, almost immediately translated into English as The Last Man. It prompted a run of projections of the end of the world, including Byron's poem 'Darkness' in 1816, the year the sun was put out by the eruption of the Krakatoa volcano, and Thomas Hood's satirical 'The Last Man' (1823), which inspired the apocalyptic painter John Martin to paint a grand vision of the last man surveying a ruined city and a dying sun, the dead body of his wife at his side. All of these led to Mary Shelley's novel The Last Man (1826), a vision of a deadly plague that races across Europe in the twenty-first century, killing everyone but the protagonist, Lionel Verney, who is left to tour the ruins of European civilization. The most important version of this story after 1945 was Richard Matheson's I Am Legend (1954), in which the last remaining human is surrounded by vampires that taunt him by night, and that he slaughters by day, becoming a legendary monster of atrocity to the new vampire population. Matheson's book was the loose basis for George A. Romero's Night of the Living Dead (1968), the first shuffling step in cinema towards millennial visions of a global zombie pandemic. It was first filmed in Italy by Sidney Salkow, as The Last Man on Earth (1964), and remade as The Omega Man (1971) and I Am Legend (2007).

Planetary horror goes for a deliberate scaling up of the Gothic effect, aiming to overwhelm the reader or viewer. But there is a further stage that ramps up

The Anthropocene binds together human history and geological time in a strange loop, weirdly weird.

this revelation: cosmic horror, associated most strongly with H. P. Lovecraft, who in his essay 'Supernatural Horror in Literature' set out a distinction between 'fear-literature' of the 'mundanely gruesome' and 'the literature of cosmic fear'.

A certain atmosphere of breathless and unexplainable dread of outer, unknown forces must be present; and there must be a hint, expressed

---

1. [opposite] 'Earthrise': photograph taken by William Anders during the Apollo 8 mission in 1968, often considered the most influential image in raising environmentalist concerns about the fragile planet.

2

3

with a seriousness and portentousness becoming its subject, of that most terrible conception of the human brain – a malign and particular suspension or defeat of those fixed laws of Nature which are our only safeguard against the assaults of chaos and the daemons of unplumbed space.

Elsewhere, Lovecraft advised that his brand of 'weird literature' was after 'a vivid depiction of a certain type of human mood' – a mood best described as that moment of ghastly dethronement, when the protagonist finally grasps the cosmic scale of what they have found, resulting in a sublime annihilation of puny human scales and concerns. The celebrated opening passage of Lovecraft's 'The Call of Cthulhu' (1928) reads:

> The most merciful thing in the world, I think, is the inability of the human mind to correlate all its contents. We live on a placid island of ignorance in the midst of black seas of infinity, and it was not meant that we should voyage far.

As he explained to the editor of *Weird Tales*, 'Cthulhu' embodied his whole aesthetic aim. This is horror that escapes the gravitational pull not only of humanity, but of the planet itself.

Lovecraft's 'The Color Out of Space' (1927) is another attempt to reach for this impossible goal of imagining the wholly other. He fights with the limits of language to describe 'the weird visitor from unknown stellar space'. It is only a *colour*, but a colour with 'hectic and prismatic variants of some diseased, underlying primary tone without a place among the known tints of the earth'. It causes everything and everyone it touches to rot or mutate into disgusting, unspeakable forms; the narrator, a surveyor for a new dam and lake, comes to welcome such complete annihilation. A tricky story to film, the deeply eccentric horror director Richard Stanley nevertheless cast Nicolas Cage at his most brilliantly wigged out in his 2019 adaptation.

To imagine the wholly other is to evoke what the theologian Rudolf Otto attempted to describe in his 1917 book *The Idea of the Holy*, for which he coined the term numinous: that teetering sense of being on the cusp of the presence of something divine. For Otto, this intertwines the *mysterium fascinosum* ('the mystery that attracts'), the redemptive promise of the transcendent, with the *mysterium tremendum* ('the mystery that repels'), an overwhelming feeling of dread and abject fear.

2. Sketch of the monstrous god Cthulhu in a letter from H. P. Lovecraft to his young friend R. H. Barlow, May 1934.
3. The globe seized by the grasping tentacles of the 'yellow danger', cover of the satirical German journal *Simplicissimus*, which by 1935 had started to toe the National Socialist party line.
4. *The Color Out of Space* (Richard Stanley, 2019).
5. John Martin, *The Last Man*, 1849.

4

5

6

7

6. Konstantin Fyodorovich Yuon, *The New Planet*, 1921, a vision of the Bolshevik Revolution as a cosmic event.
7. The tear in the space-time continuum, *Stranger Things 2* (Duffer Brothers, 2017).
8. *The Beyond* (Lucio Fulci, 1981).

A lot of early twentieth-century cosmic horror was written by spiritual searchers exploring the cross-currents of magic and the occult, such as pulp writers Abraham Merritt, Clark Ashton Smith and Walter Owen, who published *The Cross of Carl: An Allegory* in 1931, as well as Lovecraft's main inspirations, Algernon Blackwood, Arthur Machen and William Hope Hodgson. Hodgson's *The Night Land* (1912) is a nightmare vision at the end of the solar system, where the remnants of humanity quake in fear inside a vast metal pyramid called The Last Redoubt, forever beset by weird forces of darkness beyond the walls. Hodgson was to die in the mud of the fourth Battle of Ypres in 1918, and it is hard not to see his novel as an anticipatory vision of the horrors of the First World War.

Horror is useful because it does not deal 'with human fear in a human world (the world-for-us)', but with 'the limits of the human as it confronts a world that is not just a world, not just the Earth, but also a planet (the world-without-us).'

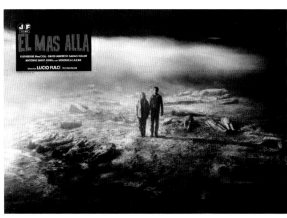

8

This era of mechanized slaughter also coincided with the Soviet 'Cosmism' movement, a mystical philosophy that fused with early Bolshevism in the 1917 Revolution. Cosmism has been defined as the utopian striving to perfect the human race, overcome death and reach the stars; it was propounded in Nikolai Fyodorovich Fyodorov's *Philosophy of the Common Task* (1903), a small book that brimmed with grand ideas about extending life, achieving immortality, exploring space and resurrecting the dead. It fed directly into early Soviet ambitions to launch rockets into space and transcend the contradictions of life on Earth, a programme advocated by rocket pioneer Konstantin Tsiolkovsky. When Lenin's body was preserved after his death in 1924, it was not just to make his memorial in Red Square the focus of the Communist state. Soviet scientists, inspired by Fyodorov, were thought to be close to cracking the problem of reanimation of the dead. Lenin still lies in state, dreaming of his return.

In the 1930s, when another global war seemed ever more likely, there was another peak of cosmic horror – including two novels by the American writer William Sloane. *To Walk the Night* (1937) and *The Edge of Running Water* (1939) both start as conventional mystery novels, but steadily dial up the feelings of dread to a moment of revelation about the true, cosmic nature of the awful enigma that drives their plots. *To Walk the Night* ends on the top of an ancient mesa in the American desert, a wholly inhuman geological landscape close to the burning stars above:

Below us spread the gigantic sweep of the desert, tarnished gold where the sun still lay, and purple blue where the shadows from the western mountains were racing across it as the sun sank behind us. Watching that great tidal wave of darkness pouring across the valley, I suddenly realized how truly the earth was a ball, hung in gulfs of space and spinning around its axis with majestic precision and power.

Another term one might use for this culminating effect of cosmic horror is vastation, which the critic John Clute picks up from the writings of the mystic Emmanuel Swedenborg to describe a belated moment of horrified understanding – 'a laying waste to a land or a psyche; a physical or psychological devastation'. It is the moment when the last plot reveal moves from the physical to the metaphysical; when a vast wasteland of nothingness opens up at the end of Lucio Fulci's nasty horror film *The Beyond* (1981), or when David Lynch moves *Twin Peaks* from a small-town murder mystery into a cosmic clash of the supernatural forces of good and evil. Vastation is when the distraught mother of the murdered schoolgirl Laura Palmer removes her face to show only the annihilating white noise of emptiness beneath.

In an unexpected moment in the 2010s, cosmic horror became a resource for speculative philosophy. Lovecraft took on a starring role in 'object-oriented ontology', which rejects the privileging of human existence and perception over that of non-human objects. For the poet and philosopher Eugene Thacker, horror is useful because it does not deal 'with human fear in a human world (the world-for-us)', but with 'the limits of the human as it confronts a world that is not just a world, not just the Earth, but also a planet (the world-without-us)'. He proposes that horror allows the 'thought of the unthinkable'. A pessimistic philosophy, in which human life itself is a malign joke by indifferent cosmic forces, has also been at the core of the stories and musings of cult horror writer Thomas Ligotti – one of the few living authors who has reached the heights of a Penguin Classics edition, in a sign of the shift of cosmic horror from the margins to the centre. His cosmic pessimism even crept into the metaphysics espoused by the cynical cop Rust Cohle in the first series of the television show *True Detective* (2014), whose writer, Nic Pizzolatto, acknowledged cosmic horror influences ranging from R. W. Chambers's *The King in Yellow* (1895)

10

9. The Cassini Planisphere, an early attempt to map the Earth using longitude and latitude, 1696.
10. The Norilsk Nickel Plant, in the closed Soviet city of Nikel on the Russian/Norwegian border. The site was the subject of the 2018 *Dark Ecology* project of architect Tatjana Gorbachewskaja, urbanist Katya Larina and writer and filmmaker Mirna Belina.

9

to Ligotti's *The Conspiracy Against the Human Race* (2010) and Eugene Thacker's anti-philosophy. As a result, cosmic horror even appeared in the literary imprint of the New York Review of Books, which released a combined edition of William Sloane's novels, *Two Tales of Cosmic Horror*, along with a collection, *Shadows of Carcosa: Tales of Cosmic Horror* (both 2015).

With *Twin Peaks: The Return* (2017), David Lynch was allowed truly mind-blowing free rein, and so cosmic horror also became a recognizable mode in visual culture. The cynical, knowing *Cabin in the Woods* (2012), which rapidly runs through all the clichés of sweet teens killed off one by one in a remote backwood, closes with a splendid, comical take on the cosmic reveal, a grand metaphysical statement that gleefully finishes with the destruction of the rest of humanity. While the television series *Stranger Things* (premiered in 2016) mutes its cosmic horror beneath a smog of nostalgia, Brit Marling's *The OA* (2016–19) has greater ambitions to evoke the sublime on the small screen. There was also a willingness in this cosmic horror cycle to reach for the *mysterium tremendum* – as in the slow reveals of *The Endless* (2017) or Jeff Nichols's *Midnight Special* (2016), both of which start inside fringe religious cults but daringly proceed to affirm at least some of their seemingly crazy beliefs.

Another strong impetus behind this revival of planetary and cosmic horror is the growing recognition that climate change has entered into a crisis phase. The pioneer ecologist James Lovelock first proposed 'the Gaia hypothesis' in the early 1970s, suggesting a model of co-evolution that rendered the Earth itself a kind of integrated and networked being. Thirty years later, the chemist Paul Crutzen proposed in a short paper in 2000 that the planet had entered a new geological epoch marked by the decisive influence of the human race on planetary systems: 'the Anthropocene'. The slow violence of unfettered development powered by fossil fuels has finally reared up in extreme stresses on weather systems and thus on many social systems across the globe. What has emerged, according to ecocritic Timothy Morton, is a 'dark ecology' that is uncanny because 'the Anthropocene binds together human history and geological time in a strange loop, weirdly weird'. Nature cannot be conceived in some pristine way outside culture, but is now always entangled.

> Watching that great tidal wave of darkness pouring across the valley, I suddenly realized how truly the earth was a ball, hung in gulfs of space.

In the first steps into this new epoch, Morton says, 'everything gains a haunting, spectral form'.

The culture of the Anthropocene registers a global weirding, a horror with a new emotional tenor. The products of this era are filled with nonspecific dread, unnerving, new, hybrid things and events that seem to make no sense. Particularly impressive are John Langan's *The Fisherman* (2016) and Paul La Farge's *The Night Ocean* (2017), the latter of which makes an obsession with H. P. Lovecraft central to its plot. The English novelist M. John Harrison has made a career from writing about foundational, existential dread, through hyperreal everyday details that gently unstitch secure meaning. We glimpse horrifying, intrusive forces in bland edgelands and anonymous suburbs in *The Course of the Heart* (1992) and *The Sunken Land Begins to Rise Again* (2020). Perhaps the most evocative of this cluster of cosmic horrors has been the *Southern Reach* trilogy of books by Jeff VanderMeer (*Annihilation, Authority* and *Acceptance*, all 2014), which deal with a strange, anomalous and possibly alien zone that opens up in the wilds of Florida and uncannily transmutes everything that enters it. The first volume, *Annihilation*, was filmed by Alex Garland, although it struggles to recover the weird emotional state of joyous catastrophe that suffuses the characters in the novel as they are slowly transformed into uncategorizable states of being.

But the idea of 'dark ecology' can also be explored in those settler literatures that occupy wilderness landscapes, supposedly 'empty wastes' that seethe with the absent presences of their indigenous populations. This can stretch from the forests of the far north, to the frontier Gothics of the American West or Siberian East, or to the south, where in Australia and Aotearoa New Zealand sacred indigenous landscapes are continually transgressed by settlement. In *Mapping the Godzone* (1998), William Schafer explores an Aotearoa Gothic, in which settlers feel unease in landscapes mapped in sacred ways that they cannot or will not read. The Gothic pokes through the tales of Katherine Mansfield or Janet Frame, and rears up in the novels of Ronald Hugh Morrieson or the early horror films of Peter Jackson. The actor Sam Neill characterized the central emotional tenor of the country's film culture as a 'cinema of unease', the title of his 1995 survey documentary.

Visiting these specific cultural instances of the Gothic begins to stitch together transmutations that seem to reach for the language of the supernatural to create an eerie, cosmic atmosphere, a creeping planetary dread of the slow violence that is the climate crisis. At this moment of revelation about the rapidly accelerating disasters of climate change, cosmic horror has once again remade the Gothic as a central genre for processing this cataclysm.

> We live on a placid island of ignorance in the midst of black seas of infinity, and it was not meant that we should voyage far.

11. [opposite] *The Last Man on Earth* (Sidney Salkow and Ubaldo Ragona, 1964), the eerie first adaptation of Richard Matheson's *I Am Legend* (1954).

IV

MONSTERS

Scale

If the Gothic teaches us anything, it is that humans are bad at processing difference. Anyone or anything that is not like us (whoever that 'us' is) has long tended to be deemed abnormal, deviant or monstrous. The fate of Frankenstein's creature emphasizes that these are always cultural and contingent norms: 'my virtues will necessarily arise when I live in communication,' he tells his creator. Sadly, even Victor Frankenstein cannot rise above his 'breathless horror and disgust' the instant his creation moves. The poor creature has set off on his journey to become the marauding, mute monster of movieland.

Since then, Frankenstein's monster, along with a panoply of nightmare beings, has served as a rallying point for those abjected by social norms. The lost female companion torn to pieces by Victor Frankenstein is recovered; the gay Hollywood director James Whale folds an allegory of monstered men into his 1932 Universal Studio adaptation of the book; in 1992, writer, film-maker and theorist Susan Stryker constructs a trans identity out of the exile and rage of Mary Shelley's creature. Here is an early lesson: the poles of the normal and the pathological can swiftly be flipped in value, and what any social order excludes as monstrous can become an unexpected point of identification for the outcast and abused.

The monstering of difference has been embedded in Western thinking at least since Aristotle argued in *Generation of Animals* (c. 350 BC) that anything that did not resemble its parents was a monster. His fascination with the endless cataloguing of 'monstrous births' suggests, however, that it is precisely the deviation that helps establish the norm. Hence monsters rear up at the edges of maps and at the boundaries of categorical thought, projections of the Other that secretly assist in the formation of cultures and communities of the same. The most overt way of figuring this is in terms of scale. The origin stories and mythologies of many cultures include giants, intermediate beings between humans and gods; in the same pantheon, one might find fairies and elves, fallen angels or 'pygmy' survivals of lost races, who cling on in marginal spaces or are caught only in the corner of the eye by those gifted with special vision. The Gothic works on these same scales of difference, running the gamut from *Godzilla* to *Gremlins*. In David Lynch's *Twin Peaks* we get both: a gentle giant and a backwards-talking, dancing dwarf, 'The Man from Another Place'.

1. [opposite] Boris Karloff as the monster in *Bride of Frankenstein* (James Whale, 1935).
2. One of the metal armatures used for the stop-animation sequences of the giant gorilla in *King Kong* (Merian Cooper and Ernest Schoedsack, 1933).

2

Gigantic

3

4

In the earliest surviving text that tells a human origin story, the Assyrian hero Gilgamesh must meet and slay 'the great demon, Humbaba the terrible', guardian of the Cedar Forest. In Norse myth and theology, the giants that rove the edges of human culture as rivals to the gods all descend from Ymir, the Screamer, the embodiment of chaos before the gods brought order to the cosmos. This distinct order of being is associated not with Asgard, the land of the gods, or Midgard, the human territory, but with Utgard, the Out-yards, the places that lie beyond the safety of the enclosure. The Jötunn, translated as 'giants' but perhaps better as 'devourers', are emblems of the formless chaos that lies swirling in the cosmic outside.

A mix of sources from Northern myth and Christianity run through the Old English poem *Beowulf*. Grendel, its monstrous outsider, is a 'God-cursed brute' (in Seamus Heaney's translation), a descendant of the outcast Cain, who killed his brother and lies outside the hall, 'haunting the marches, marauding round the heath / and the desolate fens'. But it is only in visual culture that he becomes a giant, as for instance in Robert Zemeckis's film *Beowulf* (2007), scripted by Neil Gaiman. J. R. R. Tolkien translated *Beowulf* in 1926; similarly allegorical figures, including giants, subsequently entered his own immersive fantasy world of Middle Earth. Kazuo Ishiguro's strange and wonderful novel *The Buried Giant* (2015), meanwhile, toys with legends of giants sleeping underground, ambiguous figures that might redeem as much as damn the cultures that have slowly forgotten their patient slumber.

This deep history of the giant suggests certain repeated associations: giants are nearly always male figures, enraged by their exile and driven by outsize desires to satiate their appetite for rape and violence or avenge their expulsion on the puny humans that have condemned them to the margins. These monsters are never *quite* defeated, returning to hold together human hearth and home even as they threaten it. Of course, in Sigmund Freud's remarkable speculations about the origins of monotheistic religion, to kill this gigantic, primal father only internalizes the fear of the Big Daddy, who now menaces human desires from within.

The eighteenth-century Gothic Revival was closely intertwined with renewed interest in preserving folklore – and thus with giants. One such tale, of Jack the Giant Killer, survived across the fringe cultures of Wales, Cornwall and Brittany.

3. Thor's encounter with the giant Skrymir: an illustration of the Norse myth by Louis Huard, 1891.
4. *The Modern Living Colossus*, a leaflet announcing visiting times to meet Charles Byrne, the 'Irish Giant', 1781.
5. Francisco Goya, *Saturn Devouring His Own Son*, c. 1819–23

6

7

6. 'A hero celebrated by ancient historians': wood engraving from a chapbook
   containing the legend of Jack the Giant Killer, Oxfordshire, UK, 1820.
7. David and Goliath, in an etching by Hanns Lautensack, 1551.

In the Cornish legend, Jack, a farmer's lad, rises to Arthur's round table due to a serial giant-killing spree. The last of these deaths, the beheading of Thunderbel, is source material for the obscure rhyme 'Fee-fi-fo-fum / I smell the blood of an Englishman' that appears in *King Lear* and made its way into Joseph Jacob's popular 1890 pantomime *Jack and the Beanstalk*, which completes the verse: 'Be he alive, or be he dead, / I'll grind his bones to make my bread.' As David Punter notes, the political resonances of Jack's resistance to the tyrannical giants began to be emphasized in a 1748 dramatic opera by Henry Brooke, *Little John and the Giants* – though it was 'more faery than Gothic'. Versions of the play and Jack's story were published again during the mass organization of the working classes against factory bosses during the turbulent 1810s. In 1819, the year of the Peterloo massacre, in which striking workers in Manchester were mowed down in the street, *Jack the Giant Queller* was reissued yet again.

The giant was again put to political use, though to far more ambiguous ends, in Francisco de Goya's work of the 1810s, particularly *The Colossus*, made during the Peninsular War against Napoleonic France, and *Saturn Devouring His Son*, painted at the same time as he produced his *Disasters of War* sequence. The giants in Goya's images depict an insatiable appetite for violence and destruction; like Henry Fuseli's paintings of the night hag or rampaging giants, they feed the feverish imagery of the Gothic monster.

Perhaps the fate of the real-life 'Irish Giant', Charles Byrne, first turned giants into figures of entertainment and pity. Giants were integral to the 'wonders' cruelly presented in travelling 'freak shows'. Byrne, who was 7'7'' (2.3m) tall, was a remarkable phenomenon when he appeared first in Edinburgh in 1782 and then in London, drawing swarms of visitors. He died in 1783, his gigantism likely caused by a pituitary tumour. In his last months, Byrne was terrified of being preserved after death as a monstrous specimen – quite rightly, as it turned out. His corpse was stolen on the way to burial for the collection of the London medic John Hunter, and his skeleton remains on display at the Hunterian Museum, despite campaigns to honour his wishes and lay it properly to rest.

Gigantism really returned to popular culture with the new, outsize spectacle of cinema, turbocharged by the truly gargantuan monster who stalks into view in the early 'talkie' *King Kong* (1933). The American writer

Susan Sontag declared that the trend for gigantism-obsessed B-movies offered only 'primitive gratifications', with 'absolutely no social criticism' in sight and, most damningly, that they were 'in complicity with the abhorrent'. The Gothic is not entirely comfortable with them either, and indeed *King Kong* was not at first marketed as a horror film.

King Kong used stop-motion animation mixed with live action to track the giant gorilla Kong off the maritime maps to Skull Island, a riot of prehistoric survivals and fetish worship that has its roots in Arthur Conan Doyle's *Lost World*. King Kong becomes enamoured of the sacrificial victim left for him, the scream queen Fay Wray – who in fact screamed so much

Fee-fi-fo-fum,
I smell the blood of an Englishman.

because the script and plot remained unfinished long into shooting. These perverse scenes openly elide the menace of the gorilla with the racist trope of the Black man's threatening sexual appetites for the white woman – Edgar Wallace's first draft, *The Beast*, was even more explicit about this, although the film's last writer, Ruth Rose, made the question of where sympathies lie more ambiguous. In the memorable finale, the monster is first put on humiliating display in slave stocks at Radio City Music Hall (where the film premiered, adding another layer of thrill for the first audience), and then, once he breaks his bonds, seen atop the Empire State Building. In the end, the stilted movements of the stop-motion Kong as he is cornered and fatally wounded by buzzing bi-planes make the giant an oddly sympathetic monster, hounded to death by a world of hucksters and sensation-seekers. Already, audience identifications might be more with the monster than expected, as we secretly delight as he chomps down on New York's high society.

Re-released in 1952, *King Kong* was to have a huge influence on the filmmakers at Toho Studio in Japan, then in the last year of American occupation after the Second World War. *Gojira* (1954) was directed by Ishiro Honda, who had passed through the remains of the city of Hiroshima and seen the results of the firebombing that had devastated Tokyo. At the same time, American H-bomb testing was taking place at Bikini Atoll in the Pacific. In March 1954, one such test notoriously irradiated the entire crew of the Japanese fishing trawler *Lucky Dragon No. 5.*

All of these elements directly fed into the plot of *Gojira*, which is a fusion of 'gorira' and 'kujira', or gorilla and whale, an impossible, monstrous chimera. Gojira is a prehistoric sleeping giant awakened from slumber under the ocean by nuclear testing – a being that can be slotted into a parade of Japanese monsters and water spirits. The giant beast, merely glimpsed in the first part of the film, goes on to spend fifteen uninterrupted minutes stamping on a perfect scale model of central Tokyo, a scene apparently cheered on by the first Japanese audiences.

It is common to read the monster in *Gojira* as an emanation of conscience that erupts into post-war Japan. The war guilt of active aggressors and the shame of a traumatically defeated and punished nation flows into *Gojira*, as does a more subtle re-assertion of Japanese power. When, in 1956, the film was reframed with new footage and released in America as *Godzilla: King of the Monsters*, most of the political resonances were thoroughly excised. In the (over twenty-five) Japanese sequels, *Gojira* becomes a less ambiguous figure. The creature defends Japan against persistent obtrusions of gigantic creatures, including Rodan (Giant Monster of the Sky), Dragan (Giant Space Monster), Varan (Giant Flying Squirrel Monster) or the three-headed Ghidora (Winged Membrane Dragon). This breathless sequence makes up the genre of *kaiju eiga*: Japanese monster movies.

Each cycle of *Godzilla* revivals has its own allegorical resonances. *Shin Godzilla* (2016), for instance, contains the required, spectacular destruction of Tokyo, but is really about the bureaucracy that snarls up the government response to the crisis. When it looks like the United States will step in and nuke Tokyo, it is left to a rogue group of Japanese experts who discard hierarchy to save the city from another American nuclear bomb. Reviews were not slow to read into *Shin Godzilla* a version of the disaster at the 2011 Fukushima nuclear plant, where a tsunami caused by an undersea earthquake over-whelmed its safety systems and caused widespread radiation – a context also evoked by *Godzilla*'s 2014 outing, directed by Gareth Edwards. Perhaps a renewed sense of planetary horror, rather than just the esca-lating logic of sequels, produces ever more outsize versions: *Godzilla: King of the Monsters* (2019) fea-tures nearly every rival giant monster in the back catalogue, while *Godzilla vs. Kong* (2020) brings us neatly full-circle.

8. The finale of *King Kong* (Merian C. Cooper and Ernest B. Schoedsack, 1933).

9

12

11

9. *Gorgo*, the British answer to Gojira and Godzilla (Eugène Lourié, 1960).
10. *Gojira* (Ishirō Honda, 1954).
11. *The Beast from 20,000 Fathoms* (Eugène Lourié, 1953).
12. The Americanized *Gojira*, released as *Godzilla: King of the Monsters* in 1956.

In the 1950s, American B-movies generated their own giant evocations of the existential terror of the Cold War. Half a century later, the traumatic reconfiguring of the New York skyline after the 11 September 2001 attack on the World Trade Center saturates the Peter Jackson remake of *King Kong* (2005), and resurfaces in films like *Cloverfield* (2008), a found-footage variant of Godzilla in New York, with the glimpsed gigantic monster memorably twisting off the head of the Statue of Liberty and hurling it into midtown Manhattan. Gareth Edwards's remarkable low-budget *Monsters* (2010) addresses the failed attempt by an American government to build a wall to contain the gigantic monsters that now drift across northern Mexico, a film that some even suggest might have entered the disordered dream-world of former United States President Donald Trump. The *kaiju* genre is echoed in the eccentric film *Colossal* (Nacho Vigalondo, 2016), in which petty arguments between alcoholics in a playground in small-town America are played out as the irruption of giant monsters in the centre of Seoul, South Korea – surely a sly satire on American narcissism, its grandiose self-absorption causing outsized catastrophe across the globe.

Very different, domestic-scale anxieties seem to lie behind the emergence of the Slenderman – a freakishly tall, faceless monster dressed in a formal suit, sometimes with tentacles, who crept onto the internet via Photoshop in 2009 and has preyed on children, usually in surburban woodlands, ever since. Urban folklorists have the unusual chance to track the dissemination of this 'creepypasta' legend (a form of internet 'tall tale') from its first appearance on the 'Something Awful' forum, where its mythology was built collaboratively by users, to fake footage on YouTube and into computer gaming (*Slender: The Eight Pages* in 2012 and *Slender: The Arrival* in 2013). The horror film *Slenderman* was released in 2018 to controversy over its echoes of the real-life stabbing of a twelve-year-old girl in Wisconsin by two of her friends, who adamantly believed that this would appease Slenderman and save the lives of their families, a case sensitively documented in *Beware the Slenderman* (2016). The Slenderman is a condensation of many anxieties that hover around child abuse, domestic invasion and the contaminating ubiquity of networked media. Child-killers were once created by comics, or by video nasties: now they are made by the internet.

The ability of the monster to stretch its limbs or squeeze its tentacles through every home defence makes it a distinctive conjuration of the World Wide Web itself, built from stubs of ancient story with deep cultural roots.

To be gigantic is of course a relative term. But what also terrifies is the sudden change or inversion of scale. The most gigantic monsters might, paradoxically, be invisible, as imagined in films about contagion from *The Andromeda Strain* (1971) to *Outbreak* (1995) to *Contagion* (2011), and any number of zombie films based on viral transmission, like *28 Days Later* (2002) or *World War Z* (2013). Gigantic monsters help us to think the Anthropocene. The monster here is what Timothy Morton calls a 'hyperobject': vast, global, interconnected events that are simply too big for us to represent.

Giants are nearly always male figures, enraged by their exile and driven by outsize desires.

13

14

Little Creatures

As the giant stamps up and down on signature buildings, elves carry on their impish sport at the bottom of the garden and fairies appear on the edge of the settlement, or on the fuzzy borderlands of the nation. You catch them only out of the corner of your eye – a sight that might be lucky or very unlucky indeed. The pixies, elves and fairies who were de-fanged, prettified, shrunk down and given wings in the nineteenth century were once far nastier than anything Walt Disney ever imagined.

According to Robert Kirk's extraordinary testimony in *The Secret Commonwealth of Elves, Fauns and Fairies* (collected in Scotland in 1691–92, but only published in 1815), these folk are 'of a middle nature betwixt man and angel' – the typical, intermediate location of the monster. In one common version of their origins, they were camp-followers of rebellious angels who found themselves locked out of heaven. Some fell into the sea (becoming merrows, mermen and sirens), some onto the land, where they live underground in caves, burial mounds or other 'fairy hills', and others remain 'merry dancers' in the air, where they might be experienced as ghostly figures, or reveal elaborate fairy castles or *fata morgana* in the sky.

As one might expect from this fate, fairies can be fickle in mood, sometimes helpful and sometimes impish or downright devilish. They can curdle milk and make animals sicken, bring luck, signal buried treasure and grant healing powers and second sight, and curse you if you betray their existence or interfere with fairy paths. Most dangerously, they can kidnap children and replace them with their own changelings. As late as 1895, there was a trial in Ireland over the death of Bridget Cleary, a twenty-seven-year-old woman whose husband had been persuaded that her change in personality signalled that she had been replaced by a changeling. She was tortured, held to the fire and burned to death – the common means to try to persuade fairies to reverse the switch. Young children who bore physical disabilities or showed developmental problems were also treated to this form of torture if they were suspected changelings; supernatural agency gave meaning to arbitrary and cruel changes in development or blighting illness. At their height in the 1640s, Puritan witch-hunters sometimes referenced imps and elves as likely familiars for witches. By the late nineteenth century,

13. Henry Fuseli, *Robin Goodfellow (Puck)*, c. 1799.

14. Illustrated page from a notebook kept by Rev. Robert Kirk in the 1660s, towards the book eventually published as *The Secret Commonwealth of Elves, Fauns, and Fairies*.

15. [opposite] Richard Dadd's *The Fairy Feller's Masterstroke*, painted between 1855 and 1864 while incarcerated in Broadmoor Lunatic Asylum.

the persistence of such beliefs proved perfect fodder to cast the colonial subjects of Ireland and Scotland as primitive, superstitious peasants.

Poor old Robert Kirk, meanwhile, was himself thought to have been the victim of fairy capture for revealing their ways. Walter Scott recorded in his *Letters on Demonology and Witchcraft* (1830) that on his last evening on Earth, Kirk was crossing a 'fairy mount' when 'he sunk down in what seemed to be a fit of apoplexy, which the unenlightened took for death, while the more understanding knew it to be a swoon produced by the supernatural influence of the people whose precincts he had violated'. His coffin was long rumoured to contain only stones.

The nineteenth century was a golden age of fairies. The craze for fairy paintings lasted from about 1840 to 1870, during which period depictions shifted from Henry Fuseli's grotesque, bat-winged *Robin Goodfellow-Puck* (1799) to the teeming scenes of tiny fairies in Sir Joseph Noel Paton's *Reconciliation of Oberon and Titania* (1847) or John Anster Fitzgerald's many fairy scenes, including *The Fairies' Banquet* (1859) or *Fairies in a Bird's Nest* (1860). Fitzgerald's Irishness gave authenticity to his transfixing visions, as did the likelihood that opium inspired some of these scenes. Paintings such as John Simmons's *Titania* (1866) indicated a path towards prettified erotic images of fairy queens, but the weirdest of these images came from a very dark place in the painter Richard Dadd's mind.

Dadd, a supremely gifted young painter at the Royal Academy Schools, had sketched images of fairies long before an ill-fated trip across Europe and the Middle East in 1842, on which he started to show incipient signs of mental illness. Back home in 1843, convinced that his father Robert was the devil, Dadd stabbed him to death. He remained in criminal lunatic asylums until his death in 1886, his delusions fixed and unshakeable. After over a decade in Bethlem asylum, Dadd was allowed painting equipment by the reforming doctor Charles Hood, by which time his mind had travelled to some very strange regions. He spent years perfecting two fairy paintings, *Contradiction: Oberon and Titania* (1854–58) and *The Fairy Feller's Master-Stroke* (1855–64): complete, self-contained worlds, executed with a miniaturist's skill.

The exhibition of physical and cultural difference in 'freak shows' had long featured dwarfs and little people as 'sports of nature', but in the nineteenth century,

biological and race science began to use the existence of diminutive races as natural explanations for formerly supernatural beliefs in fairies and elves. In the Hunterian Museum, next to the skeleton of Charles Byrne, is the diminutive skeleton of 'The Sicilian Fairy', Caroline Crachami. Standing only half a metre tall, Crachami was exhibited in London by 'Dr Gilligan', and spoke, so one contemporary report said, with 'a strange, unearthly voice'. She died in 1824 aged only nine, and has subsequently been diagnosed with the condition 'primordial dwarfism'. The career of Maximo Valdez Nunes and Bartola Velasquez, known as the Aztec Lilliputians, was much longer. Originally from Salvador, but presented as ancient Aztec survivals from a lost city in Central America, they were displayed in human zoos and freak shows across America and Europe for decades, and their marriage in 1867 was reported in newspapers around the world. An echo of their lives is found in Tod Browning's controversial 1932 film *Freaks*, which used real carnival sideshow performers and included a marriage ceremony.

Of a middle nature betwixt man and angel.

These cases were already making monsters of physical and racial difference. The small stature of the Sicilians or 'Aztecs' suggested to those such as Robert Knox, the anatomist and racist ethnologist, a more primitive stage of human development. Paul du Chaillu's sensationalized 'discovery' of the long-mythical 'pigmies' of Africa in the 1860s fed directly into such scientific racism. Henry Stanley's bestselling *In Darkest Africa* (1890) expresses this perception of monstrous hybridity: 'That little body of his represented the oldest types of primeval man…eternally exiled by their vice, to live the life of human beasts in morass and fen and jungle wild. Think of it!' This fascination with the Other feeds directly into the horror felt at the 'troglodytic' Mr Hyde in Robert Louis Stevenson's *The Strange Case of Dr Jekyll and Mr Hyde*, a book he called a 'Gothic gnome', or the fear associated with the 'unhallowed dwarf' Tonga in the Sherlock Holmes adventure *The Sign of Four* (1890), a 'black cannibal' from the Andaman Islands and a sidekick of Holmes's dastardly adversary.

There is a long tradition of casting people with dwarfism in horror films, continuing the nineteenth century's cruel reliance on deviation from an assumed norm to create monsters. The four siblings of the Earle family, known as 'The Doll Family', appeared

16. [opposite above] John Anster Fitzgerald, *Fairies in a Bird Nest, c.* 1860.
17. [opposite below] Ticket for Admission to see 'The Aztec Lilliputians' in London, 1855.

alongside Lon Chaney in Tod Browning's silent films *The Wicked Darling* (1919) and *The Unholy Three* (1925) before *Freaks* made them famous. Angelo Rossitto featured in *Seven Footprints to Satan* (1929), and alongside Bela Lugosi in *Spooks Run Wild* (1941) and *Scared to Death* (1947). He continued working up to his appearance with Vincent Price in *From a Whisper to a Scream* (1987). Billy Barty was a child when he first appeared in *Bride of Frankenstein* (1935), reappearing later in Roger Corman's *The Undead* (1957). Skip Martin played Hop Toad in Corman's memorable adaptation of Poe's *The Masque of the Red Death* (1964), and later in *Vampire Circus* (1971) and *Horror Hospital* (1973). Cousin Itt in the television series of *The Addams Family* was played by the circus performer Felix Silla, and Zelda Rubinstein was still playing the scary dwarf in *Poltergeist* (1982). David Lynch films from *Eraserhead* (1976) to *Mulholland Drive* (2002) are full of strange dwarfish figures who seem to control destinies from a distance. This is not a trope that has faded with the rise of disability activism, **18**

even if in *Game of Thrones*, Peter Dinklage's abused and humiliated dwarf Tyrion Lannister proves one of the series's great survivors.

Towards the end of the twentieth century, such tropes emerged again in the monstrous invaders of alien abduction narratives. In 1987, the horror writer Whitley Strieber published an extraordinary memoir, *Communion*, in which he revealed that hypnotic recovery techniques had allowed him to retrieve repressed memories of a lifetime of traumatic visitations from small grey aliens. It was made into a film with a typically eccentric performance by Christopher Walken as Strieber in 1989, and much of the tale also ended up in the narrative arc of *The X-Files* (1993–2002), which effectively mixed science fiction with Gothic horror. Although newly wrapped in the accoutrements of science fiction, many elements of these stories repeat material seen in beliefs about fairies and even Indian captivity narratives (see p. 192). Underneath a cutesy culture of fairies, we still fear the viciousness of little monsters.

18. *Freaks* (Tod Browning, 1932).
19. Daguerreotype portraits of Maximo and Bartola, The Aztec Lilliputians, made on a tour of America, *c.* 1850.
20. Encounter with a little grey alien, *Communion* (Philippe Mora, 1989).

19

20

Splice

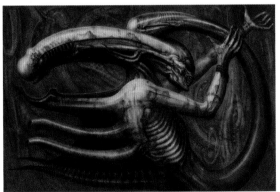

In Ridley Scott's film *Alien* (1979), a fusion of science fiction, Gothic horror and murder mystery, the audience can never quite make sense of the life-cycle of the creature that stalks the spaceship. Its eggs expel a skeletal 'Face-Hugger' that clamps onto the face like a leech or a lamprey. Then, in an epochal chest-bursting birth scene, we realise that this monster works like a parasitic wasp, the larvae eating their host from the inside out. The fanged thing that bursts from Kane is small and nasty and monstrously quick; the hapless crew hunt it with a net, like they were out hunting for butterflies. They realize too late that its adult form looms over the human crew, its smooth, eyeless skull with the sheen of a shark or the chitinous carapace of a giant bug, the body of a reptile and the swishing tail of a serpent or dragon.

The designer of this adult alien, the maestro H. R. Giger, let this beast step down from the paintings he had made of hybrid bio-mechanical forms for his book inspired by H. P. Lovecraft, *The Necronomicon* (1977). The alien can disguise itself by folding into air ducts and instrument panels, because it looks as much like a machine as a biological being. With the logic of dreams, it is an impossible splice of different parts, a rebus of dark fantasies about biological origins.

The monster theorist and medievalist Jeffrey Jerome Cohen has proposed that monsters are cultural bodies that mark 'a crisis of category'. They dwell ambiguously at what Cohen calls the 'gates of difference', potentially punishing transgression but sometimes rewarding it or provoking it too; they are what the philosopher Stephen Asma calls 'mosaic beings', elements fused together that offend the moral or natural order of things. Such creatures have deep roots in ancient cultures, from the Assyrians and Egyptians onwards.

1. [opposite] Hieronymus Bosch, *The Garden of Earthly Delights*, c. 1503–15 (detail).
2. H. R. Giger's design for the 'Facehugger' xenomorph in *Alien* (Ridley Scott, 1979).
3. H. R. Giger, *Necronomicon* (1977), one of Ridley Scott's inspirations for the fully grown xenomorph in *Alien*.

4

5

4. Spread from the Helmingham
   Herbal and Bestiary, Suffolk,
   England, *c.* 1500.
5. The Chimera of Arezzo, an Etruscan
   depiction from about 400 BC of
   the monstrous hybrid creature slain
   by Bellerophon in the Greek myth.
   It was rediscovered in 1553,
   and became part of the collection
   of the Medici family.
6. German wood relief, after a woodcut
   design by Lucas Cranach, 1512.
   The lower left depicts a creature
   half-man, half-wolf devouring a child.
7. *Aristotle's Masterpiece, Or The Secrets
   of Generation displayed in all the
   parts thereof*, a medical text about
   reproductive health, was first
   published in 1684 and remained
   popular for over a century.
   It was not the work of Aristotle.

They are called 'chimera', after the Greek she-monster who had a lion's head, a goat's body and a serpent's tail – a term still used in biology for organisms that are composed of cells from more than one genotype.

Medieval bestiaries blended classical and Biblical sources of authority, and cast monsters and marvels as meaningful signs within an ordered moral universe. Creation was supposed to work in neat oppositions and symbiosis – the cat and the mouse, or the basilisk whose gaze can kill a man yet which can be bested by the weasel. Natural history was meant to be God's orderly book of moral instruction, but mixed into this order were truly strange spliced creatures that themselves seemed to travel from hybrid places – Greek or Roman natural history and mythology, religious texts or travellers' tall tales. We might know about the sphinx, the centaur or the satyr, but less familiar, perhaps, are the griffin, a Hyperborean animal that mixed the lion and the eagle, or the manticore, which had the face of a man, but with three rows of sharp teeth, a lion's body and the tail of a scorpion. Bestiaries sometimes extended to include races of man that deviated from the assumed normal human form, found in the east or the fiery south: the one-footed Sciapodes from Ethiopia; the dog-headed Cynocephali of the Indies; the headless Blemmys, with faces in their chests.

In fact, we can distinguish two orders of extraordinary creatures from these texts. *Marvels* were rare and extraordinary animals used as proof of the diversity and ingenuity of God's creation. Wealthy men spent serious money to acquire unicorn horns, sable fur or griffin eggs for their cabinets of curiosity. *Monsters*, however, were not in the normal order of things. They were prodigies and portents of God's displeasure, ominous warning signs of something morally rotten in the state of things. Monstrous births were pored over as markers of significance: a cluster in Italy in the 1490s portended war, as they did in France during the 1560s and 1570s, when the religious war against the Protestant Huguenots was at its height, resulting in the multivolume *Histoires Prodigieuses*, which reported on all manner of horrific creatures, monstrous births, strange fish and sea monsters.

Also running through these accounts was an interest in therianthropy – the ability of humans to metamorphose into animals. This shape-shifting includes ailuranthropy (turning into a cat), cyanothropy (turning into a dog), and, most famously, lycanthropy, the ability to become a wolf. This idea is central

6

7

to many cultural and religious practices of shamanism in the north, and to the diverse classical myths of Egypt, Greece and Rome. Jacques Tourneur's atmospheric Gothic shocker *Cat People* (1942) is a memorable psychological treatment of the case of an alluring-yet-dangerous ailuranthrope from the Balkans, that breeding ground for Europe's monsters. Its Serbian heroine, Irena, is caught in a fatal attraction to and identification with the panthers of Central Park zoo, which seems openly connected to her recent marriage and anxiety about expressing her sexual desires. The film hovers unnervingly on the edge of literal and metaphorical treatment of 'animal' desire throughout.

But it is the werewolf that has been the most enduring survival of this belief, both as folklore and Gothic convention. The term derives from the Greek myth of Lycaon, a tyrant who offended the gods and was cast into the wilderness, losing the capacity to speak and reduced to howling and a thirst for human blood. It feeds into the stories of wild men and feral children that have obsessed many cultures, transgressive figures that help determine the boundary of the human. Stories of children raised by wolves or dogs are found from Siberia to Ukraine, Germany to Chile. The folklorist Sabine Baring-Gould collected many such European stories in his *Book of Werewolves* (1865), securing lycanthropy's place in the Gothic tradition.

The werewolf in folklore and Gothic fiction usually articulates a transgression of norms, whether bestial, sexual or racial. What line has been crossed to bring down this curse? It is a perfect metaphor for moments of transition, whether in structured cultural rituals, or the comedy of key life transitions (hence: *I Was a Teenage Werewolf*, 1957). Werewolves were fodder for a multitude of Gothic tales in the Victorian period, from the serial melodrama of G. W. M. Reynolds's *Wagner, the Wehr-Wolf* (1846-47) to Rudyard Kipling's 'The Mark of the Beast' (1890), and slotted neatly into the Universal Studios cycle of monster films (*The Wolf Man*, 1941). The werewolf has never been quite killed off in cinema. Where splatter-horror drives the special effects of *An American Werewolf in London* or *Wolfen* (1981), the comic potential of turning corporate masculine ego into a werewolf was the premise for Jack Nicholson's over-the-top performance in *Wolf* (1994). More recently, in the X-Men universe, the story of the mutant Logan, who transforms into Wolverine, shows that this narrative remains a powerful allegory

of a man overwhelmed by his animalistic compulsions. The comic universe – populated by Batman, Spiderman, Catwoman, the Wolverine and so on – is where therianthropic tales now find their most persistent home. Animalistic monsters concretize gigantic extremes of rage and shame in the modern world.

But this trope can also be inverted. While the folktale 'Little Red Riding Hood' is often told as a moral lesson in restraining wolfish desires, in *The Bloody Chamber* Angela Carter lets her female characters escape with the wolves, unpunished for exploring their sexual pleasures. Her werewolf stories formed the basis for Neil Jordan's film *The Company of Wolves* (1984).

Transgressive figures that help determine the boundary of the human.

The anthologist Pam Keesey collated a series of werewolf stories in *Women Who Run with the Wolves* (1996), which uses the allegory of transformation to explore lesbian identity. This has been a feature of the vampire tale, too, which can be encoded, as in LeFanu's 'Carmilla' or Stoker's *Dracula*, with all manner of 'perverse' sexual desire. Another Keesey anthology, *Vamps*, subverts the trope of the sexually predatory, vampiric female, while writers like Suzy McKee Charnas and Jewelle Gomez have used the mythology of the vampire to explore dissident sexual identities. The perverse dynamic of transformation is deployed to flip the hierarchies of self and other, normal and pathological, human and monster.

8. The werewolf head used for the groundbreaking special effects in *An American Werewolf in London* (John Landis, 1981).

9. *Cat People* (Jacques Tourneur, 1942), a psychological take on animal transformation.

10. Full wolf transformation in *An American Werewolf in London*.

11. *The Wolf Man* (George Waggner, 1941), the film that established many of the modern cinematic conventions of the werewolf.

12. *Wolverine*, Marvel Comics cover, September 1982.

13. Prop mask from *The Wolfman* (Joe Johnston, 2010), a remake of the Universal Studios classic from 1941.

14. *I Was a Teenage Werewolf* (Gene Fowler Jr., 1957).

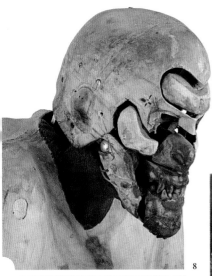

8

9

She was marked with the curse of those who slink and court and kill by night!

10

11

13

14

12

15

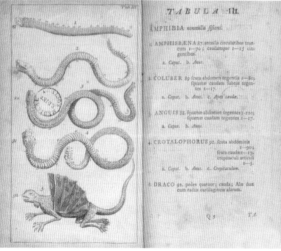

16

Hybrids

In the early eighteenth century, two developments shifted attitudes to monstrous splices. In 1720, the horticulturalist Thomas Fairchild, who kept a nursery of exotic plants in Hoxton, East London, presented the first actively *designed* hybrid flower, a wholly new form of the dianthus, to the prestigious Royal Society. It became known as 'Fairchild's Mule' (because a mule is the offspring of a horse and a donkey). Fairchild's anxiety about presenting the mechanism by which he had created this hybrid in public was typical, since he worried that his plant might be received as blasphemous, a deliberate tinkering with the order of God's creation. One hundred years before Victor Frankenstein, Fairchild was the Promethean usurper of God's power of creation, creating a monster through controlled breeding. It was the kind of evidence that Charles Darwin would later use to determine the mechanism of evolution through natural selection. Fairchild's Mule was also the first necessary step in the creation of what has since been christened the Plant Gothic.

The second development was the work of the Swedish naturalist Carl Linnaeus, whose *Systema Naturae* (1735) constructed a scientific classification system for all living things that is still used today. The taxonomies that Linnaeus created abolished the moral and religious organization of the natural world for one built on strictly observed patterns of sameness and difference. They also effectively abolished the medieval chimera. In 1735, Linnaeus actually travelled to Hamburg to inspect the 'seven-headed hydra', a famous Church relic then held in the collection of the Burgomeister of the town, and pronounced it a fake, the seven heads made of the jaws and claws of weasels glued onto snake skins. He suggested that the monks had fashioned it to match the description of the seven-headed beast of the Book of Revelation. His public pronouncement and challenge to religious authority over the artefact was deeply unpopular, and Linnaeus had to make a sharp exit from the city.

The fate of the Hamburg Hydra suggests that with the advance of scientific taxonomy, monsters were no longer possible. Science quells magic; it disenchants the world by positioning everything in it. But here we encounter the same old paradox of the rise of the Gothic romance in the eighteenth century: it irrupts at exactly the moment it ought to disappear. The Gothic becomes the repository for older beliefs,

15. Preserved samples of 'Fairchild's Mule', the first artificial plant hybrid, created by Thomas Fairchild in 1717.
16. Pages from a 1756 edition of Carl Linnaeus's *Systema Naturae*. The 'Linnean' taxonomy is still used to name and classify all living things.
17. *Little Joe* (Jessica Hausner, 2019).
18. The 'Hamburg Hydra', drawn for Albertus Seba for the *Accurate Description of the Very Rich Treasury of Natural Objects* (1734–65).

17

18

rather in the way that Freud once defined the uncanny as the return of superstitions and primordial beliefs that enlightened sceptics thought they had superseded. But it is also the case that taxonomy doesn't really abolish monsters at all.

In the 1820s, the French professor of anatomy Étienne Geoffroy St Hilaire proposed a formalization of the science of monsters: he called it teratology. Geoffroy argued that the embryo recapitulated in sequence the whole history of biological forms, from the most primitive to the present, and so monsters could be seen as sudden *arrests* along these phases of normal development. Monsters were mistakes of normal processes, but they were always explicable and identifiable; there was a law of deformation as well as formation, and the 'normal' could now be studied through these rare instances of the pathological.

The Gothic becomes one of the privileged places in culture where this revolution in thought is presented in all its traumatic potential. For all the genre's roots in theological ideas, after these biological theories of development emerged into public discourse, the monsters of the Gothic took on new resonances. Darwin, to reassure the readers of his faith-shaking theory in *On the Origin of Species*, talked about an upwards journey of evolution towards 'perfectibility'. Others, though, were less optimistic: if man could advance up the evolutionary ladder, might it not also be possible to move down? What if every respectable Dr Jekyll hid a simian Mr Hyde? Is the psychology of man spliced between the human and the bestial? Did every Dorian Gray hide a secret portrait of physical degeneracy?

H. G. Wells was the great writer of degenerate horrors in the 1890s, having been one of the first to train to teach the biological sciences under T. H. Huxley, Darwin's 'bulldog' and public defender. In *The Island of Doctor Moreau* (1896), the titular doctor vivisects beasts into grotesque forms of men, only to see them fall back into their animal state again. The disturbing splices and grafts of monstrous hybrids, built by surgery in Moreau's House of Pain, entirely undercut any secure boundary between human and animal, and even disturbingly suggest that these pitiful beastmen have a greater understanding of morality than humans. When the book was adapted to screen in 1932 as *The Island of Lost Souls*, with Charles Laughton playing an insidious Doctor Moreau, the plot was driven more by the transgressive prospect of an interracial or even interspecies sexual relationship

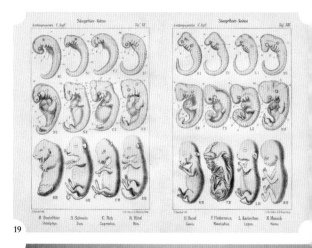

19

20

19. Ernst Haeckel's argument that human embryonic development passes through all the stages of animal evolution, here illustrated in his *Anthropogenecy* (1874).
20. *Splice* (Vincenzo Natali, 2009).
21. *The Fly* (David Cronenberg, 1986).

between the 'Panther Woman' and Edward Parker, or between the blonde leading lady and Ouran, the priapic ape. The film was censored in many countries, including Australia, where its NEN rating banned its viewing by Aboriginal audiences.

In the 1980s, the term 'Splatterpunk' was applied to another kind of splicing. A group of writers including Clive Barker and Richard Laymon emphasized bodily suffering, the opening of the flesh and the kind of intense pain that morphs into perverse ecstasy. This coincided with the last golden age of analogue special effects in horror cinema before the arrival of CGI. 'Body horror' films emphasized extraordinary bodily transformations. The constantly mutating alien of John Carpenter's *The Thing* (1982) moves through dogs, spiders and men by absorbing and transforming their genetic code, embodying the plasticity of adaptive survival. *The Fly* (1986), in which an unfortunate scientist mixes his DNA with a rogue fly in his laboratory equipment, was David Cronenberg's mainstream breakthrough after a long career making low-budget horrors that emphasized the infinitely malleable human body and its openness to alien transformation (as in *Rabid*, *Shivers*, or *Videodrome*). Grotesque bodily distortion became the capstone effect of cult films like Stuart Gordon's *Re-Animator* (1985, with two sequels), Clive Barker's *Hellraiser* (1987, with nine sequels so far) and Brian Yuzna's *Society* (1989). The trend latterly heads towards the grim cycle around *Hostel* (2005) and the *Saw* franchise (started in 2004) that became known as 'torture porn'.

There are complicated reasons for the emergence of this kind of extreme Gothic – not least in the constantly shifting line of cultural acceptability around graphic images of sex and violence, and the economics of low-budget horror sequels, cycles and imitations. But there is a biological context that brings us back to the idea of the chimera or splice. In the 1970s, a neo-Darwinian group of scientists emerged into public discourse: Richard Dawkins published *The Selfish Gene* (1976), which restated a ruthless struggle for advantage as the defining dynamic of biological existence. The monsters of *Alien* and *The Thing* are relentless, murderous competitors, perfectly honed and weaponized to triumph over the weak altruism of human beings. Ripley wins a few battles against monster and corporation in the *Alien* series, but she never quite wins the war. Such monsters embody the idea of the selfish gene –

Absorbing and transforming their genetic code, embodying the plasticity of adaptive survival.

21

a position opposed by other biologists, most notably Lyn Margulis and Stephen Jay Gould, who argued for the *social* gene and the adaptive benefits of cooperation. The ideological fight over the meaning of evolutionary monsters was restaged again in this resurgence of 'the Darwin wars'.

22

In 1984, the Human Genome Project started the process of mapping the full genetic sequence of human DNA. This enormous project, completed in 2000, has fostered a whole new panoply of monsters in the Gothic and science fiction imagination, from the alien of the *Species* films (1998–2007), to the catastrophic mix of genetic materials that produces the laboratory chimera in the film *Splice* (2009) or the ghastly giant insects and tentacular horrors that emerge out of the mist in Stephen King's *The Mist* (adapted for the screen by Frank Darabont in 2007). The science fiction films *Gattaca* (1997) and *Code 46* (2003) have explored some of the dystopian fantasies and fears of 'designer babies' that reared up around the project, and monster films based around genetic mutation have never gone away. But there has also been a sense that the revolution in molecular biology and biotechnology has allowed for the creation of artificial, laboratory life in wholly new ways, which has in turn fed quieter, different kinds of Gothic horror. It is not always the gigantic, externalized hybrid monster that we should fear. It can also be the sense that we have been insidiously manipulated or changed, whether by the genetically modified flowers that impose placid well-being on humans through their scent, as in Jessica Hauser's *Little Joe* (2019), or the mystifying chain of horrors in Shane Carruth's *Upstream Color* (2013), which seems to bind humans into a network of larvae, artificially inseminated pigs, river systems and orchids in a strange biological linkage that begins to control human actions. Increasingly, it is the realization that humans exist in complex, interdependent, cross-species assemblages that drives a more subtle kind of monster.

Monsters are cultural bodies that mark 'a crisis of category.'

22. The letter 'S' as a hybrid creature, in a twelfth-century manuscript of Pliny the Elder's *Natural History*.
23. [opposite] The transformation scene in *An American Werewolf in London*.

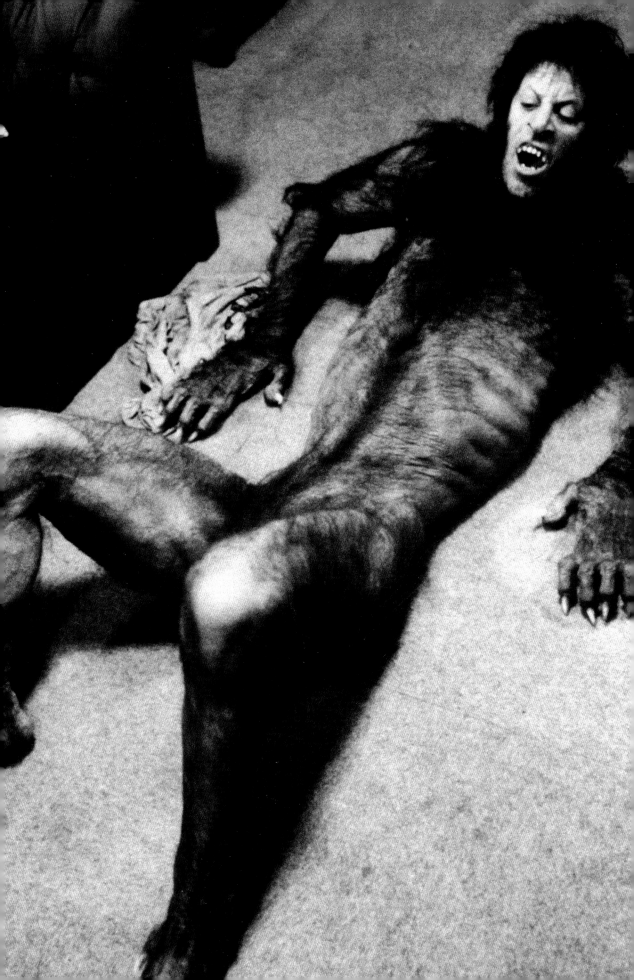

ISABELLE ADJANI   SAM NEILL

POSSESSION

un film de

ANDRZEJ ZULAWSKI

BASHA

et avec **HEINZ BENNENT**   effets spéciaux **CARLO RAMBALDI**

images de BRUNO NUYTTEN   musique de ANDRZEJ KORZYNSKI   directeur de production JEAN-JOSE RICHER

une co-production franco-allemande OLIANE PRODUCTIONS (PARIS)   SOMA FILM PRODUKTION GmbH (BERLIN)
MARIANNE PRODUCTIONS (PARIS)

INTERDIT AUX MOINS DE 18 ANS

The Tentacle

Victor Hugo, it is safe to say, did not like cephalopods – not octopuses, squid, cuttlefish, or the mythology of many-headed hydras, giant sea serpents and krakens. His novel *Toilers of the Sea* (1866), written in exile among the fishermen of the island of Guernsey, includes a whole chapter about a creature he denounces as 'the sea-vampire'. His horror seems to derive from the sense that it has no *structure*, no fixed shape, 'no blood, no bones, no flesh. It is soft and flabby; a skin with nothing inside...[a] glutinous mass, endowed with a malignant will'. Once its victim is caught in its tentacular grasp, tangled in its folds, paralysed by its venom, the devil-fish kills by sucking the blood: 'The blood spurts out and mingles horribly with the lymph of the monster, which clings to its victim by innumerable hideous mouths. The hydra incorporates itself with the man; the man becomes one with the hydra.' He waxes philosophical: the cephaloptera, he says, 'wanders ghostlike among living things', a mix of myth, sailors' yarn and biological monstrosity. He ultimately suggests that it embodies the principle of death that balances life: 'the devourers are the sextons of the system of nature.' In other words, it is the ultimate Gothic monster.

This splendid rant is hopelessly inaccurate (cephalopods do not suck blood, for starters), but proved influential. In 1873, *Scientific American* declared that 'the monster is, all in all, one of the most frightful apparitions that could be the fate of man to meet'. Reports in the press revived stories of malicious creatures swiping sailors from boats. There had long been seafaring legends about kraken and giant squid, but Hermann Melville's cosmic whale-hunt novel *Moby Dick* (1851) was at least slightly more accurate than Hugo's paroxysm of horror. In chapter 59, Captain Ahab's boat

It's bugger all like us. Alien.

1. [opposite] Film poster for *Possession* (Andrzej Żuławski, 1981).
2. Adolf Giltsch lithograph for Ernst Haeckel, *Kunstformen der Natur* (1904).

MONSTER DESTROYS HARPOON PLATFORM.

briefly sights a 'vast pulpy mass, furlongs in length and breadth' – a giant squid – in calm ocean waters. 'So rarely is it beheld', Ishmael tells us, that only the most experienced sailors 'have any but the most vague ideas concerning its true nature and form'. Stories stretching back to medieval bestiaries talked of sea creatures so vast that they were mistaken for islands. The shape of the legendary kraken of Norwegian legend, Melville's chapter ends, 'may ultimately resolve into Squid', as if fantasy will shortly be forced to take definite form by natural history.

Melville refers to the legends of sea monsters collected by Bishop Pontoppidan in his *Natural History of Norway* (1752–53). Unusually, the tales of kraken, giant squids and sea-serpents reported by writers from Pliny to Pontoppidan, and represented in art from Mycenaean culture onwards, still hovered somewhere between naturalistic fact and fantastical horror story into the nineteenth century. The Gothic has long been alive with these writhing monsters, exploiting that space of hesitation between fact and fiction, and they only intensify: Jules Verne's *20,000 Leagues Under the Sea* (1871) features the famous tussle of the submarine *Nautilus* (the nautilus is the only cephalopod to retain a hard shell) with a giant squid. In H. G. Wells's *The War of the Worlds* (1898), the Martians inside their metallic tripods are loathsome creatures that 'heaved and pulsed convulsively' with 'lank tentacular appendages', 'fungoid' skin and a head covered with 'Gorgon groups of tentacles'. They evoke the writhing, tentacular horror of the Greek Gorgon Medusa, who can petrify men stone dead with her gaze – but they have arrived on Earth to suck human blood straight into their brains, in an echo of Hugo's engulfing devil-fish. The seaman-turned-horror-writer William Hope Hodgson populated his Gothic sea tales with human-fungal-fish monsters, tentacular splices that slither and slime all over *The Boats of 'Glen Carrig'* (1907), and one of his fans, H. P. Lovecraft, took this aesthetic of disgust to its greatest extreme. The icon of the monstrous old god Chthulhu is described as being 'of a form which only a diseased fancy could conceive' – a mix of 'an octopus, a dragon and a human caricature' with 'a pulpy tentacled head'. And then there is the anatomy of the Dunwich Horror, that diabolic chimera that 'below the waist' is 'thickly covered with coarse black fur, and from the abdomen a score of long greenish-grey tentacles with red sucking mouths protruded'.

5

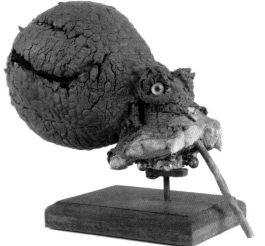

6

Oh! Boundaries and borders gone! I've vanished!

3. Illustration of a kraken attack in Arthur Mangin, *Les Mystères de l'Ocean* (1870).
4. Harper Goff, the art director for Disney's *20,000 Leagues Under the Sea* (Richard Fleischer, 1954), collected visual ideas in scrapbooks of images.
5. Illustration by Henrique Alvim Corréa for the 1906 French translation of H. G. Wells's *The War of the Worlds*.
6. Ray Harryhausen's de-tentacled original model for the monster in *It Came from Beneath the Sea* (Robert Gordon, 1955).

'When the thing breathed', the appalled narrator continues, 'its tail and tentacles rhythmically changed colour.' The story goes that Lovecraft had a phobia of eating seafood: no kidding.

In cinema, the distinctive heightened emotion of abjection – that horror of the goo that overflows and slimes over the boundaries between what should be inside and outside of the body – commonly exploits such disgust. The gigantic kraken in *It Came from Beneath the Sea* (1955), one of the classic monster movies animated by Ray Harryhausen, competes with Godzilla for destruction of iconic buildings, as its tentacles wrap around the Golden Gate Bridge and pull it into the water. This tentacular sublime

7

can equally be switched with intimate bodily invasion, as in the squiddy sex scenes of Andrzej Żuławski's *Possession* (1981), the rapidly evolving tentacular alien that stalks the *Species* films (1995–2007) for a human reproductive partner, or the monstrous creatures that overcome their biological engineers in Ridley Scott's *Alien* prequel, *Prometheus* (2012). Taking this horror of engulfment to its logical end, in the horror film *The Borderlands* (2013) the investigators of a dark tunnel notice that the walls convulse, ooze acid and constrict, and we are left to realize that they are inside the intestine of a giant, unseen monster. No wonder the old sea-dogs of Robert Eggers's film *The Lighthouse* (2019) are driven mad by the visions of slithery female creatures that wash up on their island.

Why does this kind of monster evoke such horror? Freud and his followers had a fairly unsurprising answer: sexual anxiety. In a brief note entitled 'Medusa's Head' (1922), Freud argued that the myth of Perseus cutting off the head of the Gorgon, her hair a wriggle of snakes or tentacles, was simple to decode. 'To decapitate = to castrate. The terror of the Medusa is thus a terror of castration that is linked to the sight of something.... It occurs when a boy who has hitherto been unwilling to believe the threat of castration catches sight of the female genitals.' In compensation for the *absence* of the penis, the image of the writhing hair multiplies the reassuring *presence* of the male organ. If the Medusa 'makes the spectator stiff with terror', this is oddly reassuring. Jacques Schnier later wrote a much fuller psychoanalytic exploration of the octopus as unconscious symbol, relying principally on a reading of *Toilers of the Sea* that emphasized the 'oral sadism' of the entrapment by tentacles and the steady incorporation into the maw of the sea-vampire (and still, in the end, a fear of castration).

Some feminist thinkers, objecting to the construction of woman as lack, have mocked this interpretation. Hélène Cixous wrote in 1976: 'You have only to look at the Medusa straight on to see her. And she's not deadly. She's beautiful and she's laughing.' Clearly, there is a strong cultural link between cephalopods and sexual fantasy. The notorious woodblock print by the Japanese artist Hokusai, *The Dream of the Fisherman's Wife* (1814), is an image of a woman being pleasured by an octopus, head thrown back in blissful abandon. Part of the Japanese text reads 'Oh! Boundaries and borders gone! I've vanished!' – ecstasy found where Victor Hugo saw only horror.

7. Ray Harryhausen's storyboards for *It Came from Beneath the Sea*.
8. [opposite, above left] Film poster for *It Came from Beneath the Sea*.
9. [opposite, above right] Storyboards for *It Came from Beneath the Sea*.
10. [opposite below] Attack on San Francisco, in *It Came from Beneath the Sea*.

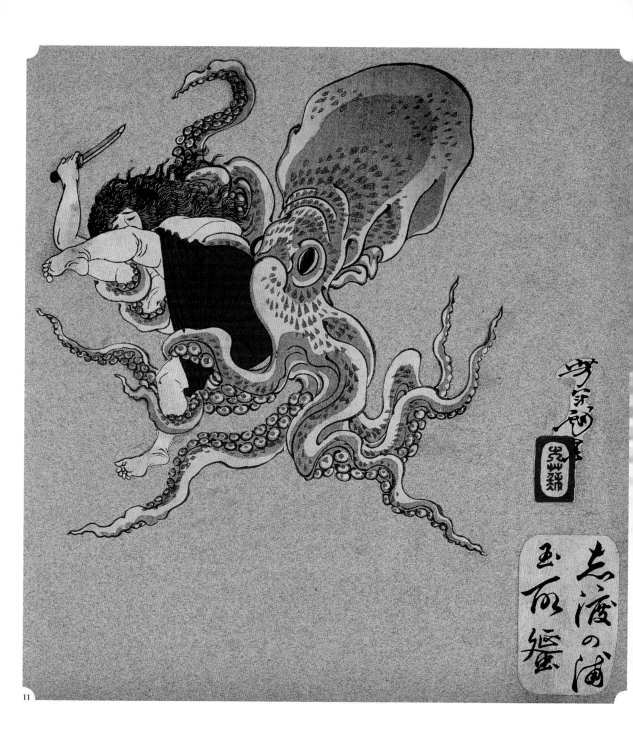

11

志渡の浦
玉取蜑

11. The innovative woodblock printer Taiso Yoshitoshi's
A Female Abalone Diver Wrestling with an Octopus, 1870s.
12. *The Dunwich Horror* (Daniel Haller, 1970).
13. *Monster from the Ocean Floor* (Wyott Ordung, 1954).

In Japan, the *shunga* (erotic print) genre leads into a whole subculture of 'tentacle porn' from the 1960s, in part a response to strict censorship laws that forbade the depiction of (human) genitalia. In the same decade, the French Surrealist Jean Painlevé released his short film *The Love Life of the Octopus* (1965), a quirky and distinctly unfrightening investigation of the weird, rather melancholy reproductive cycle of the cephalopod. The sexual imagery associated with octopuses is plainly not about castration. The tentacle sex depicted in *Possession* (1981) is transgressive in multiple ways: ambiguously incestuous, overtly across the species barrier, avowedly perverse. In the queer Mexican film *The Untamed* (2016), sex with an alien is so good that it starts to unravel you, men and women undone in ecstasy as the tentacles slide around and penetrate human bodies. Sex with the tentacular other is a writhing mass of allure and repulsion: the point where the perverse dynamic starts to flip the value of the monster. This seems more aligned to the use of the octopus in Mycenaean and Greek culture, where it was a symbol of plenitude and good fortune. Guillermo del Toro's sweet fantasy about squiddy sex, *The Shape of Water* (2018), even won an Oscar. In 2020, there was controversy over whether the South African diver Craig Foster develops an erotic relationship with an octopus in the documentary *My Octopus Teacher* (2020) – surely dependent on one's understanding of the boundaries of trans-species eroticism.

To lose the boundaries of one's self, even one's *species*, can evidently evoke the positive rather than the negative sublime. Donna Haraway notes that *tentaculum* means to feel, to try (hence the term for a related biological structure, the 'feeler'), and that what she calls 'tentacular thinking' might mean to see and feel very differently: to overflow rigid categories and 'spin out loopy tendrils' of new ideas. She inverts this monster from threat to promise, welcoming Medusas, Gorgons, Harpies and Sirens to a 'bumptious queer family'. The tentacle can signal a dissident identity and sexuality; it has also been essential to fantasy fiction by women of colour, whether Octavia Butler's *Xenogenesis* trilogy (1987–89), Nnedi Okorafor's *Binti* (2015) or Rita Indiana's *Tentacle* (2018). In Butler's allegory, the alien race that enslaves humans and forces them to breed are monstrous Medusas – but the smarter human survivors come to accept their tentacular embrace. In *Binti*, Okorafor weaves an alien race called the Meduse into another narrative that welcomes travel outside rigid identities.

12

13

China Miéville's tongue-in-cheek fantasy novel *Kraken* (2010) also refuses the abjection of cephalopods, making the *architeuthis dux*, the giant squid, 'the perfect God': 'It's bugger all like us. Alien.' In *Kraken*, the worshippers of the tentacled god that they liberate from the Natural History Museum in London are only one of the competing apocalyptic subcultures who offer rival ends of the world.

There is a clue in Miéville's off-the-cuff 'bugger all like us' that might offer a final clue about the prevalence of the tentacular in Gothic horror. The tentacle has become shorthand for the absolute Other, the very limit of human thought. In his eccentric study *Vampyroteuthis Infernalis* (The Vampire Squid From Hell, 2012), the philosopher Vilém Flusser proposes that the cephalopod has an entirely other ontology, or nature of being, from man. This is why Peter Godfrey-Smith suggests in his bestselling book *Other Minds: The Octopus and the Evolution of Intelligent Life* (2016) that the octopus is likely to be 'the closest we will come to meeting an intelligent alien'.

At these limits, the monster reaches out a tentacle, which can be received with either abject horror or sublime wonder. Denis Villeneuve's film *Arrival* (2016) stages both. The film is a serious inquiry into the problem of how to understand the absolute Other, based on Ted Chiang's knotty conceptual short story 'The Story of Your Life'. The alien visitors are 'heptapods' (seven-footed beings) that appear inside twelve spacecraft dotted around the world. The creatures emerge from a murky mist behind a screen and communicate in a language that sounds a bit like whale-song. Eventually, they begin to 'write' with squirts of ink, rather like a species of octopus (for whom ink, known as a form of defence, may also be a form of communication). The political and military response to their messages is to assume that this must be a violent alien invasion; the female linguist, surrounded by macho military glinting with weaponry, instead works out that the message 'OFFER WEAPON' really means something like 'we offer you a tool, or a gift'. Her sublime experience – open palm to open tentacle – is to be allowed access to an alien understanding where time is no longer linear but experienced as simultaneity. In the last scenes, what we assume have been intrusive, traumatic memories of a dead child are revealed to be forward glimpses in time: she will have a child, and the child will die of a rare cancer.

She steps forward to embrace this experience rather than veer in horror from it, as her husband will do. The human Lilith gives a similar message to her hybrid-alien child, whose head writhes with Medusoid tentacles and a radula for a tongue, in Octavia Butler's *Xenogenesis*:

> 'Human beings fear difference,' Lilith had told him once. 'Oankali crave difference. Humans persecute their different ones, yet they need them to give themselves definition and status. Oankali seek difference and collect it. They need it to keep themselves from stagnation and overspecialization. If you don't understand this, you will. You'll probably find both tendencies surfacing in your own behavior.' And she had put her hand on his hair. 'When you feel a conflict, try to go the Oankali way. Embrace difference.'

You have only to look at the Medusa straight on to see her. And she's not deadly. She's beautiful and she's laughing.

14

16

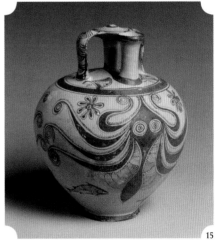

15

14. *The Shape of Water* (Guillermo del Toro, 2017).
15. Mycenaean stirrup jar featuring an octopus,
    c. 1200–1100 BC.
16. George Shaw, 'Eight Armed Cuttle Fish',
    from *Zoological Lectures Delivered at the Royal
    Institution* (1809).
17. [following spread] Katsushika Hokusai, *The Dream
    of the Fisherman's Wife*, 1814.

Formless

The formless is the piss and shit and vomit and spit that we expel. It is the gooey, gluey, slimy stuff that adheres to us, that we cannot shake off. It spreads, it travels, it cannot be contained. It is the transcendent and sublime yanked down into the ooze and the rot, the worms that writhe in the soil or the maggots that feast on decaying flesh.

The French writer Georges Bataille, who proved slightly too transgressive even for the Surrealists, included a very short essay called 'L'Informe' (The Formless) in his deliberately perverse and bewildering *Critical Dictionary*, made with friends from 1929 to 1930. He wrote: 'for academic men to be happy, the universe would have to take shape. All of philosophy has no other goal: it is a matter of giving a frock-coat to what is.' The formless includes everything that refuses to take shape, to behave as an object; the abject; things that mess up the boundary between self and other. Jean-Paul Sartre's *Being and Nothingness* (1943), written a few years after Bataille's essay, ends with a whole chapter on sliminess:

> it sticks to me, it draws me, it sucks at me. Its mode of being is neither the reassuring inertia of the solid nor a dynamism like that in water which is exhausted in fleeing from me. It is a soft, yielding action, a moist and feminine sucking.

The gender of formlessness is overt for these writers: the masculine impulse seems to want to give everything a shape, while the feminine is gooey, sticky and engulfing. What is celebrated by Bataille seems to give Sartre the shivers – what has been called by feminist Gothic scholars the fear of the 'monstrous-feminine'.

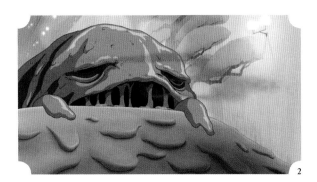

2

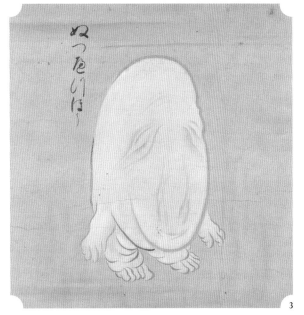

3

1. [opposite] The Slimer, from Paul Feig's 2016 *Ghostbusters* reboot.
2. Okusare, the Stink Spirit, *Spirited Away* (Hayao Miyazaki, 2001).
3. Nuppeppō, a *yōkai* spirit or ghost, depicted in anthology of monsters, *c.* 1700.

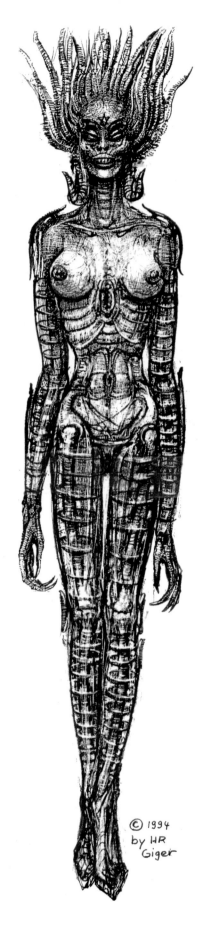

© 1994
by HR
Giger

In *The Viscous* (2020), the writer and filmmaker Freddie Mason notes that there is a whole taxonomy of fluid dynamics. These states might be arrayed in a spectrum that can lead us from fixed forms down to the most material and disgusting goo, and even to immaterial monsters so volatile that they vanish in a puff of smoke or never quite manifest in the first place. Many Gothic monsters horrify because of their refusal to keep to a single form. Dr Jekyll only alternates in a binary logic with Mr Hyde, but he predicts a future where man 'will be ultimately known for…multifarious, incongruous and independent denizens'. Further down that path, there is the well-attested ability of Count Dracula to transform into dog or wolf or bat, or to slink across thresholds as a wisp of miasmal fog. The vampire is a corpse that continues to move and flow, a contagion associated with pestilence, grave dust, wormy loam and plague rats.

The weird lifecycle of the creatures in *Alien* (1979) or *Species* (1995) means that we cannot fix them into any sure shape. Such monsters lick their lips, rub their feelers together and slime their victims with their foul and sticky ichor, as in the quivering mass of *The Blob* (1958), the half-human-half-fly in David Cronenberg's *The Fly* (1986), or the Slimer in *Ghostbusters* (1984). Slimer is formed of foul-smelling 'ectoplasm', a term coined in 1894 by the psychical researcher Charles Richet for the gooey interstitial stuff that mediums are said to extrude from their bodies in seances: neither spirit nor matter, but some horrible in-between. Many Japanese monsters are also fluid and formless, yet grossly physiological. They leave behind stains and stenches that are hard to remove, like the stink spirit in Hayao Miyazaki's Studio Ghibli animation *Spirited Away* (2003).

In Bataille's sense, all of these creatures are base and profane, and our visceral, immediate revulsion has long been exploited by the Gothic. There is something truly horrific, for instance, in the realization in Arthur Machen's 'The Novel of the Black Seal' (1895) that a local boy, an evolutionary throwback, can throw out soft pseudopods, like feelers, that leave behind the stench of snakes and patches 'all sticky and slimy, as if a snail had crawled over it'. It leads the tale's Professor Gregg to the awful secret that 'man can be reduced to the slime from which he came'. The giant snails discovered on a remote island by Professor Clavering in Patricia Highsmith's brutal horror story 'The Quest for Blank Claveringi' (1967) turn out to be man-eating in a rather memorable way.

4

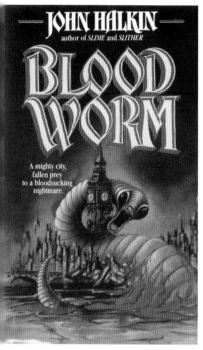

JOHN HALKIN
author of *SLIME* and *SLITHER*

BLOOD WORM

A mighty city,
fallen prey
to a bloodsucking
nightmare.

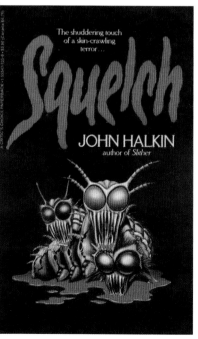

The shuddering touch
of a skin-crawling
terror . . .

Squelch

JOHN HALKIN
author of *Slither*

John Halkin
author of *SLITHER*

SLIME

Turn on the tap...and die of terror!

Edward Jarvis
author of *PESTILENCE*

The
squirming
menace...
MAGGOTS

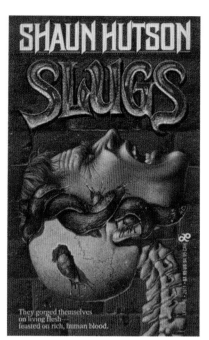

SHAUN HUTSON
SLUGS

They gorged themselves
on living flesh—
feasted on rich, human blood.

John Halkin

SLITHER

You'll never feel safe in your bath again . . .

5

4. Early drawing by H. R. Giger for the
protean monster in *Species* (Roger
Donaldson, 1995).
5. Pulp covers from the puzzling 1980s
boom in slimy horror novels.

These low-down creatures prompted a whole cluster of pulp horrors in the 1970s and 1980s, riding on the 'revenge of nature' killer-animal trend that dimly registered the new ecological consciousness. Shaun Hutson's *Slugs* (1982) is perhaps the most fondly remembered of these pulp phantasmagorias, as it formed the basis of a cult film of the same name (1986). It came alongside Edward Jarvis's *Maggots* (1986) and John Halkin's admirably consistent body of works: *Slither* (1980), *Slime* (1984), *Squelch* (1985, about killer caterpillars) and *Blood Worm* (1987). In film, we are in the body horror realms of David Cronenberg's mid-1970s shockers *Shivers* (1975) and *Rabid* (1977).

There are monsters that are so formless that they can get inside us, slither through our vulnerable orifices, explode from the body's hollow chambers or distend the skin so much that it deforms the very

6. The continual transformations of the monstrous alien in *The Thing* (John Carpenter, 1981).

morphology of the human. In the body horrors of *The Thing* (1981), *Society* (1989) or *The Color Out of Space* (2019), the human form is finally rendered so plastic that it melds or merges with others to form unspeakable gelatinous masses.

Is it both; or is it neither? Some decide in favour of the last supposition and establish an intermediate kingdom, a sort of biological No Man's Land for all these questionable forms.

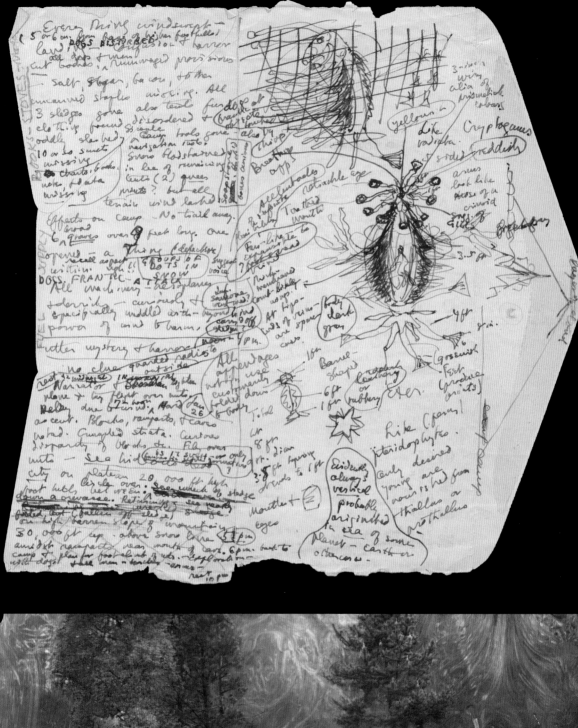

Fungi

The biological world of fungi is highly ordered, marked by open-ended cooperative assemblages, ecologies whose complexities scientists are still trying to grasp. Yet fungus disgusts not just because of its association with decay, but also because of its sheer boundlessness. When Darwin's advocate Thomas Huxley argued controversially that all living forms shared the same biological basis, he constantly bolstered his argument by turning to fungus. The *Aethalium septicum* 'appears upon decaying vegetable substances' and is surely a plant; but in other states, Huxley notes, it seems to be 'an actively locomotive creature' that absorbs other matter to feed. 'Is this plant; or is it an animal?', he asks. 'Is it both; or is it neither? Some decide in favour of the last supposition and establish an intermediate kingdom, a sort of biological No Man's Land for all these questionable forms.' Just as the taxonomy of all living things introduced by Linnaeus had seemed to establish a strict logic that abolished any chance of monstrosity, fungi travelled insidiously across these most foundational divides. Huxley's argument caused a profound shock when published in early 1869. It also introduced another level of biological horror to the imagination – that deformation might progress much further than the simian Mr Hyde, and end up back at the primordial, undifferentiated jelly of life itself.

In William Hope Hodgson's 'The Voice in the Night' (1907), a ship-wrecked man and his wife will not reveal themselves to the sailors who come across them in the dark of night. The man tells of surviving a wreck only by living on an island where a 'vile fungus...was growing riot. In places it rose into horrible, fantastic mounds, which seemed almost to quiver, as with a quiet life.' The spores begin to absorb the couple into their disgusting biome. 'Our drear punishment was upon us', the man explains, 'for, day by day, with monstrous rapidity, the fungoid growth took hold of our poor bodies.' The listeners realize with horror that the tale has been told by a fungal-human hybrid, an abhuman monster, shortly to be entirely absorbed into a fungal ecology.

H. P. Lovecraft similarly evokes the primordial jelly of protoplasm in *At the Mountains of Madness* (1936). The landscape of the far south reveals all manner of 'fossil cephalopods, corals, echini and spirifera... Mesozoic tree ferns and fungi', merely the precursor to

Disturbance-based ecologies in which many species sometimes live together without either harmony or comfort.

7. [opposite above] H. P. Lovecraft, plot notes for *At the Mountains of Madness* (1931).
8. [opposite below] *Annihilation* (Alex Garland, 2018).
9. James Sowerby, 'Fuligo Septica' in *Coloured Figures of English Fungi* (1803).

the discovery of the traces of a long-lost alien race that share some of the radial logic of the octopus and other creatures of the deep. Powerful biological engineers, the aliens had manipulated 'multicellular protoplasmic masses' and shaped from them a race of slaves: the Shoggoths. This revolting jelly is the spark for aeons of evolution on planet Earth that one day results in the human form; typically, this origin story is too much for Lovecraft's men of science to bear. Lovecraft was closely associated with the journal *Weird Tales*, a magazine that began its first issue in 1923 with a short story by Anthony Rud called 'Ooze'. Set in the sucking swamps of Alabama, it recounts the return of a scientist's horrific experiment as 'a slimy, amorphous something' that swallows him whole.

In more recent times, the science fiction imagination has fused with the Gothic to explore the 'Grey Goo' hypothesis, in which nano-technology bots run out of control and basically convert all structured matter into an undifferentiated mass of goo. First used by the futurologist Eric Drexler, it is best imagined in Greg Bear's oddly sublime tale *Blood Music* (1985), in which a research scientist saves his nano-bots from destruction by injecting them into his bloodstream, only to be entirely transformed from within, eventually taking the whole planet with him.

This sequence of male writers, like Sartre, mostly face the dissolution of decisive human boundaries with horror. But to think fungally, as the anthropologist Anna Lowenhaupt Tsing has written, is to have to embrace 'disturbance-based ecologies in which many species sometimes live together without either harmony or comfort'. In Aliya Whiteley's potent novella 'The Beauty' (2014), the women of the world have died; from their graves, woman-shaped mushroom-beings begin to rise. Lowenhaupt Tsing's pursuit of the highly valued Matsutake mushroom across the world, meanwhile, requires a form of 'multi-species storytelling' that is anti-Gothic in its embrace of impurity and mess. There is a sense in some writers of the New Weird that human survival depends on transforming our horror of impurity into an ecstatic embrace of post-human transformation, as in Jeff VanderMeer's books *Borne* (2017) and *Dead Astronauts* (2020), or the film of his 2014 novel *Annihilation* (2018).

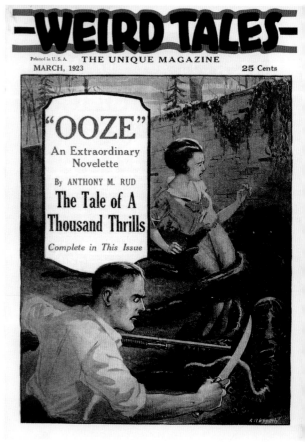

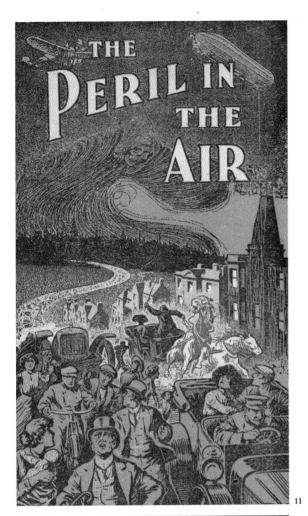

Atmospherics

Fog renders everything formless, softens outlines and abolishes all perspective. We get lost, turned around inside it. It hides the true state of things; in mystical Christian thought, the seeker is lost in the 'cloud of unknowing' and risks losing sight of the true path to God. As veils, clouds, fogs and mists distance and disorient us, they also inveigle themselves inside us, merging everything together under their soft, shapeless mantle. In *London Fog* (2015), Christine Corton suggests that 'fog's formlessness lent itself to a wide variety of representations and metaphorical usages', and it has certainly been an integral part of the wild atmospherics of the Gothic since the eighteenth century. Clouds roll in on Ann Radcliffe's sublime mountains; apparitions swim out of the mist; monsters lurk in the smog.

Step one: the fog acts to *hide* the monster from full view, prevents a full grasp of the thing and skews any sense of scale. 'There's something in the fog!' the local radio DJ shouts into the microphone in John Carpenter's *The Fog* (1980). This is a common device. Count Dracula seems to command the weather to isolate the doomed ship, the *Demeter*, in 'another rush of sea-fog, greater than any hitherto – a mass of dank mist, which seemed to close on all things like a grey pall'. The billowing fog that surrounds the summoned devil in *Night of the Demon* (1958) seems to aid its conjuration; the unnatural cloud atop the Swiss mountains in *The Trollenberg Terror* (1958) hides the crawling, tentacular aliens. A dense fog also veils the transdimensional monsters in Stephen King's *The Mist* (1980). In Frank Darabont's slow-burn film adaptation, the creatures hidden in the blank mist first begin to manifest with the appearance of a single tentacle that slides under a loading-bay door. 'Tentacles?' a disbelieving rationalist barks at the witnesses with utter contempt. Perhaps because some species of octopus can create their own clouds of confusion with defensive jets of ink, cephalopods and fogs often come together in the Gothic imagination. Doesn't fog always creep forward in a sinister, tentacular way, probing its path as though sentient?

Step two: it is not that something hides in the fog, but the fog itself. Fog billows into the prose of Charles Dickens's most Gothic novel, *Bleak House* (1853), 'where it rolls defiled among the tiers of shipping, the waterside pollutions of a great (and dirty) city'. Dickens was writing at a new stage of London's perennial problem with winter fogs, which had combined with the black soot

10. The first issue of *Weird Tales*, March 1923, announcing its intentions by leading with 'Ooze'.
11. Advert for Peps Company cough tablets, 1913.
12. *Night of the Demon* (Jacques Tourneur, 1958).
13. [following spread] *Godzilla vs. Hedorah* [the smog monster] (Yoshimitsu Banno, 1971).

of coal-fired industry and the cheap, smoky sea-coal that was used to heat homes to create a lethal combination later called 'smog'. The doubling of London's population to two million by 1830 pushed the city into regular winters of dense, cloying fogs, dark yellow because of the high sulphur content and called 'pea-soupers' after the dried yellow split-peas cooked in poor households. They became almost annual presences, squatting over the city and suffocating the population. In 1840, the poet Peter Styles wrote:

London fogs are all made up
Of strange and monstrous things,
Which nature, scorning to receive,
Back on the city flings.

Smog has become inseparable from the iconography of the late Victorian Gothic, whether in the fogs that conceal the crimes of Mr Hyde, or the dense cloud of unknowing through which Sherlock Holmes tries to shine his beacon of truth. There was also a cluster of books that featured menacing, destructive fogs or clouds. M. P. Shiel's remarkable *The Purple Cloud* (1901) killed off all but one last man; Arthur Conan Doyle's *The Poison Belt* (1913), about the Earth passing through a toxic cloud of ether, came out a year after the first use of tear gas on demonstrators, but just before the first use of chlorine gas at the Battle of Ypres in 1915. The cloying, choking fogs of chlorine, mustard gas and phosgene killed and debilitated thousands.

After the Second World War, invisible, radioactive clouds – slow, insidious, boundless and universally deadly – became another source of fear. There is a powerful sense of pathos to Jack Arnold's film *The Incredible Shrinking Man* (1957), where the protagonist encounters a strange, radioactive fog while boating, which in turn kickstarts his downward path of horrifying diminution and eventual vanishing. We are now painfully aware that with rapid development comes real-life climate horror: in the twenty-first century, old-school smogs have engulfed cities in India and China. In the 1970s, Yoshimitsu Banno monstered the smogs that afflicted industrial Japan as the sludgy Hedorah, battled by a newly environmentally conscious Godzilla.

We have reached a point where the formless has become so attenuated, so dispersed, that some narratives barely give the monster any form at all. Here we might conjure the wisps of any number of shy and retiring ghosts that leave only the most oblique marks on the material world, the wind that surges through Algernon Blackwood's 'The Willows' or the dust that may be animated by something malign in Robert Aickman's 'The Unsettled Dust' (1968).

There have been bold experiments, too, in horror films that resist monstrous spectacle and instead create malignant forces that take no shape, but tilt the material world against their victims. In *It Follows* (2013), whatever 'it' is pursues its victims by hopping from one possessed bodily form to another, constantly changing shape but always intent on chasing down the chain of sexual transmission. In the *Final Destination* films, Death never manifests in physical form, but announces its presence with just a brief gust of wind before setting out to manipulate the technological matrix of everyday modern life against us. Death can come from anywhere – from the microwave, the knife rack, the garbage grinder, the sink, the toaster, the electrical short circuit. Complex technological environments turn into catastrophic spaces, whether on highways or rollercoaster rides, in gymnasia or airport lounges. As the camera wheels in anxious 360-degree scans in *It Follows*, turning everyone populating the field of vision into a potential threat, so the *Final Destination* franchise resists the physical embodiment of the monster and makes the whole infrastructure of modernity the threat. It is 'risk society' itself that becomes the monster, and that paranoid feeling of persecution by malignant forces, so typical of the Gothic, reaches its peak exactly as the monster vanishes completely from the screen. Godzilla, stomp your heart out: a tanning bed or an airbag is good enough to complete Death's design.

14. [opposite] 'Something came out of the fog and tried to destroy us!': *The Fog* (John Carpenter, 1980).

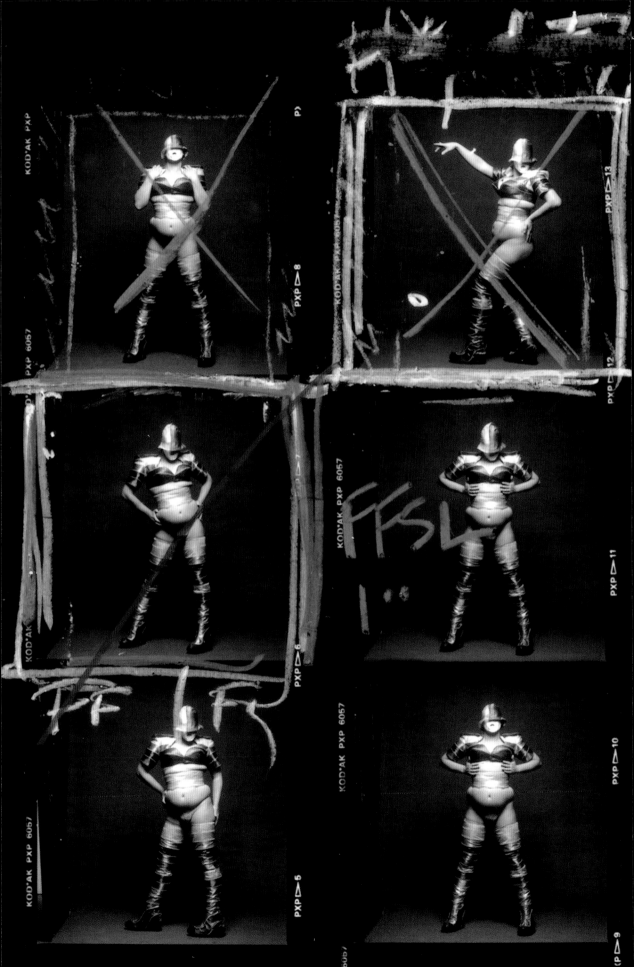

Us

In Jordan Peele's horror film *Us* (2019), the Wilson family home is invaded at night by a group of four intruders: their unnerving doubles. The duplicate suburban ideal of mum, dad and two kids stare back across the living room, only each one is altered and malignant. Adelaide's double, 'Red', comes bearing an outsize pair of scissors: she announces that they have come to cut themselves free from the lives that they have been doomed to shadow as 'The Tethered' and take the family's place. This murderous eruption into the home presages a nationwide rebellion of this underground underclass. An allegory of the structural underpinning of affluent America by invisible yet identical others looms into view, but the most disturbing sections of the film are these opening, uncanny moments of domestic confrontation. This relies on a long Gothic tradition of uncanny doubles or doll-like substitutes. Rather than the spectacular difference of a slimy tentacular other, *Us* belongs to a quieter but no less Gothic recognition, this time delivered in Red's hoarse, strangulated whisper: the worst monsters are very likely to lie within us.

A shadow has fallen across the repetition of 'home sweet home', making it subtly non-identical with itself. It is from this apparent safety, or in the mirror image that is supposed to reflect myself back to me, that disquiet begins to bubble up. We are entering the uncanny valley.

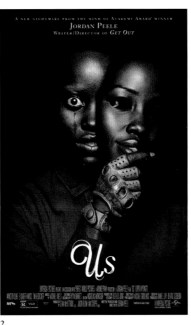

2

In my death, see by this image, which is thine own, how utterly thou hast murdered thyself.

1. [opposite] Fergus Greer, *Leigh Bowery Session III, Look 15*, 1990.
2. *Us* (Jordan Peele, 2019).

That class of the frightening which leads back to what is known of old and long familiar.

3

Sigmund Freud defined the *unheimlich* (the unhomely or uncanny) as 'that class of the frightening which leads back to what is known of old and long familiar'. From the beginning, the Gothic romance has invested in figures of the double: dark, usurping others in plots replete with structural echoes. The German term *doppelgänger* ('double-walker') was first coined in the 1796 Gothic novel *Siebenkäs* by Jean Paul (Johann Paul Richter), and defined as 'the name for people who see themselves'.

The doubling of the physical self with forms of soul or spirit is central to many early religious and cultural belief systems. Dualistic in Christian thought, there are more complex forms of doubling in other beliefs, ranging from the division of the Egyptian soul into multiple elements, including the *ka*, the life-force, the shadow, and the *ba*, the personal soul, to the distinct elements of the self in Norse belief, which include the *hugr*, the mind, and the *fylgja*, the follower or attendant spirit, often in animal form, whose fate is inextricably tied to its human owner. The Gothic romance appeared in eighteenth-century England alongside the resurgence of Celtic folklore, and its rich array of doubles strongly influenced early attempts to evoke the supernatural.

The strongest superstition of this kind was undoubtedly that of the *fetch*, associated with peasant culture in Ireland and Scotland. To encounter a fetch, a double of a close relative or, more unnervingly, oneself, could be taken as a signal of luck, but much more often as a portent of death. In Ireland, the brothers John and Michael Banim published a tale called *The Fetches* in 1825, but rather typically prefaced it with a 'real life' account of a fetch, deliberately confusing the boundaries of fact and fiction. 'In Ireland', the preface explains, 'a fetch is a supernatural fac-simile of some individual, which comes to insure to its original a happy longevity, or immediate dissolution; if seen in the morning, the one event is predicted; if in the evening, the other.'

In Catherine Crowe's influential collection of ghost sightings and testimonies, *The Night Side of Nature* (1848), there is a whole chapter devoted to 'Doppelgangers or Doubles'. She accumulates testimonies from contemporaries and the archive, including John Donne's famous account of his vision, while in Paris, of his wife carrying a dead child at the exact time she suffered a stillbirth back in London. Crowe makes a clear distinction between the idea of the lingering spirit of the dead

3. Catherine Crowe, *The Night Side of Nature* (1848), an influential collection of 'true' ghost stories and supernatural events.
4. [opposite] 'The features seemed to melt and alter': One of S. G. Hulme Beaman's illustrations for the 1930 edition of *The Strange Case of Dr Jekyll and Mr Hyde*.

Fac Simile. See P. 366.

September 8.— My first night of trial in this place is overpast! Would that it were the last that I should ever-gee in this vile world! Of the horrors of hell are equal to those I have suffered, eternity will be of short duration there, for no creature can support them for one single Month, or week. I have been buffeted as never living creature was. My vitals have all been torn and every facility and feeling of my soul racked, and tormented into callous insensibility. I was even hung by the locks over a yawning chasm to which I could perceive no bottom, and then — not till then, did I repeat the tremendous prayer! — Jesus instantly at liberty; and what I now am, the Almighty knows! Amen.

THE PRIVATE MEMOIRS

AND CONFESSIONS

OF A JUSTIFIED SINNER:

WRITTEN BY HIMSELF:

by James Hogg

WITH A DETAIL OF CURIOUS TRADITIONARY FACTS, AND
OTHER EVIDENCE, BY THE EDITOR.

LONDON:

PRINTED FOR LONGMAN, HURST, REES, ORME, BROWN,
AND GREEN, PATERNOSTER ROW.

MDCCCXXIV.

and the apparition of the double, which she speculates may be an ability of the *living* spirit to detach from the constraints of the physical body and travel across the ether to communicate to loved ones, particularly at moments of extremity. Crowe refers to the 'well known' instance when Lord Byron was seen by friends in London while suffering a life-threatening fever in Patras, or Goethe's account, in Book XI of his autobiography *Poetry and Truth*, of how, cantering along at speed on his horse at night, he came face to face with himself riding in the opposite direction. The sting in the tail of this story is that this is the very path Goethe was to take eight years later, and in the very outfit he had seen eight years before.

This idea of the double as a projection of mental energy was also central to the early work of the Society for Psychical Research in the 1880s, who sidestepped the question of supernatural belief by arguing that the apparition of doubles of oneself or others sent to loved ones were best thought of as 'phantasms of the living', not of the dead. They collected thousands of examples from their correspondents and even issued a 'Census on Hallucinations' to gather statistical evidence. Superstitions about fetches and their like were both Gothicized and psychologized in the course of the nineteenth century, the golden age of the double.

German Romantics, in particular, returned again and again to this psychologized double; alongside Jean Paul's *doppelgänger*, Heinrich von Kleist's play *Penthesilea* (1808), in which the central character's sexual frenzy splits her identity, was also influential. Adelbert von Chamisso's *Peter Schlemihl* (1814) used the form of a folktale for the story of Peter's Faustian bargain to sell his shadow to the devil; two years later, E. T. A. Hoffmann's 'A New Year's Adventure' (sometimes known as 'The Lost Reflection', 1816) briefly introduces the bereft character of Peter Schlemihl before focusing on Erasmus Spikher, a man who trades his reflection in pursuit of his mad lust for the ravishing Giuletta. Spikher is condemned to wander the earth outside human society, briefly trying to pair up with Schlemihl 'so that Erasmus Spikher could provide the necessary shadow and Peter Schlemihl could reflect properly in a mirror'. When Spikher is told that Giuletta, another demonic lure, will 'eternally own your dream-ego', Hoffmann reveals the direct influence of G. H. Schubert, whose lectures and book *The Symbolism of Dreams* (1814) explored

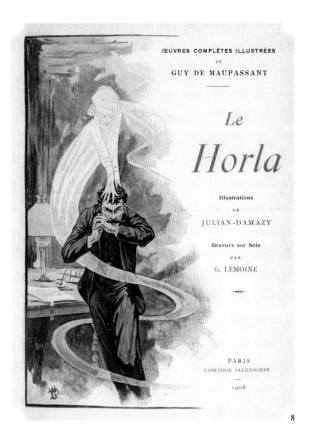

ŒUVRES COMPLÈTES ILLUSTRÉES
DE
GUY DE MAUPASSANT

Le
Horla

Illustrations
DE
JULIAN-DAMAZY

Gravure sur bois
PAR
G. LEMOINE

PARIS
LIBRAIRIE OLLENDORFF
1908

8

What was abolished internally returns from without.

5. Title page and frontispiece of the first edition of James Hogg, *The Private Memoirs and Confessions of a Justified Sinner* (1824), a major influence on Robert Louis Stevenson.
6. One of many adaptations of Oscar Wilde's *The Picture of Dorian Gray* (Massimo Dallamano, 1970).
7. The German Expressionist *Student of Prague* (Henrik Galeen, 1926), in which a reflection escapes the mirror and wreaks havoc.
8. Guy de Maupassant's psychological horror 'Le Horla', about an oppressive invisible tormentor, illustrated by Julian-Damazy in 1908.

the extraordinary capacities of mind allegedly revealed by early Mesmeric experiments in inducing trance states. Claims of Franz Mesmer's early hypnotic treatments swept Europe at this time. New, even supernatural abilities of clairvoyance and mind-reading were reported, with Schubert and others exploring the idea that the somnambulistic self was able to split from the body. Hoffmann began to pour out stories devoted to strange doubles: his most famous, 'The Sandman' (1816), became the basis for Freud's theorization of the *unheimlich*. His tale 'The Lost Reflection' had a clear influence on Edgar Allan Poe's 'William Wilson' (1839) and Hans Christian Andersen's folktale 'The Shadow' (1847), and was one of the source texts for the German Expressionist film *The Student of Prague* (itself a double, with versions made in 1913 and 1926), the first version of which was scripted by Hanns Heinz Ewers, a writer, editor and translator of Gothic tales in his own right.

Something clarifies in these repetitions: 'William Wilson' tells the story of the appearance of a double who is initially admired, even loved, by the protagonist, but who slyly begins to undermine him, love curdling into persecution. In the last scene, Wilson denounces his double at a masquerade, plunging his sword 'repeatedly through and through his bosom', before realizing too late that he is confronting only his own mirror image. The last words of the double are:

> You have conquered, and I yield. Yet, henceforward art thou also dead – dead to the world, to Heaven and to Hope! In me didst thou exist – and in my death, see by this image, which is thine own, how utterly thou hast murdered thyself.

This trajectory of love for the double becoming deathly persecution is familiar from several key works of the nineteenth-century Gothic, among them James Hogg's *The Private Memoirs and Confessions of a Justified Sinner* (1824), Fyodor Dostoevsky's *The Double* (1846), Stevenson's *The Strange Case of Dr Jekyll and Mr Hyde* (1885) and Guy de Maupassant's brilliant evocation of lunatic delusion, 'Le Horla' (1887).

The insistent repetition of this story prompted the psychoanalyst Otto Rank to publish *Das Doppelgänger* in 1914, after seeing *The Student of Prague*. Rank starts by toying with the possibility that the splitting of the ego is a form of narcissism that protects the ego from the fear of death by splitting itself in two. But the structure of this Gothic tale pushes Rank to see

the double in a darker way: as a product of paranoia. Freud also explored paranoia, proposing that it works by projecting a forbidden internal wish outward, creating a double that embodies the secret and becomes a relentless persecutor: 'What was abolished internally returns from without.'

The Gothic romance has, the critic Eve Kosofsky Sedgwick has pointed out, always been full of stories of men pursued by other men. Is this hidden desire, which then turns into its opposite: a persecution unto death? Sedgwick called this driver of the Gothic plot 'homosexual panic'. This perhaps maps too closely back from Oscar Wilde's version of the double plot in *The Picture of Dorian Gray* (1890), but it also takes in all those missing reflections and shadows in German Romanticism. Wilde's story veered close to being explicit about the criminalized 'love that dare not speak its name' that brought Wilde to ruin when he was put on trial in 1895. It, too, ends with Dorian plunging a knife into his closeted double, the portrait hidden

9

9. *Five-Way Portrait of Marcel Duchamp*, 1917, a confounding multiple self-portrait of the Dadaist and conceptual artist.
10. Claude Cahun, *Self-Portrait*, 1928. Cahun, a photographer and Surrealist, continually played with elusive ideas of self and other.

in his rooms, which kills the secondary self but takes the now weaker primary self along with it. A more subtle allegory of 'homosexual panic' has been read into a number of Henry James stories, most disturbingly in his late tale 'The Jolly Corner', where the decidedly perverse Spencer Brydon chases his own ghost through the rooms of an empty house, only to come face to face with a mutilated version of a different, monstrous self.

In the twentieth century, Freud became ubiquitous, and psychological doubles proliferated everywhere. The Surrealists in Paris were fascinated by strange doublings and splittings, as well as by gender and sexual identity, played out in the double exposures and reversed images of Man Ray, the mirrors and masks of Claude Cahun's self-portraits, the 'critical-paranoiac' splittings of Dalí, Hans Bellmer's uncanny dolls, or the 137 versions Marcel Duchamp made of his own silhouette. They continually sought to catch themselves out with their own untameable, unconscious selves.

Later in the century, there was something of a return to the exact physical double, prompted by advances in scientific understanding of reproduction. Once again, Gothic narratives could act out the anxieties attendant on these emergent sciences. The idea of total bodily replacement by a soulless physiological double climbed out of pulp horror in the mid-twentieth century. In the superlatively paranoid film *Invasion of the Body Snatchers* (1955), a psychiatrist at first believes he is treating the rampant psychotic delusion that individuals in Santa Mira are being replaced by their exact doubles. He has to confront the truth that the alien invasion is proceeding by creating 'pod people'. The film is pitched perfectly between the paranoia of the Cold War (the 'reds' really are under the bed) and the fear, often voiced by liberal commentators in 1950s America, that capitalism and suburbia were producing a nation of cookie-cutter drones. The shocking last lines, 'You're next! You're next!', shouted at the traffic by the desperate psychiatrist, left a lasting impression. The film was remade in 1978, in 1993 and again in 2007, suggesting a continuing anxiety about coercive forms of social similitude.

In a slightly different mode, Ira Levin's satirical novel *The Stepford Wives* (1972; filmed 1975) is laced with the Gothic. In the affluent village of Stepford, where wealthy New Yorkers arrive to escape the terrors of the city, the bland women drift through supermarkets in weirdly

10

They continually sought to catch themselves out with their own untameable, unconscious selves.

11

12

dissociated states, seemingly building on the malaise that Betty Friedan identified in many women in *The Feminine Mystique* (1963). The plot eventually reveals another conspiracy lurking behind the surface of American privilege: the women are being replaced by exact robotic doubles, made by a former Disneyland executive in charge of animatronics at the theme park. The threat of feminism, it seems, is being neutralized by the production of robot women passively compliant to their husband's every desire. *The Stepford Wives* relies on the uncanny effect of mechanical automata – another transposition of these devices, which caused sensation when they were first displayed across Europe in the eighteenth century, into the Gothic register.

Even later, the idea of the mechanical double is left behind by the emergence of the exact biological clone. Michael Crichton's 1973 film *Westworld* features mechanical robots in a staged environment for wealthy tourists, Yul Brynner playing the memorably malfunctioning 'Gunslinger'. By its remake as a television series in 2016, the 'hosts' in *Westworld* had become biologically manufactured 'wetware' creations, entirely the same as humans but constrained by their neural programming to suffer endless traumatic servitude under their masters. When they begin to develop autonomous consciousness, their rebellion is to realize their already fully human biological condition. In the splendidly wacky television series *Orphan Black* (2013–17), meanwhile, poor old Sarah Manning discovers a proliferating number of identical clones of herself (all played by Tatiana Maslany) operating across the globe, the product of an illegal human cloning project that is now trying to eliminate the remaining bodies of evidence. Although tonally pitched towards the black comedy of science fiction paranoia, more typical of Philip K. Dick's ramshackle stories of mechanical and biological doubles and psychotically split selves, *Orphan Black* continually exploits a sense of uncanny sameness.

But what if you looked in the mirror and no longer saw your faithful self, but some monstrous other? This primal scene of self-alienation has long been integral to the Gothic, with a long history of haunted or faithless mirrors that split self from self, from Dr Jekyll's full-length mirror to the malignant haunted mirrors of *Dead of Night* (1945) or Mike Flanagan's disturbing *Oculus* (2013). In more recent Gothic, the mirror's misrecognition of the self has been used to explore gender identity. Self becoming other

13

11. Robot Nanette Newman, *The Stepford Wives* (Bryan Forbes, 1975).
12. *Blade Runner* (Ridley Scott, 1982).
13. Into the uncanny valley with 'Aiko Chihira', the robot greeter built by Toshiba, at a department store in Nihonbashi, Japan, 2015.

(or, indeed, self) is discovered *over there*, in the mirror. In what Jolene Zigarovich names the Trans Gothic, bodies do not simply align with gender. It is horror for Buffalo Bill in Thomas Harris's *The Silence of the Lambs* (1988; filmed 1991), stitching a woman's body suit out of his female victims, its patchwork forever failing to fix his sliding identity. And it is horror for the rapist Vicente in Pedro Almodovar's highly stylized Gothic film *The Skin I Live In* (2011), who is transformed by a mad doctor into the perfect image of a woman, Vera, in an act of revenge. Vicente discovers her-/him-/them-self as Vera in a Gothic mansion, in a locked recovery room, in the mirror.

The Gothic has all too frequently monstered its trans characters, its multiply interstitial, fluid, inter-sexed, transitional beings; but, as we've seen before, its perverse dynamic can also flip these values, to make the monster a place of identification. In 'My Words to Victor Frankenstein Above the Village of Chamounix' (1994), Susan Stryker finds 'deep affinity' with Frankenstein's provisional yet self-affirming monster, ending her monologue with a call to her 'fellow creatures': 'Heed my words, and you may well discover the seams and sutures in yourself.' The tropes of the Gothic render the trans body of Jack Sheppard in Jordy Rosenberg's pastiche eighteenth-century romp *Confessions of the Fox* (2020) a place of pleasure in the self; the queer theorist Jack Halberstam continually circles back to the Gothic as a mode for rendering gender instability as riotously productive. The Gothic also has a long affiliation with drag, with iconic figures from The Boulet Brothers (creators of the *Search for the World's First Drag Supermonster*) to performance artist Leigh Bowery expanding and taking inspiration from its tropes.

You're next! You're next!

Since George A. Romero's *Night of the Living Dead* reimagined the zombie as a horde of shambling dead in 1968, perhaps the key figure of the horrific double has been the zombie. The monster is no longer necessarily a loquacious and seductive aristocratic vampire, of vast age and singular wisdom, but an anonymous, shuffling mass of everyday people like us. All that has happened is a slight shift in status, the undead caught in the no man's land between the absolute categories of the living and the dead. In *Dawn of the Dead* (1978), the small group of human survivors look down on the zombies drifting around the car park of a shopping mall. They spill aimlessly up and down the escalators inside the mall and pound on the glass doors of the chain stores, as if mildly impatient for the Black Friday stampede for bargains to begin.

Is there anything weirder in twenty-first-century Gothic culture than the emergence of the zombie parade? The first took place in Sacramento in California in 2001, but they have since been replicated around the world, united through the celebration of International Zombie Day (13 October). On these zombie walks, tens of thousands of fans around the world dress up as their undead selves, choosing to identify not with the small heroic band of human survivors in the standard zombie plot, but with the masses who have succumbed to the zombie plague. This identification flips two centuries of monstering the other, and instead embraces the other as a version of the self-same. It turns out that after all these twists and turns in the labyrinths of Gothic culture, what we most want to confront is the enigma of ourselves. We have travelled a long and winding road to come back to this most Gothic of objects. As Emily Dickinson wrote: 'Ourself behind ourself, concealed – / Should startle most –'.

14. [opposite] Hans Bellmer, *The Doll*, 1935. Bellmer obsessively photographed this *poupée*, rearranging its parts in different perverse scenarios.

15. [following spread] The engulfing mass of zombies in *Dawn of the Dead* (George Romero, 1978).

FURTHER READING

Aguirre, Miguel, *The Closed Space: Horror Literature and Western Symbolism* (1990)

Aldrich, Megan, *Gothic Revival* (1994)

Apel, Dora, *Beautiful Terrible Ruins: Detroit and the Anxiety of Decline* (2015)

Asma, Stephen, *On Monsters: An Unnatural History of Our Worst Fears* (2009)

Atwood, Margaret, *Strange Things: The Malevolent North in Canadian Literature* (2004)

Balmain, Colette, 'Pan-Asian Gothic', in *Globalgothic*, ed. G. Byron (2013), 119–32

—— *Introduction to Japanese Horror Film* (2008)

Barrell, John, *The Dark Side of the Landscape: The Rural Poor in English Painting 1730–1840* (1980)

Bataille, Georges, *Visions of Excess: Selected Writings 1927–39* (1985)

Blake, Linnie, *The Wounds of Nations: Horror Cinema, Historical Trauma and National Identity* (2008)

Brooks, Chris, *The Gothic Revival* (1999)

Bulfin, Ailise, *Gothic Invasions: Imperialism, War, and Fin-de-Siècle Popular Fictions* (2018)

Burnham, Michelle, 'Is there an Indigenous Gothic?', in *A Companion to the American Gothic*, ed. C. Crow (2014), 223–37

Camaroff, Joshua, and Ong Ker-Shing, *Horror in Architecture* (2013)

Campbell, Neil, *Post-Westerns* (2013)

Carter, Michael, et al., *Writing Britain's Ruins* (2017)

Clute, John, *The Darkening Garden: A Short Lexicon of Horror* (2006)

Cohen, Jeffrey Jerome, *Of Giants: Sex, Monsters, and the Middle Ages* (1999)

—— (ed.), *Monster Theory: Reading Culture* (1996)

Creed, Barbara, *The Monstrous-Feminine: Film Feminism Psychoanalysis* (1993)

Curtis, Barry, *Dark Places: The Haunted House in Film* (2008)

Davidson, Peter, *The Idea of the North* (2005)

Derounian-Stodola, Kathryn Zabelle (ed.), *Women's Indian Captivity Narratives* (1998)

Dillon, Brian (ed.), *Ruins: Documents of Contemporary Art* (2011)

Eastburn, Melanie (ed.), *Japan Supernatural: Ghosts, Goblins and Monsters 1700s to Now* (2019)

Eastlake, Charles, *A History of the Gothic Revival* (1872)

Erb, Cynthia, *Tracking King Kong: A Hollywood Icon in World Culture* (2009)

Flusser, Vilém, and Louis Bec, *Vampyroteuthis Infernalis: A Treatise*, trans. A. Pakis (2012)

Foster, Michael Dylan, and Jeffrey A. Tolbert (eds), *The Folkloresque: Reframing Folklore in a Popular Culture World* (2015)

Foucault, Michel, *The Order of Things: An Archaeology of the Human Sciences* (1970)

Franks, Benjamin, et al (eds), *The Quest for the Wicker Man: History, Folklore and Pagan Perspectives* (2006)

Godfrey-Smith, Peter, *Other Minds: The Octopus and the Evolution of Intelligent Life* (2017)

Groom, Nick, *The Vampire: A New History* (2018)

—— *The Gothic: A Very Short Introduction* (2012)

Halberstam, J. Jack, *Skin Shows: Gothic Horror and the Technology of Monsters* (1995)

Haraway, Donna, *Staying With the Trouble: Making Kin in the Chthulucene* (2016)

Harle, Matthew, and James Machin (eds), *Of Mud and Flame: The Penda's Fen Sourcebook* (2019)

Harries, Elizabeth Wanning, *The Unfinished Manner: Essays on the Fragment in the Later Eighteenth Century* (1994)

Hearn, Lafcadio, *Inventing New Orleans: The Writings of Lafcadio Hearn*, ed. S. F. Starr (2009)

Hell, Julia, and Andreas Schönle (eds), *Ruins of Modernity* (2010)

Higgins, Charlotte, *Red Thread: On Mazes and Labyrinths* (2018)

Hoskins, W. G., *The Making of the English Landscape* (1955)

Hutton, Ronald, *The Pagan Religions of the Ancient British Isles* (1991)

Lewis, Michael (ed.), *American Wilderness: A New History* (2007)

Lovecraft, H. P., *Supernatural Horror in Literature* (1973)

Luckhurst, Roger, *Zombies: A Cultural History* (2015)

—— *The Mummy's Curse: The True Story of a Dark Fantasy* (2012)

Macaulay, Rose, *The Pleasure of Ruins* (1953)

Mann, Sally, *Still Life: A Memoir with Photographs* (2016)

Mason, Freddie, *The Viscous: Slime Stickiness Fondling Mixtures* (2020)

Matless, David, *Landscape and Englishness* (1998)

McCorristine, Shane, *The Spectral Arctic: A History of Dreams and Ghosts in Polar Exploration* (2018)

McFarland, Thomas, *Romanticism and the Forms of Ruin: Wordsworth, Coleridge and Modalities of Fragmentation* (1981)

McVeigh, Stephen, *The American Western* (2007)

Mighall, Robert, *A Geography of Victorian Gothic Fiction* (1999)

Miller, William Ian, *The Anatomy of Disgust* (1997)

Mockett, Marie Mutsuki, *Where the Dead Pause, and the Japanese Say Goodbye* (2015)

Morton, Timothy, *Dark Ecology: For a Logic of Future Coexistence* (2016)

Mowl, Timothy, *William Beckford* (1998)

Murphy, Bernice, *The Rural Gothic in American Popular Culture: Backwoods Horror and Terror in the Wilderness* (2013)

Nash, Roderick, *Wilderness and the American Mind* (1967)

Newland, Paul (ed.), *British Rural Landscapes on Film* (2016)

di Palma, Vittoria, *Wasteland: A History* (2014)

Parnell, Edward, *Ghostland: In Search of a Haunted Country* (2019)

Peirse, Alison, and Daniel Martin (eds), *Korean Horror Cinema* (2013)

Pinkerton, Nick, 'Southern Gothic', *Sight & Sound*, May 2015

Quill, Sarah, *Ruskin's Venice: The Stones Revisited* (2015)

Reyes, Xavier Aldana, *Body Gothic: Corporeal Transgression in Contemporary Literature and Horror Film* (2014)

Said, Edward, *Orientalism* (1979)

Sax, Bora, *Imaginary Animals: The Monstrous, The Wondrous, and the Human* (2013)

Scovell, Adam, *Folk Horror: Hours Dreadful and Things Strange* (2017)

Sedgwick, Eve Kosofsky, 'Toward the Gothic: Terrorism and Homosexual Panic', in *Between Men: English Literature and Male Homosocial Desire* (1985), 83–96

Shoard, Marion, 'Edgelands', in *Remaking the Landscape: The Changing Face of Britain*, ed. Jennifer Jenkins (2002), 117–46

Smith, Andrew, and William Hughes (eds), *EcoGothic* (2013)

Snodin, Michael, *Horace Walpole's Strawberry Hill* (2009)

Street, Susan Castillo, and Charles L. Crow (eds), *The Palgrave Handbook of the Southern Gothic* (2016)

Sugg, Richard, *Fairies: A Dangerous History* (2018)

Tchen, John Kuo Wei, and Dylan Yeats, *Yellow Peril! An Archive of Anti-Asian Fear* (2014)

Thacker, Eugene, *In the Dust of This Planet* (2011)

Tromans, Nicholas, *The Lure of the East: British Orientalist Painting* (2008)

Tsing, Anna Lowenhaupt, *The Mushroom at the End of the World: On the Possibility of Life in Capitalist Ruins* (2015)

Tsing, Anna, et al (eds), *Arts of Living on a Damaged Planet: Ghosts and Monsters of the Anthropocene* (2017)

William Tsutsui, *Godzilla on My Mind: Fifty Years of the King of Monsters* (2004)

Chet Van Duzer, *Sea Monsters on Medieval and Renaissance Maps* (2013)

Joseph-Vilain, M., et al (eds), *Postcolonial Ghosts* (2009)

Anthony Vidler, *The Architectural Uncanny* (1992)

Mark Wallinger, *Labyrinth: A Journey through London Underground* (2014)

Raymond Williams, *The Country and the City* (1973)

Sam Wiseman, *Locating the Gothic in British Modernity* (2019)

Ben Woodard, *Slime Dynamics: Generation, Mutation, and the Creep of Life* (2012)

Worpole, Ken, with Jason Orton, *The New English Landscape* (2013)

Young, Robert, 'The Pattern Under the Plough', *Sight & Sound*, August 2010

Zigarovich, Jolene (ed.), *TransGothic in Literature and Culture* (2017)

PICTURE LIST

a=above, c=centre, b=below, l=left, r=right

1 Photo Harry Ransom Centre, University of Texas. © Man Ray 2015 Trust/DACS, London 2021
4–5 *Arrival*, 2016, Director Dennis Villeneuve, FilmNation Entertainment/ Lava Bear Films/21 Laps Entertainment. AF Archive/Alamy Stock Photo
6 The Rosenbach of the Free Library of Philadelphia
8 Wellcome Collection, London
10–1 James Brittain-VIEW/Alamy Stock Photo
12 Mauritius images GmbH/Alamy Stock Photo
13 Getty Research Institute, Los Angeles
14 Photo English Heritage/Heritage Images/Getty Images
15a,c,b, 16 J. Paul Getty Museum, Los Angeles. Digital image courtesy of the Getty's Open Content Program
17a F1online digitale Bildagentur GmbH/ Alamy Stock Photo
17b *Dune*, 1984, Director David Lynch, Dino De Laurentiis Corporation. Universal/ Kobal/Shutterstock
18a Getty Research Institute, Los Angeles
18b Metropolitan Museum of Art, New York. Purchase, Friends of European Sculpture and Decorative Arts Gifts, 2015
20a akg-images/VIEW Pictures/Hufton and Crow
20b Photo Morgan Library & Museum/Art Resource, New York/Scala, Florence
21 Keith Corrigan/Alamy Stock Photo
23 Robert Proctor/Alamy Stock Photo
24 Zack Frank/Shutterstock
25 Photo John Bethell/Bridgeman Images
26a Tate, London
26b Private Collection
27a © Yves Marchand & Romain Meffre
27b Harvard Art Museums/Fogg Museum, Gift of Mrs. Henry Osborn Taylor in memory of her father William Bradley Isham
28a © Andrew Moore
28b Detroit Institute of Art. Founders Society Purchase, William H. Murphy Fund
29 Chicken/Alamy Stock Photo
30a Getty Research Institute, Los Angeles
30b Photo Bernard Hoffman/The LIFE Picture Collection via Getty Images
31a Photo Harrison/Fox Photos/Hulton Archive/Getty Images
31b, 32a © Rebecca Barthoy
32b Wellcome Collection, London
33a Eastern State Penitentiary Library, Philadelphia
33b Sarah Thornton/Alamy Stock Photo
35a © Yves Marchand & Romain Meffre
35b *It Follows*, 2014, Director David Robert Mitchell. Northern Lights/Animal Kingdom/Two Flints/Kobal/ Shutterstock
36 Tate, London
38 Getty Research Institute, Los Angeles
39a Yale Centre for British Art, Paul Mellon Centre
39b Image courtesy Stephen Friedman Gallery, London and James Cohen Gallery, New York. © Yinka Shonibare CBE. All Rights Reserved, DACS/ Artimage 2021
40–1 Adam Eastland/Alamy Stock Photo
40 Amherst College Archives and Special Collections
41 National Gallery of Victoria, Melbourne. Felton Bequest, 1939
42a British Library, London
42l Metropolitan Museum of Art, New York. Fletcher Fund, 1924
42r Amherst College Archives and Special Collections
45 J. Paul Getty Museum, Los Angeles. Digital image courtesy of the Getty's Open Content Program
46 *The Shining*, 1980, Director Stanley Kubrick. Warner Bros/Hawk Films/ Kobal/Shutterstock
47 Museo Nazionale Romano Palazzo, Rome. Photo Giancarlo Costa/ Bridgeman Images
48a Courtesy of Cleveland Museum of Art
48b Courtesy the artist and Hauser & Wirth. © Mark Wallinger. All rights reserved, DACS 2021
49a Photo Thierry Bal
49b Digital image, Museum of Modern Art, New York/Scala Florence. © Man Ray 2015 Trust/DACS, London 2021
50a Courtesy the artist and 303 Gallery, New York; Galleria Franco Noera, Turin; Matt's Gallery, London; and neugerriemschneider, Berlin
50b Tallandier/Bridgeman Images
51 Sonia Halliday Photographs/ Bridgeman Images
52 Mary Evans/Diomedia Images
53a Jason Rohrer
53b, 54 Arcadeimages/Alamy Stock Photo
55 British Library Board. All Rights Reserved/Bridgeman Images
56 *The Amityville Horror*, 1979, Director Stuart Rosenberg, Cinema 77 Professional Films, Inc. American International Pictures/Kobal/ Shutterstock
58, 59al, 59ar Courtesy of Lewis Walpole Library, Yale University
59b, 60, 61a, 61b Getty Research Institute, Los Angeles
62–3 *The Haunting*, 1963, Director Robert Wise. MGM/Kobal/Shutterstock
64 *Psycho*, 1960, Director Alfred Hitchcock, Shamley Productions. Paramount/Kobal/Shutterstock
65a Digital image, Museum of Modern Art, New York/Scala Florence. © Heirs of Josephine Hopper/Licensed by Artists Rights Society (ARS) New York/DACS, London 2021
65l Westmacott/Alamy Stock Photo
65r Metropolitan Museum of Art, New York. Harris Brisbane Dick Fund, 1924
66a *Paranormal Activity*, 2007, Director Oren Peli. Blumhouse Productions/ Kobal/Shutterstock
66b Society for Psychical Research/Mary Evans Picture Library
67 Arcadeimages/Alamy Stock Photo
68 *The Uninvited*, 2009, Directors Guard Brothers. DreamWorks Pictures/Kobal/ Shutterstock
69 From the Saul Bass papers, Margaret Herrick Library, Academy of Motion Picture Arts and Sciences. © Saul Bass Estate
70–1 © Clarence John Laughlin Archive at the Historic New Orleans Collection, 1981.247.1.974
72 British Library, London
74 Wellcome Collection, London
75a *Street of Crocodiles*, 1986, Directors Quay Brothers. Mary Evans/Ronald Grant/Diomedia Images
75b *The Swarm*, 1978, Director Irwin Allen. Warner Bros/Kobal/Shutterstock
76–7 From the Production artwork collection, Margaret Herrick Library, Academy of Motion Picture Arts and Science.
78 *Squirm*, 1976, Director Jeff Lieberman. The Squirm Company/Kobal/ Shutterstock
80–1a *The Relic*, 1997, Director Peter Hyams. Richard Jr Foreman/Paramount/ Cloud Nine/Polygram/Kobal/ Shutterstock
80–1b *The Host*, 2006, Director Bong Joon-Ho. Sego Entertainment/ CHEONGEORAM/Album/Alamy Stock Photo
82-3 *Phase IV*, 1974, Director Saul Bass. Alced Productions/Paramount/Kobal/ Shutterstock
84–5 Photo Pitts Rivers Museum, University of Oxford, 1911.32.8
86a British Library Board. All Rights Reserved/Bridgeman Images
86b *The Blair Witch Project*, 1999, Directors Daniel Meyrick and Eduardo Sánchez, Artisan Entertainments. Artisan Pics/ Kobal/Shutterstock
87 Photo Pitts Rivers Museum, University of Oxford, 1917.53.600
89 *Rosemary's Baby*, 1968, Director Roman Polanski. Paramount/Kobal/ Shutterstock
90 *The Wicker Man*, 1973, Director Robin Hardy, British Lion Films. Studio Canal/Shutterstock
91, 92–3 *An American Werewolf in London*, 1981, Director John Landis, PolyGram Pictures, The Guber-Peters Company. Mary Evans/Diomedia Images
93 *A Girl Walks Home Alone at Night*, 2014, Director Ana Lily Amirpour. Say Ahh Prods/Spectrevision/Logan/Black Light District/Kino Lorber/Kobal/ Shutterstock
95a Royal Armouries Museum, London
95b *Witchfinder General*, 1968, Director Michael Reeves, Tigon British Film Productions, American International Pictures. Mary Evans/Ronald Grant/ Diomedia Images
96 British Library Board. All Rights Reserved/Bridgeman Images
97a *Kill List*, 2011, Director Ben Wheatley. Film4 Productions/UK Film Council/ Screen Yorkshire/Rook/Warp X/ Kobal/Shutterstock
97b *The Village*, 2004, Director M. Night Shyamalan. Touchstone/Blinding Edge/Kobal/Shutterstock
99a *Bait*, 2019, Director Mark Jenkin. Courtesy Early Day Films & BFI Distribution. Photo Thom Axon
99b *Penda's Fen*, 1974, Director Alan Clark, British Broadcasting Corporation. © BBC Photo Library
100 *The Addiction*, 1995, Director Abel Ferrara, October Films. Mary Evans/ Diomedia Images
100–1 *Zombi Child*, 2019, Director Bertrand Bonello, My New Pictures/Les Films du Bal. Film Movement/Kobal/ Shutterstock
102–3 *The Village of the Damned*, 1960, Director Wolf Rilla, MGM. Mary Evans/Diomedia Images
104 *Troll Hunter*, 2011, Director André Øvredal. Film Fund Fuzz/ Filmkameratene/Kobal/Shutterstock
106a *Pan's Garden* by Algernon Blackwood (Macmillan and Co., 1912)
106b *The Great God Pan* by Arthur Machen (John Lane, 1894)
107 Dmitry Naumov/Alamy Stock Photo
108a *Little Otik* or *Greedy Guts*, 2000, Director Jan Švankmayer. Athanor/ Kobal/Shutterstock
108b Private Collection
110–1 *The Witch*, 2015, Director Robert Eggers. Parts And Labor/Rt Features/ Rooks Nest/Upi/Kobal/Shutterstock
112–3 *The Evil Dead*, 1981, Director Sam Raimi, Renaissance Pictures. Mary Evans/Diomedia Images
115 Library of Congress, Washington, D.C.
116 J. Paul Getty Museum, Los Angeles. Digital image courtesy of the Getty's Open Content Program
117 *Wendy and Lucy*, 2009, Director Kelly Reichardt. Field Guide/Film Science/ Glass Eye/Kobal/Shutterstock
118 National Gallery of Victoria, Melbourne, Felton Bequest, 1940
119a © British Library Board. All Rights Reserved/Bridgeman Images
119b *Picnic at Hanging Rock*, 1975, Director Peter Weir. David Kynoch/Picnic Productions/B.E.F. Film Distributors/ South Australian Film Corporation/ Kobal/Shutterstock
120a Brooklyn Museum, New York
120b *Frankenstein*, 1932, Director James Whale. Universal/Kobal/Shutterstock
121 *The Hills Have Eyes*, 1977, Director Wes Craven. Blood Relations Company/ Kobal/Shutterstock
122 J. Paul Getty Museum, Los Angeles. Digital image courtesy of the Getty's Open Content Program
123a *The Wind*, 2019, Director Emma Tammi. Divide/Conquer/Soapbox Films/IFC/ Kobal/Shutterstock
123b J. Paul Getty Museum, Los Angeles. Digital image courtesy of the Getty's Open Content Program
124a *Mad Max*, 1979, Director George Miller. Kennedy Miller Productions/Kobal/ Shutterstock
124b *Two Thousand Maniacs*, 1964, Director Herschell Gordon Lewis. David F. Friedman-Lewis Production/Kobal/ Shutterstock
125 *Wake in Fright*, 1971, Director Ted Kotcheff. Group W Films/NLT/Kobal/ Shutterstock
127 *The Happiness of the Katakuris*, 2001, Director Takashi Miike, Shochiku. Everett Collection Inc/Alamy Stock Photo
128 Photo Hulton Archive/Getty Images
129 © Martin Parr/Magnum Photos
130 *Memories of Murder*, 2003, Director Bong Joon-Ho, CJ Entertainment/Sidus Pictures. Mary Evans/Ronald Grant/ Diomedia Images
131a The Artist and MARUANI MERCIER Gallery
131b *Neighbouring Sounds*, 2012, Director Kelber Mendonça Filho, CinemaScópio. TCD/Prod.DB/Alamy Stock Photo
132a *Halloween*, 1978, Director John Carpenter, Compass International Pictures, Falcon International Pictures. Mary Evans/ Ronald Grant/Diomedia Images
132b Photo Kim Gottlieb-Walker
133 *Twin Peaks*, 1990-1, Director David Lynch, Lynch/Frost Productions, Propaganda Films, Spelling Television. Mary Evans/Diomedia Images
134 *Get Out*, 2017, Director Jordan Peele, Blumhouse Productions, GQ Entertainment, Monkeypaw Productions. Moviestore/Shutterstock
135a *The Stepford Wives*, 1975, Director Bryan Forbes, Palomar Pictures. Columbia/Kobal/Shutterstock
135b Courtesy George A. Romero Archival Collection, 1962-2017, SC.2019.03, Archives & Special Collections, University of Pittsburgh Library System
136a *Buffy the Vampire Slayer*, 1997-2003, Director Joss Whedon, Mutant Enemy Productions, Sandollar Television, Kuzui Enterprises. Richard Cartwright/20th Century Fox TV/ Kobal/Shutterstock
136b *Donnie Darko*, 2001, Director Richard Kelly. Dale Robinette/Flower Films/ Gaylord/Adam Fields Prod/Kobal/ Shutterstock
137 *The Invasion of the Body Snatchers*, 1956, Director Don Siegel. Allied Artists Pictures/Kobal/Shutterstock
139 *Parasite*, 2019, Director Bong Joon-Ho, Barunson E&A. Curzon Artificial Eye/ Kobal/Shutterstock
140–1 Photo Trustees of the British Museum, London
142 Metropolitan Opera Archives, New York
143 Photo Arni Magnusson Institute, Reykjavik/Bridgeman Images
144a Museo Nazionale Romano Palazzo, Rome
144b Heritage Images Partnership Ltd/ Alamy Stock Photo
145 National Library, Madrid
147a Photo National Maritime Museum, Greenwich
147b *Midsommar*, 2019, Director Ari Aster, Square Peg, B-Reel Films. Moviestore/ Shutterstock
148a, 148b Library of Congress, Washington, D.C.
149a *Frankenstein*, 1994, Director Kenneth Branagh. David Appleby/Tri-Star/ American Zoetrope/The IndieProd Company/Japan Satellite/Kobal/ Shutterstock
148l, 148r Photo National Maritime Museum, Greenwich
151 Library of Congress, Washington, D.C.
152 Photo Herbert Ponting/Scott Polar Research Institute, University of Cambridge/Getty Images
153 National Postal Museum Collection, Smithsonian, Washington, D.C.
154 *The Thing*, 1981, Director John Carpenter, The Turman-Foster Company. Universal/Kobal/Shutterstock
155a *Alien vs. Predator*, 2004, Director Paul W.S. Anderson, Davis Entertainment Company, Brandywine, Impact Pictures, Stillking Films. Jurgen Vollmer/20th Century Fox/Kobal/ Shutterstock
155c Photo Historica Graphica Collection/ Heritage Images/Getty Images
155b Museums Victoria, Donation from Sally Douglas
156 Cornell University Library, New York
157 Propstore.Com/Shutterstock
158–9 © Clarence John Laughlin Archive at the Historic New Orleans Collection, 1981.247.1.888
160a, 160b Courtesy Gagosian. © Sally Mann
161 *Birth of a Nation*, 1915, Director D.W. Griffith, David W. Griffith Corporation. Epoch Producing Company/Kobal/ Shutterstock
162 George A. Romero Archival Collection, 1962-2017, SC.2019.03, Archives & Special Collections, University of Pittsburgh Library System
163a *Two Thousand Maniacs*, 1964, Director Herschell Gordon Lewis. David F. Friedman-Lewis Production/ Glasshouse Images/Shutterstock

163b *Deliverance*, 1972, Director John Boorman. Warner Bros/Kobal/Shutterstock
164–5 *Night of the Living Dead*, 1968, Director George Romero. Image Ten/Kobal/Shutterstock
166a *Atlanta*, 2018, RBA, 343 Incorporated, MGMT. Entertainment. FXP/Kobal/Shutterstock
166b *Southern Comfort*, 1981, Director Walter Hill. Cinema Group Ventures Phoenix (II). Studio Canal/Shutterstock
167a HarperCollins
167b Prisma Archivio/Alamy Stock Photo
169 Photo Rex Hardy Jr./The LIFE Picture Collection via Getty Images
170 *The Mask of Fu Manchu*, 1932, Director Charles Brabin, Cosmopolitan Productions. MGM/Kobal/Shutterstock
171 Museum of Fine Arts, Boston
172a British Library, London
172b The Rosenbach of the Free Library of Philadelphia
173 A Girl Walks Home Alone at Night, 2014, Ana Lily Amirpour. Say Ahh Prods/Spectrevision/Logan/Black Light District/Kino Lorber/Kobal/Shutterstock
174al *The Mummy*, 1932, Director Karl Freund, Universal Pictures. Photo LMPC via Getty Images
174ac *The Mummy*, 1959, Director Terence Fisher. Everett Collection Inc/Alamy Stock Photo
174ar *The Mummy*, 1959, Director Terence Fisher. Hammer Film Productions/Kobal/Shutterstock
174bl, 174bc *The Mummy*, 1932, Director Karl Freund. Universal/Kobal/Shutterstock
174br *The Mummy*, 1959, Director Terence Fisher. Hammer Film Productions. Everett Collection Inc/Alamy Stock Photo
175 *Under the Shadow*, 2016, Director Babak Anvari, Wigwam Films. Moviestore/Shutterstock
176, 177a British Museum, London
177b Photo SSPL/Getty Images
178a The Hand of Fu Manchu by Sax Rohmer (A. L. Burt Company, 1917, c. 1920s reprint, USA)
178b The Insidious Dr. Fu-Manchu by Sax Rohmer (A.L. Burt Company, 1913)
179a Yellow Shadows, by Sax Rohmer (Cassell, 1925, first printing, UK)
179b Daughter of Fu Manchu, by Sax Rohmer (Doubleday Doran, 1931, c. 1931 reprint, USA)
180a *The Ring*, 1998, Director Hideo Nakata, Ringu/Rasen Production Company. Omega/Kadokawa/Kobal/Shutterstock
180b *Kwaidan*, 1964, Director Masaki Kobayashi, Bengei Pro, Ninjin Club. Toho/Kobal/Shutterstock
181 National Gallery of Victoria, Melbourne. Purchased through The Art Foundation of Victoria with the assistance of Coles Myer Ltd, Governor, 1993
182 Minneapolis Institute of Art
183a *Spirited Away*, 2001, Hayao Miyazaki. Studio Ghibli/Kobal/Shutterstock
183l *The Host*, 2006, Bong Joon-Ho. Sego Entertainment/Chungeorahm Film/Kobal/Shutterstock
183r *The Grudge*, 2002, Director Takashi Shimizu. Pioneer LDC/Nikkatsu/Oz Company Ltd/Kobal/Shutterstock
184l Arcadeimages/Alamy Stock Photo
184r *Thirst*, 2009, Director Park Chan-wook. Moho Film/Focus Features International/Kobal/Shutterstock
185a, 185b Metropolitan Museum of Art, New York. Purchase, Mary and James G. Wallach Family Foundation of Gift, in honor of John T. Carpenter, 2013
187 *Bubba Ho-Tep*, 2004, Director Don Coscarelli. Silver Sphere Corporation/Kobal/Shutterstock
188a Photo Transcendental Graphics/Getty Images
188l *Westworld*, 1973, Director Michael Crichton. MGM/Kobal/Shutterstock
188r Smithsonian Museum, Washington, D.C.
189 Library of Congress, Washington, D.C.
190–1 © Norman O. Dawn Collection, Harry Ransom Center, University of Texas
192a Private Collection
192b Smithsonian American Art Museum, Washington, D.C. Gift of Mrs. Joseph Harrison, Jr.
193a Smithsonian American Art Museum, Washington, D.C. Transfer from National Museum of Natural History, Department of Ethnology, Smithsonian Institution

193c Library of Congress, Washington, D.C.
193b *The Revenant*, 2015, Director Alejandro González-Iñárritu. 20th Century Fox/Regency Enterprises/Kobal/Shutterstock
194a *Curse of the Undead*, 1959, Director Edward Dein, Universal Pictures. Everett Collection Inc/Alamy Stock Photo
194b *Billy the Kid vs Dracula*, 1966, Director William Beaudine. Circle Productions/Kobal/Shutterstock
196a *The Wild Bunch*, 1969, Director Sam Pekinpah, Warner Bros. -Seven Arts. Kobal/Shutterstock
196b *Priest*, 2011, Director Scott Stewart, Tokyopop, DMG Entertainment. Buckaroo Entertainment/Kobal/Shutterstock
197a *The Three Burials of Melquiades Estrada*, 2005, Director Tommy Lee Jones. Javelina Film Company/Dawn Jones/Europa Corp/Sony/Kobal/Shutterstock
197b *No Country for Old Men*, 2007, Director Coen Brothers, Scott Rudin Productions, Mike Zoss Productions. Paramount/Miramax/Kobal/Shutterstock
199 New York Public Library
200 NASA
202a Howard Lovecraft Collection, Brown University Library, Rhode Island
202b Chronicle/Alamy Stock Photo
203a *The Color Out of Space*, 2019, Director Richard Stanley, Spectre Vision. TCD/Prod.DB/Alamy Stock Photo
203b Photo National Museums Liverpool/Bridgeman Images
204a Tretyakov Gallery, Moscow. © Konstantin Fyodorovich Yuon/DACS, 2021
204b *Stranger Things*, 2017, Director Duffer Brothers, 21 Laps Entertainment, Monkey Massacre. Netflix/Kobal/Shutterstock
205 *The Beyond*, 1981, Director Lucio Fulci, Fulvia Film. Mary Evans/Ronald Grant/Diomedia Images
206 Ksenia Ivanova/For The Washington Post via Getty Images
206-7 Photo DEA Picture Library/De Agostini via Getty Images
209 *The Last Man on Earth*, 1964, Directors Sidney Salkow and Ubaldo B. Ragona, Associated Producers Inc. American International Pictures/Kobal/Shutterstock
210-1 Nathaniel Noir/Alamy Stock Photo
212 *Bride of Frankenstein*, 1935, Director James Whale. Universal/Kobal/Shutterstock
213 Private Collection
214a Library of Congress, Washington, D.C.
214b Wellcome Collection, London
215 Image Museo Nacional del Prado, Madrid. Photo MNP/Scala, Florence
216a McGill Library's Chapbook Collection
216b Art Institute of Chicago, Stanley Field Fund
218-9 *King Kong*, 1933, Directors Merian C. Cooper and Ernest B. Schoedsack. Radio Pictures/Kobal/Shutterstock
220al *Gorgo*, 1960, Director Eugène Lourié. King Brothers/Kobal/Shutterstock
220ar *Gojira*, 1954, Director Ishirō Honda, Toho Productions. Everett Collection Inc/Alamy Stock Photo
220bl *The Beast from 20,000 Fathoms*, 1953, Director Eugène Lourié, Jack Dietz Productions. Warner Bros/Kobal/Shutterstock
220br *Godzilla, King of the Monsters*, 1956, Director Ishirō Honda. Toho Productions/Kobal/Shutterstock
222a Museum zu Allerheiligen, Schaffhausen. Photo Fine Art Images/Bridgeman Images
222b Edinburgh University Library Special Collections
223 Tate, London
224a Private Collection. Photo Maas Gallery, London/Bridgeman Images
224b Wellcome Collection, London
226 *Freaks*, 1932, Ted Browning. Metro-Goldwyn-Mayer/Kobal/Shutterstock
227a Amherst College Archives and Special Collections
227b *Communion*, 1989, Director Philippe Mora. Pheasantry/Allied Vision/Kobal/Shutterstock
228 Museo Nacional del Prado, Madrid
229a propstore.com/Shutterstock
229b Image courtesy of and © Museum H.R. Giger

230a Yale Centre for British Art, Paul Mellon Centre, New Haven
230b Archaeological Museum, Florence. Photo Scala, Florence. Courtesy of Ministero Beni ed Att. Culturali e del Turismo
231a Private Collection
231b Wellcome Collection, London
233a propstore.com/Shutterstock
233al *The Wolf Man*, 1941, Director George Waggner. Universal/Kobal/Shutterstock
233ac *Cat People*, 1942, Director Jacques Tourneur. RKO Radio Pictures/Kobal/Shutterstock
233ar propstore.com/Shutterstock
233bl *Wolverine*, 1982 (Marvel Comics)
233bc propstore.com/Shutterstock
233br *I Was a Teenage Werewolf*, 1957, Director Gene Gowler Jr. American International Pictures/Kobal/Shutterstock
234a Oxford University Herbaria, Sher-0569-50
234b Photo Corbis/Getty Images
235a *Little Joe*, 2019, Director Jessica Hausner, Coop99, Essential Filmproduktion, The Bureau, Arte, BBC Films, British Film Institute. Magnolia Films/Kobal/Shutterstock
235b Paul D Stewart/Science Photo Library
236 Eth-Bibliothek Zürich/Science Photo Library
236-7 *Splice*, 2009, Director Vincenzo Natali. Gaumont/Kobal/Shutterstock
237 *The Fly*, 1986, Director David Cronenberg, Brooksfilms, SLM Production Group. 20th Century Fox/Kobal/Shutterstock
238 British Library, London
239 *An American Werewolf in London*, 1981, Director John Landis. Polygram/Universal/Kobal/Shutterstock
240 *Possession*, 1981, Director Andrzej Zulawski, Gaumont. Photo 12/Alamy Stock Photo
241, 242a Library of Congress, Washington, D.C.
242b, 243a Private Collection
243b Photo Andy Johnson. © Ray and Diana Harryhausen Foundation
244 Photo Andy Johnson. © Ray and Diana Harryhausen Foundation
245l *It Came from Beneath the Sea*, 1955, Director Gordon Robert Gordon, Clover Productions. Columbia/Kobal/Shutterstock
245r Photo Andy Johnson. © Ray and Diana Harryhausen Foundation
245b *It Came from Beneath the Sea*, 1955, Director Gordon Robert Gordon, Clover Productions. Columbia/Kobal/Shutterstock
246 Wellcome Collection, London
247a *The Dunwich Horror*, 1970, Director Daniel Haller, Alta Vista Films. American International Pictures/Kobal/Shutterstock
247b *Monster from the Ocean Floor*, 1954, Director Wyott Ordung, Palo Alto. Lippert/Kobal/Shutterstock
249a *The Shape of Water*, 2017, Director Guillermo del Toro. Fox Searchlight Pictures, TSG Entertainment, Double Dare You Productions. Moviestore/Shutterstock
249l New York Public Library
249r Metropolitan Museum of Art, New York. Purchase, Louise Eldridge McBurney Gift, 1953
250-1 Photo Trustees of the British Museum, London
252 *Ghostbusters*, 2016, Director Paul Feig. Columbia/Feigco/Kobal/Shutterstock
253a *Spirited Away*, 2001, Director Hayao Miyazaki. Studio Ghibli/Kobal/Shutterstock
253b Harry F. Bruning Collection of Japanese Books and Manuscripts, L. Tom Perry Special Collections, Harold B. Lee Library, Brigham Young University.
254 Image courtesy of and © Museum H.R. Giger
255al *Blood Worm* by John Halkin (Publishers Guild Press, 1987)
255ac *Slime* by John Halkin (Hamlyn, 1983). Cover art by Terry Oakes
255ar *Slugs* by Shaun Hutson (Leisure Books, 1982)
255bl *Squelch* by John Halkin (Critic's Choice, 1985)
255bc *Maggots* by Edward Jarvis (Legend, 1986). Cover art by Terry Oakes
255br *Slither* by John Halkin (Hamlyn, 1980).

256–7 *The Thing*, 1981, Director John Carpenter, The Turman-Foster Company. Universal/Kobal/Shutterstock
258a Howard Lovecraft Collection, Brown University Library, Rhode Island
258b *Annihilation*, 2018, Director Alex Garland, Skydance Media, DNA Films, Scott Rudin Productions. Paramount/Moviestore/Shutterstock
259 The LuEsther T Mertz Library, New York Botanical Garden
260 Private Collection
261a Wellcome Collection, London
261b *Night of the Demon*, 1958, Director Jacques Tourneur, Sabre Film Production. Columbia/Kobal/Shutterstock
262–3 *Godzilla vs. Hedorah*, 1971, Director Yoshimitsu Banno, Toho Studios. Mary Evans/Ronald Grant/Diomedia Images
265 *The Fog*, 1980, Director John Carpenter. Debra Hill Productions/Kobal/Shutterstock
266 © Fergus Greer
267 *Us*, 2019, Direcotr Jordan Peele, Monkeypaw Productions, Perfect World Pictures. Universal/ILM/Kobal/Shutterstock
268 British Library, London
269 British Library Board. All Rights Reserved/Bridgeman Images
270a British Library, London
270l *The Picture of Dorian Gray*, 1970, Director Massimo Dallamano. Terra-Filmkunst/Sargon Film/Kobal/Shutterstock
270r *The Student of Prague*, 1926, Director Henrik Galleen, Sokal Film-GmbH. Photo Hulton Archive/Getty Images
271 British Library, London
272-3 © Association Marcel Duchamp/ADAGP, Paris and DACS, London 2021
273 Jersey Heritage Trust Collection
274a *The Stepford Wives*, 1975, Director Bryan Forbes, Palomar Pictures. Columbia/Kobal/Shutterstock
274b *Blade Runner*, 1982, Director Ridley Scott, The Ladd Brothers, Shaw Brothers, Blade Runner Partnership. Mary Evans/Diomedia Images
275 Photo Chris McGrath/Getty Images
277 © ADAGP, Paris and DACS, London 2021
278–9 *Dawn of the Dead*, 1978, Director George Romero, Laurel Group. United Film/Kobal/Shutterstock

INDEX

Illustration references are in **bold**.

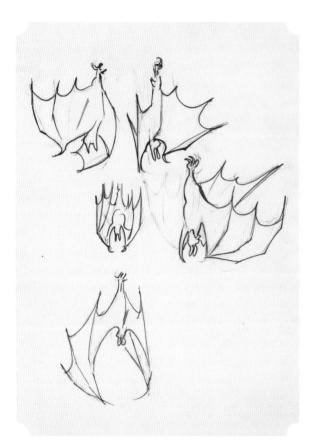

Roger Luckhurst is the author of *The Invention of Telepathy, 1870–1901* (2002), *The Mummy's Curse: The True History of a Dark Fantasy* (2012), and *Zombies: A Cultural History* (2015), and has edited several classic Gothic novels by Bram Stoker, Robert Louis Stevenson and H. P. Lovecraft. He is the Geoffrey Tillotson Professor of Nineteenth Century Studies at Birkbeck College, University of London.

ABOVE: Concept drawing for *Batman* (Tim Burton, 1989).
ON THE COVER (right to left, front to back): George Shaw, 'Eight-armed Cuttle Fish', from *Zoological Lectures Delivered at the Royal Institution of Great Britain*, London, 1809 (detail). New York Public Library; Augustus Pugin, Decorative grill from the Palace of Westminster, c. 1845-59 (detail). Metropolitan Museum of Art, New York. Purchase, Friends of European Sculpture and Decorative Arts Gifts, 2015; Haitian voodoo priest Louis Romain making the first gesture in the greeting ritual, 1937 (detail). Photo Rex Hardy Jr./The LIFE Picture Collection via Getty Images
ENDPAPERS: Niall Sweeney
P. 1: Postcard from Man Ray to Georges and Germaine Hugnet, postmarked 14 March 1960.
PP. 4–5: *Arrival* (Denis Villeneuve, 2016).
P. 6: Bram Stoker's working chapter plan for *Dracula, c.* 1890.

Published in the United States and Canada in 2021 by Princeton University Press, 41 William Street, Princeton, New Jersey 08540
press.princeton.edu

First published in the United Kingdom in 2021 by Thames & Hudson Ltd, 181A High Holborn, London WC1V 7QX

Published by arrangement with Thames & Hudson Ltd., London

Gothic: An Illustrated History © 2021
Thames & Hudson Ltd, London

Text © Roger Luckhurst

Designed by Niall Sweeney, Pony Ltd

Library of Congress Control Number 2021937908

ISBN 978-0-691-22916-4

Printed in China by RR Donnelley

10 9 8 7 6 5 4 3 2 1

FSC
www.fsc.org
MIX
Paper from
responsible sources
FSC® C144853